Brave New World™

By Matt Forbeck

O, brave new world, that has such people in't.
—William Shakespeare, *The Tempest*

Pinnacle™ Entertainment Group, Inc.

Credits

Written and Designed by: Matt Forbeck
Editing: Hal Mangold
Cover: Zeke Sparkes
Interior Art: Jim Callahan, Mike Chen, Kim DeMulder, John Grigni, Don Hillsman, Ashe Marler, Nick Napolitano, Richard Pollard, Kevin Sharpe, and Mike Sellers
Computer Coloring: Chuck Croft, Chris Impink, Kevin Sharpe, Zeke Sparkes, and Matt Tice
Graphic Design: Matt Forbeck, Charles Ryan, and Zeke Sparkes

Special Thanks to: Amber Bucheit, Rachel Butterworth, Ken Carpenter, Frank Chafe, Martin Forbeck, Marcelo Figueroa, Leticia Hayler, Michelle, Caden, and Shane Lacy Hensley, Christy and John Hopler, Ann Kolinsky, Ray Lau, Jim Pinto, Dave Seay, Matt Tice, Jennifer Wick, Maureen Yates, John Zinser, and John and Mary Zinser.

Playtesting: Eric Allan, Chet Bacon, Mario Lee Bansen III, Kevin Boerwinkle, Arron Cattle, Jim Crocker, Marcelo Figueroa, Paul Filsinger, John Goff, Kevin Gormely, James Gormley, Andy Grim, Chris Hawkins, Michelle Hensley, Shane Lacy Hensley, John Hopler, Eric Hurst, Mark Ingraham, Charles Ingram, Gilbert Isla, Patrick Kapera, Vince Knuffman, Michael A. Letendre, Lucy Lewis, Shannon R. Lewis, Chris Libey, Ashe Marler, Aaron McConnell, Greg McNutt, Scott Michael, Andrew Morris, Brock Moses, Randy Moses, Tim Nanzer, Jason Olivier, Jason Park, Jim Pinto, Jess Ray, C. David Ross, Robert Scott, Alan Seyberth, Ralph Shelton, Eric Sofer, Bob Sohl, Zeke Sparkes, Annaleise Stehwein, Rob Stehwein, William Steinmetz, Simon Stroud, Kevin Swibaker, Matt Tice, John Wick, James Williams, Dave Wilson, and Kevin Wilson.

Dedicated to: Marty, who's made my world a little braver.

Pinnacle Entertainment Group, Inc.
P.O. Box 10908
Blacksburg, VA 24062-0908
www.peginc.com
deadlands@aol.com
(800) 214-5645 (orders only)

Stop by www.peginc.com for regular, free updates!

Printed in the USA

PINNACLE ENTERTAINMENT GROUP, INC.™

TABLE OF CONTENTS

TABLE OF CONTENTS

BRAVE NEW WORLD™
#0
1999
PATRIOT'S LAST STAND!
PINNACLE
FORBECK SHARPE BAUMGARTNER DREIER SPARKES TICE

SHE WAS JUST ANOTHER KID ON THE RUN FROM DELTA PRIME.
SHE'D JUST GOTTEN HER DELTA POWERS, AND SHE DIDN'T KNOW WHAT TO DO.
LIKE THE SONG SAYS: "NOWHERE TO RUN TO, NOWHERE TO HIDE."
UNTIL SHE RAN INTO ME.
OF COURSE, SHE DIDN'T JUST RUN INTO ME.
YOU LOOK LIKE YOU COULD USE A HAND.
I WAS *LOOKING* FOR HER.
EEEEEE!!!
SHE DIDN'T SEEM TOO PLEASED ABOUT THAT.

IT'S OKAY, KID. TRUST ME.
SINCE I'M AT THE TOP OF DELTA PRIME'S 10 MOST WANTED LIST, I SUPPOSE I CAN UNDERSTAND.
I'M WITH THE DEFIANCE.
BUT YOU'RE--!
NO BUTS.
IF YOU WANT TO GET AWAY FROM THOSE PRIMERS CHASING YOU, I'M YOUR ONLY HOPE.
HERE. YOU'LL NEED THIS.
www.deltatimes.com
NOW KEEP YOUR MOUTH SHUT AND FOLLOW ME.
thup
KEEP YOUR HEAD DOWN.
IF YOU'RE LUCKY, YOU MIGHT STILL MAKE IT HOME IN ONE PIECE.

AH, HELL! GET BACK, KID. THIS COULD GET NASTY.
I RECOGNIZED THE CHOPPER IMMEDIATELY.
IT WAS ASSIGNED TO EDDIE HAMILTON, A PRIMER WHOSE CODENAME WAS "CHARGE."
I KNEW HIM WELL.
HELL, I'D TRAINED HIM.
AND I KNEW THERE WAS ONLY ONE WAY TO DEAL WITH HIM.
KA-ZWAP!
BA-DA-BOOOM!
SOMEDAY THEY'LL CORRECT THAT FLAW IN THE FUEL TANK.
OMIGOD! YOU KILLED HIM!

I WOULDN'T BE TOO SURE OF THAT.
GET OUT OF HERE, KID!
RUN!
FORGET IT, OLD MAN!
krkle-KRAK!
SHE'S DOOMED, AND SO ARE YOU!
GIVE IT UP, PATRIOT! YOU'RE OUT OF YOUR LEAGUE!
I THOUGHT I TAUGHT YOU BETTER THAN THAT, EDDIE.
NEVER COUNT A MAN DOWN UNTIL HE'S OUT!

ka-ZWAM!
KRUNCH!
DEAR GOD! EDDIE!
YOU'VE GONE SOFT, OLD MAN. I'LL WRITE THAT ON YOUR TOMBSTONE.
TIME'S UP, PATRIOT!
WHAT ARE YOU TALKING--?
DAMN.

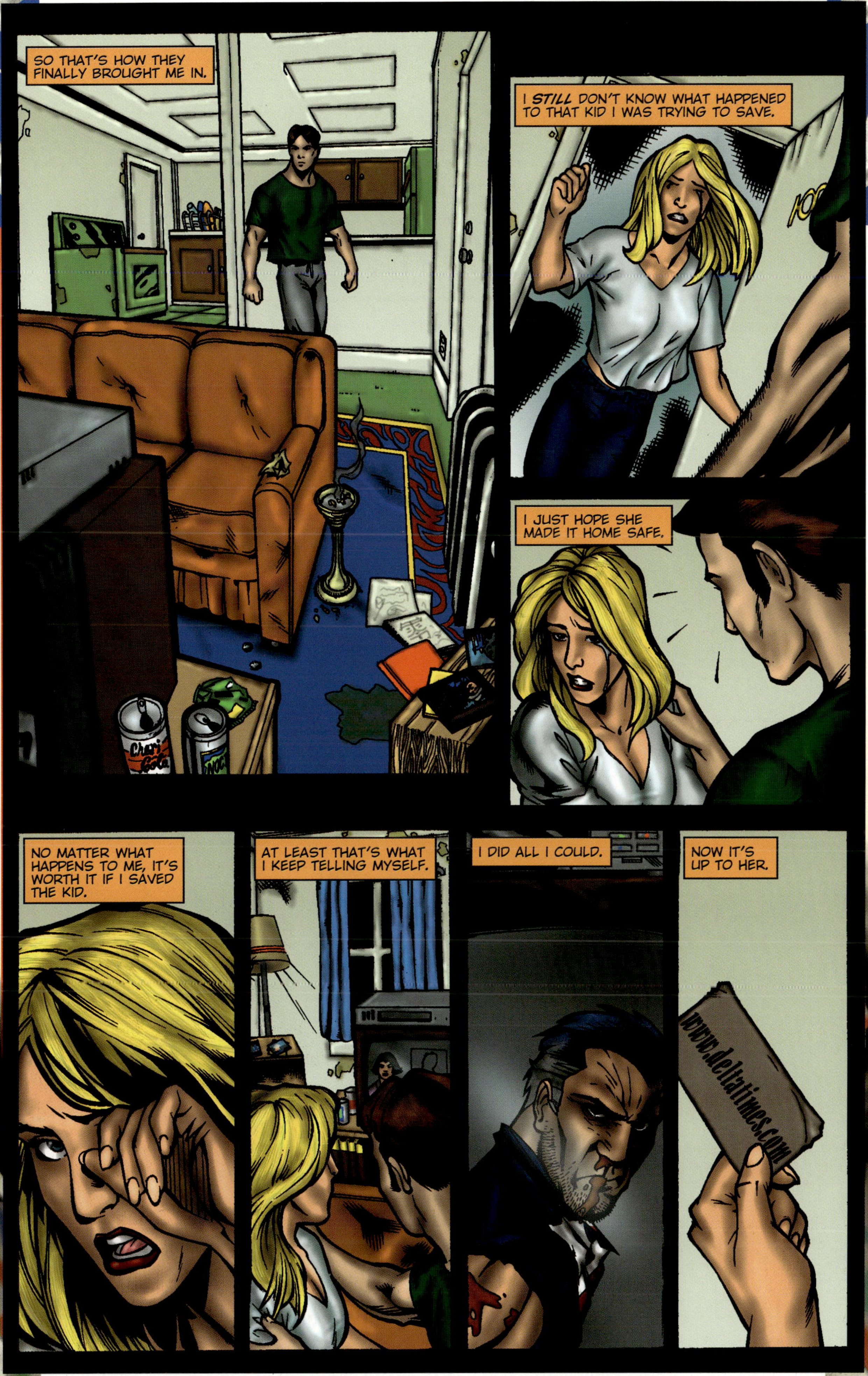
SO THAT'S HOW THEY FINALLY BROUGHT ME IN.
I STILL DON'T KNOW WHAT HAPPENED TO THAT KID I WAS TRYING TO SAVE.
I JUST HOPE SHE MADE IT HOME SAFE.
NO MATTER WHAT HAPPENS TO ME, IT'S WORTH IT IF I SAVED THE KID.
AT LEAST THAT'S WHAT I KEEP TELLING MYSELF.
I DID ALL I COULD.
NOW IT'S UP TO HER.
www.deltatimes.com

Web Sailor Pro 4.20 Beta
Favorites
History
Stop
Home
www.deltatimes.com
dle.gov
us.com
WWW.DELTATIMES.COM
The truth can't be silenced!
Features
Memorial
Archives
Crew
Events
Links
Features || Memorial || Archives || Crew || Events || Links
http://welcome_to_deltatimes/page 12

WELCOME

Since you've got the address for this site, there are three possibilities.

One, you're a hacker who was poking around and managed to find this place.

Two, you're with some kind of governmental organization, probably one that wants to shut us down.

Three, you were given this address by someone who knows about it and thinks you might need it.

If it's number one, congratulations. Now get the hell out.

If it's number two, congratulations to you too. And better people than you have tried to take down the *Delta Times* and failed miserably. Take your best shot.

If it's number three, hey, you're the people we're really here for. Come on in.

Anyhow, I'm going to assume that you're a member of that third group of people, the one I'm trying to reach. If that doesn't suit you, learn to live with it.

WHAT WE'RE ABOUT

The *Delta Times* is an irregularly published webzine. Our mission is to serve the members of the underground delta community, more loosely known as the Defiance.

To that end, we've got a series of web books that we've written about all sorts of delta-specific concerns. Things like "How to Shut Your Powers Off," "Secret Identities and You," "Life in Crescent City," and so on. These books are constantly being revised and updated with the latest information we can get our little, muckraking hands on.

Who We Are

Sorry, kid, that information's released on a need-to-know basis only. If you think being able to find our website means you've got a "need to know," then I'd like to know what flavor of crack you're smoking.

The *Delta Times* has a pretty small staff, but we're soundly dedicated to the cause. Most of our articles and information comes to us from our readers—fellow deltas, of course—making us the hub in a loose network of underground deltas.

My name's Truth. (No, it's not my real name. Go to the link on secret identities, for chrissake.) Yeah, as in me, Justice, and the American Way. Around here, we think the American Way's taken a forced holiday, and he shanghaied Justice on his way out of town.

These days, the only thing that's left is Truth, and only if you know where to find it. (Here's a hint for you slow types: www.deltatimes.com.)

Who You Are

You're what's popularly known as a delta. The eggheads use all sorts of terms for it: homo delta, superiors, paranormals, and so on. In the end, it all comes down to the same thing.

You've got powers "far beyond those of mortal men." In the old days, people like you were called superheroes—or supervillains, as often as not—but that's not turn-of-the-millennium enough for most.

Maybe you just got your gifts, or maybe you've been hiding them for years. Hell, you could even be a Delta Primer thinking about working for the other side. If you already know some of what I'm going to cover here, skip over it. I'm writing for the newbies.

What a Delta Is

I could rattle off all sorts of dry data about who first used the word "delta" to describe people with superhuman powers (it was Dr. Theodore Weiss) and the meaning of the Greek letter from which the term originally comes ("change"), but that's not what you're here for. You can get that kind of information anywhere.

Even so, let's hit the basics first.

A delta is a person who has innate powers that can't be explained by what we currently know as the laws of physics. Maybe they can fly or shoot beams from their eyes or bounce bullets off their ski n. Whatever. None of this stuff is what even the dullest knife in the drawer could call normal.

You can tell some deltas from just looking at them. They've got wings or scales, or their skin is blue, or their eyes have no pupils. Most deltas, though, you couldn't pick out in a crowd. They look just like you or me.

Well, like me at least. I can't speak for you.

Most of us have powers of a more subtle nature than what you might see on most TV shows. Those that don't are the kind who get hauled in quickly.

It doesn't take the government goons in Delta Prime much to figure out the nine-foot-tall woman's a delta, and she can't have too many places she can hide. Fortunately, most of us aren't quite so obvious, much to the frustration of even President Kennedy's most experienced goons.

Some deltas can read minds or smell evil or even cast spells like a modern-day Merlin. Me, for instance, I can always tell when someone is telling the truth. It's a handy skill in my line of work, but it's not as infallible as you might think. Still, it means that if you read it here, you know it's true!

Delta History

As the saying goes, if you want to know where you're going, you've first got to figure out where you've been. Bear with me here, kid. You may have learned some of this in school, but there's more to the story than you've been told.

The fact is, Kennedy and his cronies in that lousy excuse for a puppet show we call Congress have a vested interest in you not knowing the truth. This is a human story, after all, about living breathing people and the trials of their unusual lives.

Kennedy doesn't want you to think of deltas as humans. To him, we're the "delta menace," the "nation's greatest threat." We're anything but human.

After all, it's not as easy to hate someone you think of as human.

The First Delta

You probably know this, but the first confirmed delta was a man named Peter Payne. Old Pete was a soldier in WWI, fighting on the side of the Allies. He was an American, of course, a black man from Detroit who'd volunteered to take up a gun against the Kaiser's men.

Pete rose quickly through the ranks of the enlisted men, and it wasn't long before he made sergeant. He was a good leader, demanding yet always looking out for his men's best interests. While rescuing a fallen soldier in an open stretch of no-man's land, Pete was shot and killed by a German sniper.

Okay, he wasn't exactly killed, but he probably should have been. The bullet that had his name on it punched right between his shoulder blades and lodged near his heart.

Pete lay there in that nameless French field, the life draining out of him, when he suddenly realized the pain had left him.

"I thought for sure I was a goner," Pete told me when I interviewed him about it a few years back. Even at over 90 years old, he was still going strong, looking as fit as a man half his age, the same determined gleam in his eyes.

"But I picked myself up and looked down at the ground, and there was a bullet lying there in a pool of what I guessed was my own blood. I reached down to pick the damned thing up, but my hand passed right through it—just like a ghost."

There's more to the story, of course, but that's for another time and place. Anyhow, that's how the Silver Ghost got his start: on a shot-up field in the heart of Europe.

A State Secret

Pete kept his newfound powers to himself as long as he could. He knew that once the Army brass found out about them they'd haul his ass off the battlefield and stick him in a lab someplace where the eggheads would stick him full of more pins than a porcupine.

Still, given the fact Pete was commanding a platoon of soldiers in the middle of the Great War, there wasn't much chance of him keeping his amazing abilities quiet for long. Within three months, his CO got word of what had happened, and Pete's fears all came true.

It didn't take the scientists long to get stumped by Pete and his powers. No one had any idea how the man could simply fade in and out of solidness like, well, a ghost. When the brass got the eggheads' report, they made an executive decision.

Behind Enemy Lines

A man with Pete's abilities was too incredible to keep holed up in a secret bunker for the length of the conflict. And, hey, the War to End All Wars was on. The US Army quickly put him to use.

Pete spent the final months of the war working as an Allied spy. Able to slip in and out of any building at will, he was literally unstoppable. Estimates at the time were that his presence cut the war short by months.

The fact that Pete even existed was the US Government's most tightly held secret. The Germans had no chance of stopping a man capable of doing the impossible, especially if they wouldn't even have thought of preparing for him.

Once the war was over—and even after other deltas started popping up everywhere—Pete became the Department of War's most successful spy. It wasn't until the '30s that he actually adopted a costumed identity, long after the existence of deltas had become common knowledge.

Pete spent his entire life in service to the government, right up until one of his grandchildren became a delta in her own right. Knowing what the federal government had become like over the course of the century, Pete kidnapped the young lady from her parents and spirited her off to a safehouse he'd set up in a third-world country he knew from his own Delta Prime days.

That's where I caught up with Pete. He was lounging on a beach on an island off the coast of a country whose petty dictator he'd personally helped prop up over two decades earlier. His granddaughter was still with him then. Pete's gone now, and his sweet little girl's all grown up. She's one of us now.

A Defiant.

The Golden Years

From the final days of World War I until the dawn of World War II, it was a good time to be a delta. Throughout the Roaring '20s and even the Great Depression, more and more deltas came to light.

In those idealistic times, most of them were heroes, fighting for the common good, but even then there were villains—evil deltas bent on using their powers to further their own despicable ends. They scared the hell out of people, even back then, but in those nobler times they didn't seem quite as vicious as they do these days.

That's probably just me looking back at a past I never knew through nostalgia-colored lenses. I'm sure that people back then were just as good or evil as those who walk, run, or fly over the streets of America today. Still, there seemed to be a kind of innocence then that we're sorely lacking today.

Back then, if people were afraid, they lived in fear of villains, people who weren't too shy to wear their evilness on their sleeves. They weren't afraid of deltas just because they were deltas.

Of course, it wasn't because people were smarter in those days, or more forgiving. The fact is they just didn't know any better. The dangers were the same. The government hadn't gotten around to "educating" the public about them quite yet.

After all, the movie-house serials of the day showed reel after reel of patriotic American heroes putting down threat after threat to life, liberty, and the pursuit of happiness. They were the good guys, and they were on the side of mom and apple pie.

One of the most successful of these heroes was a man known as the Yankee.

The Man Who Made a Difference

Most of the early, so-called crimefighters were nothing more than superpowered vigilantes, deltas who had been pushed too far by a criminal of some sort and then decided to take matters into their own hands. Their methods of stopping crime were often illegal and occasionally deadly. The masks they wore did as much to hide their guilt as protect their privacy.

The radio dramas lauded them, and people across America thrilled to the tales of their adventures. But deep inside, I think people knew they were rooting for the wrong kind of people.

The Yankee, though, was different. Unlike many other deltas, he had a personal code against killing, and he followed it to a fault. He was also careful to build a case against criminals so they could be tried in a court of law. Contrary to the vigilantes, he actually believed in the Bill of Rights.

The Yankee was deputized by the city of Chicago as a law-enforcement officer, making him the first delta to be openly sanctioned by any American government. He worked alongside Eliot Ness to take down Capone. He put gangster after gangster behind bars, and he always made sure to collect enough evidence to make sure they stayed there.

Of course, this also made the Yankee a target for every power-mad delta to come down the pike. Chicago quickly became a magnet for all sorts of madness, and it wasn't long before the mayor regretted his decision. By that time, though, it was too late. The Yankee played the public like a harp, taking every opportunity he could to show how a good man—a good delta even—could make a difference.

The people loved him.

A Life to Live By

The Yankee became a role model for lots of other deltas—at least the community-minded ones. They dressed like him, gaudy costumes and all. They wore masks like him, even though many of their identities were common knowledge. Best of all, they acted like him, and by all accounts, he was a true gentleman.

Even through the tough times of the Great Depression and the years after, Yankee and his kind never lost hope. They kept fighting on against all comers, and by doing so they gave the rest of us hope as well.

They had a kind of idealism that you only find in very young children these days. From all accounts, they honestly believed that they were fighting the good fight to make the world that much safer for the rest of us.

These days, of course, most of the regs seem to have forgotten that deltas were ever heroes. Sure, we've got the hard-asses at Delta Prime and the occasional prima donna from Triumph, Inc., doing the superhero thing in the bubblegum vein, but the Yankee and his kind were the real thing.

That's something I'm not sure we'll ever see again.

The Last Great War

Nothing lasts forever, of course, and it wasn't long before the Golden Years came to an end. For decades, Americans had ignored what was happening abroad. We were still working our way out of the Great Depression. Worrying about what some little German corporal was doing across the ocean didn't seem all that important.

That didn't last.

America was dragged into the growing conflict in Europe and Asia soon enough by the sneak attack at Pearl Harbor. Dozens of Japanese Zeroes and deltas ambushed the American naval base at dawn, nearly razing it to the ground and decimating the Pacific fleet. Our response was swift. Within the week, we declared war on Japan and the rest of the Axis powers. Our troops were on their way abroad soon after, led by the all-new Delta Squadron.

There are those who claim that FDR knew about the attack coming on Pearl Harbor, but he let it happen to get the American public fully behind the war effort. Even with my powers, I've never been able to verify that theory (FDR's long dead and in no mood to answer my questions), but the very existence of Delta Squadron seems to support it.

Super Soldiers

Both the Axis and the Allies put a lot of effort into figuring out where deltas come from and how they could make more of them. Both sides' programs had some success at this, but never enough for them to actually produce what they really wanted: an army of super-soldiers.

When the call to arms finally came for the USA, the Army suddenly pulled Delta Squadron out of its five-star hat. Out of nowhere, we had deltas no one had ever heard of pulling together to take the fight to the Nazis. Mixed in among them, though, we had some of the greatest deltas ever known, and Yankee was in the vanguard.

Just because we had ourselves a mess of deltas didn't mean the Germans were just going to turn tail and run back to Berlin. They had plenty of deltas of their own.

For the first time in history, deltas were a major force in a war. While men battled on the battlefields below, deltas fought alongside them and soared overhead. When deltas clashed, the heavens shook with their fury.

During World War II, the world changed in many ways. For most deltas, having superpowers was no longer a game. It was deadly serious.

In the end, it was a delta who put an end to the war. Actually, that's not entirely true.

It was the first alpha.

Captured!

The Yankee was right there when it happened. Over the years, he'd had a lot of sidekicks, younger deltas willing to work alongside him for a while. He taught them what he knew about crimefighting, and they watched his back. It was a good arrangement that lots of other deltas mimicked over the years.

In the fall of '43, the Yankee was deep behind enemy lines when he and his then-current sidekick, a young man known as Sparky, were captured by Kapitan Krieg, one of the Nazis' most powerful deltas. Krieg personally flew his defeated foes to Auschwitz, where the Nazis had set up a special concentration camp for their delta prisoners.

Under the watchful eye of the camp commander, the Yankee and Sparky were subjected to horrors beyond imagination. The Nazis were going out of their way to exterminate not only Jews, gypsies, and gays, but also every delta in Europe that wouldn't wear a swastika armband with pride.

Never one to bow to fascist dictators of any stripe, the Yankee quickly organized a revolt against the guards.

Alpha Genesis

It was a bloody fight. Only a handful of deltas were strong enough to join the Yankee in his desperate gambit. To make matters worse, the Nazis called in Kapitan Krieg, who was there in a moment. He massacred them all.

Actually, one of the delta rioters survived the attack: Sparky.

At first, it seemed that Sparky was truly dead. The Nazi guards even tossed his lifeless body into one of their massive ovens to destroy any shred of evidence that any of the dead deltas had ever been in their "care."

As the flames consumed the Yankee and the rest of the brave souls that Krieg struck down, Sparky died in that fire alongside them.

Superior woke up in his place, and the world was forever changed.

The Turning Point

Moving almost faster than the eye could follow, Superior zoomed around and killed each and every Nazi in the entire camp.

Some he murdered with his bare hands. Others were incinerated by beams blazing from his eyes. Still others met their end by more creative means.

While being held in the camp, Sparky had thought about killing Nazis for a long, miserable time. Superior finally got to carry those fantasies out, and he did so mercilessly.

Literally within minutes, the young man once known as Sparky had liberated the camp and set the prisoners free. A cheer went up from the P.O.W.s who could scarcely believe their luck.

Moments later, Kapitan Krieg—the Nazis' most powerful delta, the man who was responsible for the deaths of dozens of deltas—flew down into the camp to put down what he thought was another uprising.

He had no idea what he was in for. When he saw the young man who'd been known as Sparky, he laughed at the boy's impudence and promised him a quick death.

Superior tore Krieg limb from limb. He hung his head on the camp's front gate.

Heady with his newfound power, Superior flew directly to Berlin. There, he punched his way straight into Adolf Hitler's bunker. Moments later, Superior emerged with der führer's body.

Before anyone really knew it, the war was over.

The Superior Age

If the rest of us superpowered people are deltas, than Superior was clearly an alpha, a whole new class of delta, a man with powers far beyond anyone on the planet. Of course, while he may have been the first alpha, he certainly wasn't the last.

Soon after the end of WWII, the Russians reported that they had "developed" alphas of their own. None of them were powerful enough to take on Superior on his own, but as a team, they could surely give him a run for his money.

The alpha race was on.

Still, America started in the lead, and because of Superior we never lost it. To this date, there's never been a delta—alpha or otherwise—as powerful as him. Sure, he faced some challenges over the years, but he overcame them all. There was really no stopping him.

The years directly after WWII were a fine time for America. We were *the* superpower in the world, with no one able to seriously challenge us, even the up-and-coming Russians.

In 1949, America—heady with its power—got its first wakeup call. On October 12, the Russians detonated an atomic bomb deep in Siberia. Their test put the world on notice not to mess with the Soviet Union.

Even with all his vaunted powers, Superior couldn't be sure that he would survive a nuclear explosion, and that went double for every other delta in the world. The American nuclear program had been put on the back burner after Superior's arrival. The Department of War had decided that deltas (and especially alphas) were the face of modern warfare. After the Soviet nuclear test, though, development of America's own atomic technology moved right up onto the hot part of the stove again.

The Red Scare

The sudden realization that America wasn't alone at the top put the fear of Godless communists into the heart of most every American, and it wasn't long before someone decided to take advantage of that. In 1950, the notorious Senator Joe McCarthy from the fair state of Wisconsin led off a witch hunt to track down and imprison or blackball every "unloyal" American he could get his hands on.

The crux of the matter was that the government needed to know if every US citizen was a loyal American or a Soviet spy—at least that was the way McCarthy put it. His solution to this problem was simple: the House Un-American Activities Committee (HUAC).

With anti-Soviet sentiment at an all-time high, HUAC set to work. They started out going after Hollywood, successfully forcing the entertainment industry to blackball any creative types who even leaned to the left. Heady with their successes in that arena, they set after the deltas.

Declaring that a criminal like the Red Reaper was a commie was a no-brainer. Hell, the man wore a hammer and sickle on his chest and spouted revolutionary jargon as he "alleviated capitalist pigs of their tools of oppression." (Roughly translated: He robbed the rich and gave to himself.)

A lot of innocents got caught up in the inquisition. Even a few members of the Delta Squadron were called on to testify against themselves or their fellows. With one exception, they uniformly refused.

Some, like the Good Knight, actually served time for contempt of Congress. Others, like the Samurai, left the country as soon as he received his summons.

Apparently there was even talk of hauling in Superior before HUAC, but no one had the balls to actually send him a summons. His approval ratings were running higher than President Truman's, and any representative who tried anything against Superior knew he could kiss his seat good-bye come the next election.

Still, that didn't stop them from bringing in Patriot in late '53. Patriot, though, knew his rights and wasn't afraid to talk about them—eloquently and at length. At the end of his opening speech, nearly all of the HUAC members were hanging their heads in shame.

In 1954, HUAC was disbanded. The country finally got its collective head back together—helped along by the announcement that America finally had a working nuclear weapons program of its own. Still, the fear of unrestrained deltas within our midst never really faded, and McCarthy remained a figure of some power in the Senate, still railing against the threat that deltas posed to our national security.

The Great Tragedy

McCarthy's campaign against the deltas waxed and waned over the years, but it all came to a head on November 22, 1963.

You know the story, I'm sure. President Kennedy, the First Lady, and the governor of Texas were riding in a motorcade through the streets of Dallas, Texas, when a squad of the Devastator's Dreadnauts came zooming in over the horizon and blasted the President's car straight to hell.

Superior was on the scene in mere moments, and he made quick work of the Dreadnauts. When it was all over, the First Lady and the governor were dead, but the President was still breathing. Superior lifted the President in his arms and whisked him away to Walter Reed Memorial Hospital in DC, where he could be treated by the top delta healers in the nation.

The President lay in a coma for three days before he awoke. When he did, life was about to change for every delta in America.

With the disaster in Dallas still fresh in Kennedy's mind, he zapped a bill down to Congress. An emergency session ratified it in days, and the President signed it into law within the week. It was the Delta Registration Act.

The Delta Registration Act

Like most laws, the DRA's complex enough to have lawyers arguing over it for decades (as they are to this day), but the heart of it's simple enough. Anyone with superpowers of any kind must register with the Federal government so that his or her movements can be traced at all times.

You don't need the ACLU to tell you this is a blatant violation of the Bill of Rights, but when people are scared, they do strange things, and dear God were they scared.

Just because you're a delta doesn't mean you're on the side of angels. We're people like anyone else—with the exception of our unearthly powers, of course. If you prick us (well, if you can manage it with some of us), we bleed. Some of us dedicate our lives to helping those who need it. Others use their abilities to take what the world doesn't want to roll over and give them.

The point is that for every crimefighting, world-helping delta out there, there was at least one other clown causing problems: robbing the wealthy, knocking over banks, and killing innocent people. This scared the hell out of regular folks, who weren't really able to defend themselves against these superpowered threats.

The incident in Dallas just brought all of that into sharp focus.

I mean, when you saw the pictures of John-John saluting his mother's casket, how could you help but feel for the entire Kennedy clan? When the DRA came down the pike, Congress passed it almost unanimously.

It went into effect immediately.

Superior was the first delta to register, and lots of others followed his lead.

All known deltas were immediately tracked down by the government and asked to register. Those who refused were tossed into jail. Of course, not all of them went quietly.

Delta Prime

That's where Delta Prime came in. Kennedy knew the DRA was going to see some resistance, so he tapped Superior himself to found a new organization dedicated to policing America's delta population. It was pretty obvious the regular cops weren't going to be up to the job. With a lot of the vigilantes refusing to register, the government needed to have some way to enforce the DRA.

To that end, Superior created a new bureau of the Justice Department, and he called it Delta Prime. The first Primers, as they're called, included a number of the members of the old Delta Squadron, plus any other deltas whose loyalty was theoretically beyond reproach. Their first directive was (and still is) to arrest every unregistered delta.

DP's second directive is to support any Federal law enforcement agency in any matters in which delta involvement is suspected. As you might see, this is an extremely broad-based mandate. As such, it's entirely open to abuse, which is exactly what happened.

The Witch Hunt Begins

Sure, the people who refused to register were lawbreakers, but this was honestly just a tool. What the Justice Department operatives really wanted (and got) was an excuse to lock up any unregistered they could find, just for being a delta.

So what if the feds didn't actually have any proof that the man in question had committed a real crime? Just being unregistered was crime enough.

As the saying goes, "When you make superhuman powers illegal, only outlaws will have superhuman powers." Of course, not everyone refused to sign. Some of those deltas became some of the most zealous and capable hunters around.

Now, most people don't have much of a problem with locking up people like the Mass Murderer or the Dreadnauts for any reason, proof or not, but it's still a matter of civil rights. This became totally apparent when the Primers went after a number of crimefighters who, for reasons of their own, absolutely and openly refused to register.

Identity Crisis

So, if you've got nothing to hide, why not register? That's the question most Americans ask when they hear about some delta being hauled in for violating the DRA.

For one, it's a violation of basic privacy rights. Two, there's a reason a lot of crimefighters (and criminals) wear masks. Here's a clue: They don't want people to know who they are.

There are lots of reasons for this. Most often it's that the hero wants to lead a normal life when he's not in his union suit. Deltas who don't lead double lives have to worry about things like old enemies, paparazzi, and even just curious neighbors bothering not only them but those they love. When you work behind a mask, none of that stuff is a problem.

Of course, there's the fact that most delta crimefighters are simply vigilantes, unsanctioned by any government. Sometimes they bend laws to get the job done. Keeping an identity secret prevents them from having to answer for that—right or wrong.

Also masked deltas can't ever appear in court. The Constitution gives every person the right to face her accuser, and a person in a mask doesn't count.

Sometimes this can prove to be more of a hindrance than a relief. Sure, nobody likes having to appear in court, but without eyewitness testimony, lots of criminal deltas go free—or at least they did back then.

In those rough-and-tumble days, more than one delta crimefighter made up for that problem by skipping right past the theoretical judge and jury, appointing themselves the executioners. They carried the sentence out right there on the spot, and more than one criminal counted himself lucky to even be able to walk away from his so-called just desserts.

The Defiance Movement

There were a number of legitimate deltas who had a real beef with the DRA, and rather than sign up, they went underground. Some of them continued to operate the way they always had, taking down the criminals while avoiding the Primers and the police. Others simply hung up their masks and vowed never to use their powers again.

More than a few deltas, though, decided to fight the whole thing. They went underground and formed a loose organization called the Defiance. (I guess they thought it was catchy. There's no accounting for taste.)

Despite what the feds might want you to believe, and no matter what you might see on TV or in the movies, the Defiance isn't really all that together. We'd like to be the efficient espionage and subversion machine we're popularly made out to be, but it just isn't so.

Sure, there's a cadre of hardcore members who make a lot of noise every so often—enough to get on the evening news—but most of us are simply deltas who want to get by without anyone knowing who we are. We're not so different from the regs, after all.

Most Defiants don't know more than a few other members. In the old days, they all communicated through an underground newspaper called *The Delta Times.* It was sent to P.O. boxes and to general delivery addresses across the country. It was pretty crude, but it worked.

These days, we use the worldwide web to get people connected. We shuttle around from server to server, all of which are located far beyond the long arm of Delta Prime. Being who they are, Primers don't usually let things like pursuing stalwart webmasters like myself across international borders give them more than a moment's pause. Still, they haven't caught me yet.

More than one of my predecessors as publisher of this fine periodical is spending his days watching the world from a cage, but they haven't caught me yet. I'm hoping to someday even top the record-setting run of the paper's founder, the Yellow Journalist. Wish me luck.

And if you're feeling nostalgic, drop YJ a line. He's doing his time in New Alcatraz, right in the heart of Chicago Bay. He's always glad to hear from new Defiants.

Defiant Behavior

Despite the fact that most of the Defiants are good people, that's not true of all of us. Dozens of delta criminals fought tooth and nail against the newly formed Delta Prime. Battles broke out all across the nation in nearly every major city.

No one fought more viciously than the Devastator himself. Delta Prime cornered him and his Dreadnauts in his underground lair deep beneath New York City. Just when it looked like they were finally going to bring the bastard to justice, he set off a self-destruct device that brought down the roof on his den. It destroyed very shred of evidence in the place, along with four city blocks.

This all happened in the middle of the day, and the office skyscrapers above the Devastator's headquarters were packed full of people. The death toll numbered in the thousands.

Martial Law

When he learned of the incident in Manhattan, President Kennedy declared martial law across the entire country. From then on, only his word was law, although he promised to listen to the words of Congress and the Supreme Court on an advisory basis. Eventually he ignored that and simply appointed his own handpicked toadies to fill these posts, all the way from the federal government on down.

To this day, Kennedy rules our fair nation by decree. Over the years, his power base has solidified to the point that most people figure that the only way Kennedy's ever going to leave office is feet first. At a spry 82, Kennedy looks like he's not planning on leaving us any time soon.

Now I'm not one to advocate murder—even assassination—but there have been others who have tried to finish the job that incarnation of the Dreadnauts started in Dallas in '63. In those early days, most of them were put down by Superior. A special Secret Service detachment of Delta Prime took care of the rest.

Anyhow, Kennedy started out ruling with an iron fist, and he hasn't mellowed much over the years. If anything, matters have gotten worse.

Life as an American delta was pretty tough in the '60s and mid-'70s. With the support of a terrified American public behind him, Kennedy launched a witch hunt for unregistered deltas that made HUAC look like a Girl Scout meeting. FBI agents knocked down the doors of any suspected deltas and hauled them off to jail in the middle of the night. The concept of due process went right out the window, and soon the prisons were jammed with superpowered inmates.

Lots of deltas were killed while "resisting arrest." In truth, the Primers had simply decided that some deltas were just too dangerous to risk another encounter like the Manhattan Incident. Rather than chance it, they simply chose to save the country the bother of having to feed, clothe, and house the deltas, much less the expense of keeping watch over them until they died in prison.

You'd think the American public wouldn't have put up with that sort of crap. After all, millions of Americans have put their lives on the line to protect things like the Constitution and the Bill of Rights.

Instead, John Q. Public rolled over and exposed his throat to the Primers.

Some Defiants take this as a reason to hold a lot of anger for ordinary people—the "regs" as they call them (rhymes with "dregs"), but I don't agree. I don't hate regular folks. I pity them.

Figure this: These people are scared out of their wits. Even most deltas are scared. The world's changing overnight, people with superhuman powers are walking the earth, and lots of innocent people are dying.

Aren't you scared too? I know I am.

Hell, before you found out you're a delta, you might have felt the same way. Your friends and family probably still do, especially if you haven't told them anything yet.

Kennedy didn't take control of the country so much as we gave it to him. We've only got ourselves to blame.

Anyhow, delta or not, life during those days was pretty damn awful.

It got worse.

The Fortress

With all the deltas being brought in by Delta Prime, the US government needed a place to hold them. Traditional prisons weren't much use against people who could walk through walls or simply blast them down. Kennedy's answer? The Fortress.

The Fortress is a massive, maximum security prison specially outfitted with state-of-the-art restraint devices. The place is staffed by registered deltas of all stripes, all working in concert to keep the bad guys locked up, making the world safe for decent, God-fearing folks.

Forgive my sarcasm. Sure, some of the Fortress' inmates are murderous scum who need to be locked up—permanently—but there are a lot of

political prisoners in there as well, people whose only crime was failing to register with the feds. Friends.

Either way, no one's been able to break out of the Fortress to date. Its walls are reinforced with all the means that science and (I'm told) magic can offer.

The place has been so successful over the years that it's been duplicated in country after country across the world. These days, the place is packed solid, so much so that the feds built New Alcatraz just to hold the overflow.

The exact location of the Fortress is a closely guarded secret. All I can tell you is that it's located somewhere in Nebraska, in the heart of the National Grasslands. I've been out that way before, and even in the places where they've got roads, there's a whole lot of space between towns.

The Bicentennial Battle

You've probably heard this story before, but maybe from a different point of view—say through the government-controlled media. Either way, it's worth repeating, so bear with me.

It was July 4, 1976. The Devastator, along with the latest incarnation of his Dreadnauts, made his last stand on the top of the Sears Tower in downtown Chicago. He just happened to be standing on top of a doomsday bomb as well, and he threatened to set it off unless Superior surrendered to him once and for all.

Of course, Superior wasn't going to go quietly. He brought every alpha in Delta Prime along with him to the Windy City, and they took the fight straight to the Dreadnauts.

Delta Prime cleaned the sides of the Sears Tower with the Dreadnauts, and it wasn't long before Superior confronted the criminal mastermind atop the world's tallest building. Of course, it was then that the Devastator set his bomb off.

Eyewitnesses report that there was a brilliant flash of white light, and then the city of Chicago just disappeared.

That's right. Into nothing.

The Aftermath

That wasn't the end of it, of course, In fact, everything within 25 miles of the Sears Tower just disintegrated. According to the teams of scientists who scoured the area in the months after the disappearance, there was nothing left behind—not even a whole lot of dust.

Airplanes that were above the radius of destruction disappeared too, as did the soil for about half a mile down. The nearby coastal waters of Lake Michigan left with it.

If nature abhors a vacuum, Mother Earth had never seen something so abhorrent. The rest of Lake Michigan rolled into the perfectly round-shaped hole, and the resulting tidal wave wiped out every building within a mile of the shore of what would thereafter be known as Chicago Bay. Floods destroyed everything within another mile or so of that, and the resulting tornadoes from the air sweeping in from all directions extended the radius of destruction even further.

The property damage was incalculable. The loss of life was staggering. Literally millions of people died, and many more were hurt. Since the Devastator disappeared along with everyone else, it seems like we may never know how or why.

The Vanishing

At exactly the moment of the destruction of Chicago, every free alpha in the world vanished. No one realized this at first. There wasn't any kind of announcement about it. The people simply disappeared.

Some of the missing alphas were missed right away, especially those who were busy saving lives when they went missing. The lack of some others wasn't felt for days, particularly if they were in hiding in the first place. Eventually the world put it all together, and the shock rang through the globe like an earthquake.

No one can say how a bomb set off in Chicago could affect people all around the world, but it did. The Devastator was known to be a master of the occult as well as science. Perhaps his doomsday device combined the two in a way that traditional science could never hope to explain.

Most people didn't know how to react. On one hand, they'd finally gotten rid of all those dangerous alphas. On the other hand, all the "good" alphas were gone too, Superior—the mightiest of them all—among them.

The worst part was that only the free alphas disappeared. All those in the maximum-security, delta-only prisons still remained. Apparently the devices that keep the deltas in also kept the effects of the Devastator's bomb out.

There haven't been many alphas cropping up since then either. Deltas still get into the same kinds of crunches as before, but there's no magic "have another chance" card out there anymore.

If you're a delta and it looks like the end is here, well, it probably is. Life's hard like that.

The Delta Wars

With the alphas gone, you might have thought things would get better. You know: fewer deltas, fewer problems. At least with the alphas gone you'd expect to have smaller problems. But that's not really what happened. Actually it was the exact opposite.

You can say lots of things about Superior (fascist pig, tool of the state, whatever), but the man kept the world together. While he was around, no one was going to try anything crazy, like launching a nuclear attack. First of all, he might have been able to stop it before it started. Second, he'd promised to kill the leaders of any country that started a nuclear exchange.

It wasn't an idle threat. Just ask the Germans.

Sure, we had all sorts of little brushfire wars over the years, and sometimes Superior would let nations duke it out as long as American interests weren't threatened. But nothing major.

Hell, he even put an early end to the Korean and Vietnam conflicts.

Without Superior's calming (read: oppressive) influence, all hell broke loose.

Post-Superior Life

In the last 20-odd years, this planet's been ravaged from one end to the other. Deltas of all stripes battle in the streets, and armies of deltas struggle on battlefields across the world.

To see what this means to the average American, all you've got to do is look at any major city. Tops of buildings stand razed off, with new girders stretching toward the sky like bones in a regenerating limb. Windows stand boarded up where they've been shattered by explosions or having the odd delta knocked clean through the building. Monuments lay in ruins. Wrecked cars litter the place.

In short, the world's a mess.

The low point, of course, came back in '89 when there was a total nuclear meltdown in the Russian city of Chernobyl. That was bad enough, but it got worse.

It turned out that a supposedly covert Delta Prime team was seen battling their Soviet counterparts in Crimson Pride just before the disaster. Before the mushroom cloud had settled over the city, the Kremlin had "determined" that Primers were at fault, and they launched a reprisal at Atlanta. Within the hour, the capitol of the South was a smoking crater.

Of course, we couldn't tolerate that, so we blasted back, taking out Kiev. We also destroyed Minsk, and it turn we lost San Francisco before the madness finally came to a glow-in-the-dark kind of end.

Our Ravaged Planet

That's enough history for now, and it should give you a good idea why most people would just as well shoot a delta as give her the time of day. The fact is that—even when we're good people—we're dangerous.

Even if you never actually harm anyone with your own powers, you're a magnet for trouble. Most people killed by deltas weren't intentionally murdered. They were just innocents caught in the crossfire.

Before you became a delta, you probably felt the same about us as everybody else. Best to keep away from us. Far, far away.

Well, kid, there's no running from yourself.

Decisions

Now that you know a bit about your heritage, it's time to decide who you're going to be. It's not as simple as choosing between good and evil.

This is real life.

That means no one can tell you what to do. Okay, they can tell you all right, but there's nothing that says you've got to listen.

That said, listen to this.

You've basically got two choices: register or don't. After that, things become more complicated.

Signing On

You've seen the posters and the ads. Superior leans into the frame and points out at you. In Superior's long-gone tones, the booming voiceover tells you: "It's your duty, and it's the law. Register now!"

The law is pretty clear about this matter, and with Kennedy still running the country by decree, you don't have to worry about a long court trial. If you're a delta (or even a suspected delta—some of us have powers that aren't all that obvious), then you've either got to sign up or rot in jail.

Strictly speaking, you've got to register within seven days of discovering your powers. If you fail to do so, you're eligible to spend the rest of your life rotting in a high-tech cell in either the Fortress or New Alcatraz.

The Pros

The feds have all sorts of reasons why you should register.

It's your duty. Hey, it's the law, right? Never mind that it's one that was handed down by a government that hasn't been elected for over 30 years.

It's for the safety of your neighbors. This way, whenever there's a problem with a delta in the area, people know which house to burn down. They skip right past the regs and knock down your door instead. Your neighbors are safe—as long as they don't live next door to you. Deltas have a notoriously bad effect on property values.

It's to protect yourself. The theory here is that if you're registered and something happens that could be traced back to powers of your kind, you can provide the police with an alibi. Then they can cross you off the list of potential suspects. Or they can just lock you up, and with the courts the way they are these days—few juries, mostly judges appointed by Kennedy and his goons—you have no recourse other than taking matters into your own hands.

It's for your own good. If you register, you're eligible to use your powers openly without fear of being hauled in for that reason alone. If the police need to, they can always find a different reason, but that one's off-limits. Best of all—and this is the one bonus even I can't argue with—you don't have to spend the rest of your life either on the run or waiting for one of your neighbors to turn you in.

The Cons

No privacy. Everyone knows you're a delta. The DRA doesn't keep that information secret. Even if you join up with Delta Prime or Triumph, Inc., (the world's largest, privately owned employer of deltas), your family and friends have to deal with the stigma of being associated with you.

Your movements are tracked. If you even leave town, you've got to tell Delta Prime when you're leaving and where you're going to. It's the only way for people to feel safe around someone like you, it seems.

Everyone you know is in danger. Like I said before, everyone knows you're a delta. This includes every killer, every psycho, and every jackass with a chip on his shoulder that you've ever run across. And with just a little bit of research, they can find out where you live. Even if you're with Delta Prime, they can still find your family and friends

The draft. When you're registered, the government can draft you for any reason it sees fit. This may only be on a mission-by-mission basis, but it can involve long-term deployment too. This is another reason the DP needs to know your location at all times.

No rights. When you sign up, you give your life over to the feds. Kiss the Bill of Rights good-bye. Come to think of it, since Kennedy tore the damn thing up when he declared martial law 36 years ago, it hardly matters.

Employment Opportunities

So if you've signed your life away, what next? As a registered delta, you've got several options: Delta Prime, the Delta Academy, corporate work, freelance, or a normal life.

Delta Prime

Hey, if you're looking to become the tool of an oppressive, fascist government, go ahead and Hancock that dotted line. Compared to other deltas, Primers lead a pretty good life. Uncle Sam feeds you, clothes you, and tells you what to think and do.

You even get a steady paycheck. Sure, it's stable and legal and all that, but don't kid yourself. You are working for the Man.

By "the Man," of course, I mean Kennedy. Is there anyone else?

As part of DP, you can be a covert operative doing all sorts of wetwork (read: killing) and other spy stuff. Or you can be one of the costumed puppets they let run around to "inspire" the regs. Either way, you're sure to find yourself facing off against delta criminals and major threats of all kinds.

I've got to admit that the Primers have done some good over the years. They've managed to save the planet more times than I'd care to count. Of course, each and every one of them had to sell their souls to do it, but that's the price you pay.

Delta Prime's got offices and operatives all over the country, although their main headquarters is on the outskirts of Alexandria, VA, just spitting distance from DC.

The Delta Academy

If you're under 18, Delta Prime doesn't want you. In that case, the feds want you in the Delta Academy instead.

The Academy is located right in downtown Crescent City, in the band of buildings that went up around the rim of the circle where Chicago used to be. In fact, from the top of this diamond-shaped structure, you get a beautiful view of Chicago Bay.

Delta Prime encourages the parents of any registered delta minors to send their kids to the Delta Academy so they can be trained in how to control their powers. There's also the added benefit of the fact that they won't be running around loose in whatever town they were growing up in. Teenagers are dangerous enough with cars. With superpowers, they're a real headache.

Before you start calling me an old crank, let me tell you that I'd never send a kid of mine to the Academy. Sure, it's safer for everyone involved, but it also means the feds can get their hooks into the kid during his formative years.

There's a reason the military doesn't like admitting people after they reach a certain age. The older you get, the more you already know who you are, and the less willing you tend to be to take orders without question.

The same's true with deltas. Get a kid into the Academy when he's 13, and by the time he gets out, he's ready and willing to sign up with Delta Prime for life.

The Academy takes children in at any age, although it's rare to see a delta younger than eight. It does happen, though, and it can be a real problem. Just imagine a superpowered kid in the middle of his "terrible twos." Boggles the mind.

Corporate Work

Just because Delta Prime wants you doesn't mean you want them. Maybe you're more interested in a fat paycheck than in saving the world. If so, there are a number of corporations out there that would be happy to hire someone with your particular skills.

The bidding for deltas can get pretty fierce at times, even surpassing the salaries of top athletes. And why not? A well-known delta's endorsement is worth at least as much as one from nearly any reg, no matter how talented.

By the way, if you're thinking of hiring on with a pro regs sports team, forget it. All reg teams have strict rules against using the talents of any kinds of deltas, whether on the field or off.

However, if you're interested in a real challenge, you can always try your hand at deltaball. Of course, after that incident in LA a few years back, you don't get to play in front of live crowds anymore, but the TV audiences are huge.

The largest employer of deltas in the nation is, of course, Triumph, Inc., the corporation founded by Rex Shepherd after he retired from the hero game back in 1960. As the world's richest man, Shepherd controls a lot of power, and not just because of his money. He's got a number of the most powerful deltas on the planet under contract, and with the kind of checks he's writing, when he says, "Fly!" they ask, "How high?"

There's a catch though. Even if you sign on full-time with Triumph, the feds can still call on you at any point. Shepherd and Kennedy seem to have some kind of deal that keeps this from happening too often. When it does, it usually just means that a Triumph delta gets detached to a DP squad for a certain period of time or the length of a single mission. Then the Triumphant gets to go back to her luxury apartment while the Primers head back to the barracks.

Freelancers

If you like, there's nothing stopping you from going into business for yourself. If you're a real do-gooder, you don't even have to charge for your services. Or you can only bother charging those who can afford it. Some people even have insurance that covers unexpected charges for having their bacon hauled out of the fire, and you

can make a good living off that, as long as you've got yourself an accountant to handle the intricacies of the billing process.

Don't think about trying to defraud the insurance companies though. They've got their own teams of delta investigators, and if they even suspect you've been cheating them out of their premiums, they're happy to punch your one-way ticket to the Fortress. More than one innocent freelancer has found himself in a holding cell this way, so it's a riskier way of earning a living than you might think.

Of course, you can just hire out your services on a job-by-job basis. The real problem here is that if you ever make a real name for yourself, you can expect one of two things to happen—and maybe both. Either a corp like Triumph, Inc., is going to make you an offer you can't refuse, or Delta Prime's going to do the same thing.

As a freelancer, the trick is to keep your profile low enough that you don't attract too much attention, while at the same time you have enough clients that you don't starve.

I've got a lot of respect for freelancers. Anyone who can actually register and still try to maintain her own destiny has a long, crooked road to walk. I prefer life in the shadows.

Some freelancers even try to maintain a secret identity so they can have a normal life. Unfortunately, it's not a secret from the Primers, and they have a habit of not giving a damn about any freelancer's personal life. When they need you, they usually just show up wherever you are and haul your ass out along with them, secret IDs be damned.

A Normal Life

I hope you didn't skip all the way down to this entry first off. If so, go on back and keep reading.

It's a joke.

No registered delta ever gets a normal life.

A Secret Life

Your other option, of course, is to hide your light under the biggest bushel you can find. Literally, there's no one forcing you to run on down to the nearest Delta Prime office and show them why you're not a reg anymore. Of course, you've got to face the consequences if you're caught.

Pros

Why in God's name would you want to be a Defiant? (That's what people are going to call you if you don't register, no matter if you're part of the Defiance Movement or not.) That's a damn good question.

Freedom. Once you register, your life is no longer your own. In a very real way, you're on a federal leash held by Delta Prime. Sometimes the leash is long, and sometimes it's short, but when they want to yank you around, they've got you, and good.

Privacy. Complying with the DRA doesn't mean you just walk into the nearest Delta Prime office and say, "Hey, I'm a delta." You've got to basically bend over and let them creep up inside you with a microscope. Now, they don't have to tell all your neighbors that you've registered, but when the DPs show up on your doorstep to search your house and question your relatives and neighbors, people are going to talk.

Safety. When you lose your privacy, you lose your safety. Say you're a Primer and you foil some madman's plan for poisoning Manhattan's water supply. Then you find the bastard and spank him in front of the entire, couldn't-be-less-grateful city. Do you think your family's safe from him or his friends anymore? Do you think you're going to be able to relax in your own house? As a Primer, you can't control who knows who you are. Sure, some Primers wear masks, but that doesn't mean you can't figure out who they are with a little legwork. Trust me.

Be your own delta. This country was founded on the idea that all men are created equal. That you've got rights to life, liberty, and the pursuit of happiness. When you sign that line, you give all that up. You surrender yourself over to Kennedy's government, one which hasn't seen an election in over 35 years. You become complicit in the country's betrayal of those ideals.

Cons

Now, as much as I believe in being a Defiant, it's not for everyone. No matter how you want to slice it, it's a hard life. Here's why.

A double life. Sure, you think you can keep quiet about who you are, but it's tough. Some delta powers are nearly impossible to hide. Even with those you can conceal, you're going to be tempted to use them from time to time. My only advice here is, if you ever do use your powers, make sure no one sees you. If you can't do that, wear a mask. Gloves help too. In fact, even if you're sure no one can see you, cover up anyhow. You never know. There's a reason all those goofs are running around in costumes out there.

Trust no one. If you don't tell the feds you're a delta, make damn sure you don't tell anyone else. If anyone figures out that you're a delta—or has even good reason to suspect you're a delta—your life, as you know it, is over. Parents have even been known to turn in their children, and vice versa.

Life on the run. Chances are good that eventually somebody's going to figure you out and turn you in. Unless you like your chances in the Fortress, you'd better hit the road. If you're determined to stay in the States, you're pretty much doomed to living life on the run. At the very least, you have to set up a new life somewhere far away and hope no one tumbles to who you are. Leaving the country's always a possibility, but most places aren't much better, and Delta Prime's chase units don't really give a damn about international borders anyhow.

Prison. If you do get caught, you're looking at one hell of a long term in either the Fortress or New Alcatraz. The phrase you'll hear a lot of is "life without parole." Of course, if you're willing to play ball once you've been caught, the government might allow you to join Delta Prime instead, but only if they really need you. And guess who gets the most dangerous assignments from there on out?

Death. If you piss off enough people before you're caught, you might never be lucky enough to see the inside of a prison. Lots of times, the Primers will decide to save the kangaroo courts around here the bother of a trial. The next thing your loved ones know, you were killed "resisting arrest." Even if you manage to get your day in court, if you killed anyone in the course of evading arrest, you're doomed. It's a one-way ticket off this mortal coil for you.

Career Choices

Assuming you make the right choice and piss on the DRA, your life's not over yet—at least until you get caught. For now, you've still got a few options: keep quiet, tell the world, run, get a mask, or join the Defiants. Or you can try some combination of these.

Keeping Quiet

The first thing you need to do is learn to keep your mouth shut. I don't care if you're dying to tell your parents, your spouse, or your best friend. Don't.

First, the more people who know your secret, the harder it is to keep it. It only takes one person to make a single slip of the tongue, and you can kiss your life good-bye.

Second, it puts the person holding your secret at risk too. They've just become accessories to your crime, and lying about it may not do them or you any good. Some courts have people with powers like mine that they haul out to verify testimony in high-profile cases, and if a fugitive delta isn't high-profile, I don't know what is.

Telling the World

Have you actually listened to a word I've said? If you really want to just drop your pants like this, you're on your own.

Okay, there are some deltas like Bill King who have stood up and openly proclaimed who they are, but they're unique cases. You've got to have a certain kind of personality to pull it off, and it doesn't hurt if everyone you've ever cared about is dead. Otherwise, you can count on having them harassed by the government, the press, and any enemies you might make.

Of course, if you don't have anyone you care that much about, you're all set. Just make sure you don't develop any other friendships in the future either, unless you're sure they can handle themselves at least as well as you can.

Just because you've told the world doesn't mean you're off the hook. Now you've got to deal with the fact that everyone who watches the news or reads a newspaper now probably knows what you look like. And when they spot you, they're a lot more likely to call the feds than shake your hand.

In short, unless you've got a death wish, forget about this.

Life on the Run

If you really want to keep your friends and family safe, think about hitting the road. Living on the streets isn't a whole lot of fun, nor is couch surfing—if you've got the kind of friends who don't mind harboring a fugitive for a few nights at a time. However, you really cut down on the chances of someone getting to know you well enough to discover your secret and turn you in.

Chances are that folks back home are going to figure you were killed or ran away or simply dropped off the face of the earth. Sure, this isn't going to make them happy, but it's better than having Delta Prime or the latest incarnation of the Dreadnauts show up on your family's doorstep. If that happens, you can be sure it won't be a social call.

Life on the run's lonely though, and it's not for everyone. When you find yourself getting homesick, you need to remind yourself that if you stuck around your home might have been destroyed. At least this way the rest of your family can enjoy it.

It's not always a choice, of course. Lots of closet deltas get forced into leaving town when their secret is revealed.

The worst part about life on the road is that sooner or later your luck is going to run out. Someone—maybe even someone you don't even know—is going to recognize you or see you using your powers or whatever, and she's going to turn you in. The only thing you can hope then is that you can run far enough or fast enough to get away.

I've been living "on the run" myself now for over nine years. No, it's not a whole lot of fun, but it sure as hell beats rotting away in New Alcatraz.

I've actually met some deltas who've been on the run since the DRA was first handed down, if you can believe that. You'd think that more than 35 years of looking over your shoulder would have an effect on most people, but these folks seem to have weathered it just fine. Of course, the ones who flaked out were captured years ago, right?

Keep thinking that. It makes the long nights a bit easier.

At least it does for me.

Get a Mask

Masks are pretty common in the delta trade. Not everyone wears them, but those that do have their reasons, and they're usually damn good ones.

As I said before, the world can be pretty hard on someone who's a confessed delta, and that's true no matter if you're registered or not. One way to get around this is to wear a mask.

There's a long-standing tradition of masked deltas, going all the way back to the Silver Ghost himself. When you think about it, wearing a mask makes a lot of sense. If no one knows who you really are, you get to go home at the end of the day and put your troubles away. Otherwise, with a little detective work, those troubles can track you home and blast your place to splinters.

The flipside of this is that normal citizens don't always trust people in masks. After all, you can't really tell who's behind the mask, and you can't even be sure if it's the same person from day to day. While protecting your identity and your privacy, a mask also removes a certain amount of accountability.

Wear one or not. It's your choice. If you're a Defiant though, I recommend it.

Joining the Defiance

Despite what the government-censored newshounds might try to shove down your throat, the Defiance isn't really the ruthlessly efficient organization you might be hoping for (assuming you're a closet delta). Other than the *Delta Times* and a few mailing lists, there's no real way to contact a whole bunch of deltas at once.

Remember, we're an oppressed people. As soon as we rear our heads enough to pop up on Delta Prime's radar, we're either outlawed or co-opted directly into the government (or a government-condoned corporate venture).

By DP's definition, joining the Defiance Movement is easy. All you've got to do is develop delta powers and not tell the feds.

In reality, it's both that easy and a whole lot harder.

Sure, we (if I can speak for Defiants everywhere for a moment) take all comers, but there isn't really a "we" to speak of.

There are pockets of more-organized deltas scattered all over the place, but we don't have much in the way of mechanisms to coordinate with each other. Yeah, every now and then some crackpot stands on top of the Empire State Building and declares himself the leader of free deltas everywhere. He'd get his ass laughed out of the country if Delta Prime wasn't so busy thumping on him.

So, hey, you want in, you're in.

Being a Defiant

Welcome to the club, you poor bastard.

Like the song says, "You can check out any time you like, but you can never leave." Once you're a Defiant, you're marked for life. The only hope you have is that if you're ever caught you can manage some kind of plea bargain with your captors. Otherwise, you're looking at life in a high-security cell. And this isn't *The Shawshank Redemption*, and you're not Tim Robbins. You're not getting out.

Being a Delta

It's kind of strange actually. It's as if becoming a delta does something to your head. You hardly ever hear about a delta who swears off using his powers so he can live a quiet life in the suburbs. I'm not saying it doesn't *ever* happen, but some of us just seem to get too heady with our powers to contain ourselves.

Give a man a mask and the power to bounce bullets off his chest, and even the most shy and retiring bookworm can become a glory hound.

For some it comes from a sense of responsibility. You've got these amazing powers, after all, and there are people out there who could use your kind of help. If you're not going to save them, who will? Delta Prime? They're too busy more often than not.

Other deltas just have something to prove—usually to themselves. They act like they just won the superpowers lottery, and they've got to share their winnings with the world.

These are the kind who get on my nerves, even though they've got their place. Usually they change their tune after some other delta (Primer or otherwise) kicks the crap out of them. It's not so fun being a delta when you're laid up in a shed somewhere, hoping you can heal up before anyone finds you.

Still others are a bit more subtle, using their powers to suit their own ends, if and when they're necessary. These are the most dangerous kind, since it's often hard to know just who it is you're dealing with and what she's capable of.

Halos and Horns

Just because you spat on the DRA doesn't mean you're a saint. If you're a Defiant, then by definition you're a criminal. The real question is what kind of criminal you are.

Some of us take to Robin-Hooding, while others simply line their own pockets. Some want to save the world, while others are the people the world needs saving from. Most of the time, you can't tell the two kinds apart, at least on the surface.

Remember what I said before about not being able to trust anyone? Well, that's doubly true with other Defiants. If they tell you they're good people, just misunderstood, take it with a grain of salt.

It's hard to imagine how the regs might "misunderstand" a bank robbery, right?

On the other hand, if someone comes right out and tells you he's bad news, listen to him. Don't try to change him. Just walk the other way. Unless of course he's threatening to hurt someone. Then I'll leave it up to you and your conscience as to what you should do.

There's a whole subsection of deltas who just let the power go to their heads. They think they're above things like laws and human life. They treat the rest of the world like their playground, brothel, and toilet all rolled into one. And woe to anyone who gets in their way.

These are the guys who give the rest of us a bad name. If you're one of them, all I can say is you'd better hope the Primers get to you before the Defiants do. If you're lucky, the Primers will cart you off to jail. The Defiants don't have that option.

A Defiant Life

Now that you're leading a double life or a life on the run—or both—there are some adjustments you're going to have to make.

If You're Not a Good Liar, Learn

Every time you put on a mask, you're living a lie. You're telling the world that this new identity you've created for yourself is not the real you. In fact, you're saying the mask has absolutely nothing to do with the person behind it.

Also, you're going to need to be able to come up with plausible excuses on the fly. Why are you never around when your alter ego is? (Lots of other people aren't around either, sure, but if the question's put to you, you'd better have a good answer.) Where have you been for the last few hours/days/weeks? Where did you get all of those bruises?

Choose Your Friends Carefully

Eventually, the questions are going to catch up with you, and then you're going to have to decide what to do. Can you confide in the questioner? If you can, your life just got a whole lot easier. There's nothing like having someone to back up your stories.

Of course, as soon as you tell your confidant what's going on, you've made her an accomplice to your crime. Think long and hard on that before you break down.

Sometimes it's better if the confidant isn't actually a friend. Defiants have a lot more support out there than you might guess. I've even known of the rare occasion in which a cop or even a Primer has kept a Defiant's secret, for reasons of their own. Of course, you can hardly count on that kind of treatment, but sometimes there's just no other way out.

Choose Your Enemies Carefully Too

Lots of deltas are more defined by who they hate than who they love. When you're bouncing around, trying to make the world safe for humans and deltas alike, always try to figure out whose toes you might be stepping on.

If you're not able to handle getting into a battle with someone like the Wiseguy, walk away while you still can.

In fact, run like hell.

The people you piss off are the people you really need to watch out for. These are the people who are going to spend day and night trying to hunt you down and kill you.

If your friends figure out who you are, they might forgive you. With your enemies, you can forget about it. They're not only not going to forgive you. If you really got them torqued, they're going to come to your hometown and start killing people on the off chance you might know one of the victims.

Either way, it's not going to be pretty. Do yourself a favor and avoid this scene entirely. Keep your mask on.

Delta Prime Is Your Enemy

If you have any doubts, don't. These are the people you want to steer clear of at all costs. You may not have anything against them, but the reverse just isn't true.

It's nothing personal on their part, and that almost makes it worse. It's easy to understand why someone you've pissed off is trying to put an end to your life as you know it. When you're dealing with something as large and relatively indifferent as the federal government though, things sometimes get strange.

For the most part, these guys are just doing their jobs, and if not for a simple twist of fate, you might be working on their side, or they might be on ours. Sure, there's the occasional federally sanctioned psychopath out there—the G-Man leaps to mind—but they're mostly deltas doing what they've got to do, just like you.

That said, you can't expect any mercy from the Primers. It's their job to track you down and bring you in, and they're good at it. When it comes down to you or them, well, I know which side I'd come down on, but it's your choice—and your life.

Contacting Others

This is the worst part about being a Defiant. Finding other Defiants you can trust can be a stone-cold bitch.

You never know about anyone. Most times, two Defiants who meet on the street each do an about-face and do their best to forget their paths nearly crossed.

Sometimes you can find a friend out there, but it's rare. If you do, hold on to her as long as you can. Such people are rarer than diamonds.

Hell, the only saving grace is the internet. Without it, finding and working with other Defiants would be nearly impossible. As it is, it's the best thing going.

The first thing you need to know about is, of course, *The Delta Times*. We're the best source of timely Defiant information in the world, and we're a target because of it.

Delta Prime would love to shut us down, and they've tried more than once. We're strictly outlawed in the US, but fortunately there are nations out there with less-oppressive regimes, and some are beautiful places too.

In fact, more than one nation has granted deltas tax-exempt status in an effort to lure superpowered expatriates within their own borders. They appreciate unregistered help, even if the US doesn't.

Even so, lines on a map aren't much to stop Primers with a real mad-on. We've got ourselves up on several mirror sites around the world, and we shift around from server to server on an almost weekly basis.

Given a chance, I think Kennedy would shut down the entire internet. It's been a thorn in his side since its development in the way that it promotes the free (and anonymous) exchange of ideas. It started out as a government-run means of transmitting data years back, and now it's grown into the most important part of the global economy's infrastructure.

Even if Kennedy wants to, there's no putting that genie back in the bottle.

Anyhow, there are a number of Defiance mailing lists out there too. Most of these are divided up according to who's on the list and why they need to know each other. There are a couple general interest ones, and if you go back to the home page, you can sign up for one right there.

The Liberators, for instance, have a famous list that's been cracked by DP more than once. It's by invite only, and don't bother asking me how to join. I'm not on it either.

One last bit of advice about the internet. It's impossible to tell who's going to read what you write on the internet, so be careful out there. By the same token, try to be polite to the people you meet. You never know which of them can blow your brain to pieces just as easy as looking at you.

Our Mission

When I say "our," in one sense I mean "my," but in another way I'm talking about Defiants everywhere. Your take on this whole issue might differ from mine, and that's fine. This is how I see things though. Take it as you will.

Our mission is to restore democracy to America. Nothing less will do.

By that, I mean we need to rescind the state of martial law which has strangled the people of this country for the past 35-plus years. We need to repeal the Delta Registration Act or—better yet—have it struck down by the Supreme Court as being completely unconstitutional. We need to kick Kennedy's withered ass out of office and have free elections to put a government of the people, by the people, and for the people back in office.

There are those who advocate using only peaceful means to accomplish this, but most Defiants think we're long past that point. It's up to you to figure out what side you're on.

Check out the Declaration of Independence for a clue on how I feel about the whole thing. "There comes a time in the course of human events," wrote Jefferson, and I think that time has come again.

That time is now.

A Challenge

No matter which side of this debate you come down on—even if you're a Primer lurking around this site—get involved in the discourse. As a thinking human being (assuming you're not a Primer), it's your duty.

The greatest power of the web is the free exchange of ideas. If Kennedy has his way, he'll figure out a way to take that away from us somehow, so make use of it while you still can.

After all, when the time for words is over, with what are we left?

See you in the future.

REGISTER NOW

Chapter One: What You Need to Know

Welcome to *Brave New World*, a roleplaying game set in a modern-day America in which the history is not our own—which you should have figured out by now if you've read this far.

This Is a Roleplaying Game

In *Brave New World*, one person known as the Guide gathers together a bunch of players to create a story or an adventure.

As a player, you play the role of a *Brave New World* hero you come up with. (That's why it's called "roleplaying," Sherlock.) We'll get to how you create a character in a moment.

Of course, having a hero without a story means you're all dressed up with no place to go. After all, what's a hero without a plot to unravel?

That's where the Guide comes in.

The Guide's job is to come up with a story for the heroes to interact with. This means coming up with a plot, some settings, and all the other characters the heroes might encounters, anyone from earthshaking villains to grifters on the street.

We could go on at length about the philosophical ramifications of roleplaying games and the wonderful kinds of vicarious experiences they can provide for those who really invest themselves in their heroes, but that's all a load of crap—sorry: sophistry.

It's a game, and it's all about fun.

So let's figure out how this thing works.

The Gist of It

You've roleplayed before. Anytime you made a gun out of your hand and chased your buddies around the yard, going "Bang! Bang!", you were actually roleplaying. You took on the role of someone with a gun who was going to take down his foes, and so did your friends.

The problem with those kinds of games is sometimes when you shot someone, she didn't always fall down

like she was supposed to. Sometimes she just stood there and shouted, "You missed!"

This usually led to an argument that often fell into a vicious circle of "Did not!" and "Did too!", which quickly took all the fun out of the whole thing. Hey, you're there to pretend, not bicker with your little sister, right?

Okay, you're a bit older now, and we've got some ways for you to get around that frustration and keep the make-believe going. They're called rules, and that's what this part of the book's all about.

Now, instead of pointing your finger at someone and hoping she falls down when you shout "Bang!", you tell the Guide, "I'm going to blast down that Dreadnaut with my lightning bolts!" (Of course, you're not actually blasting anyone. You're just speaking in your hero's voice—"in character," so to speak.)

The Guide guesstimates about how hard he thinks it is for you to hit the Dreadnaut with your bolt, and he sets a number (called a Target Number) and hands you some dice. You roll the dice, and if you get that number or higher, you blast the Dreadnaut into next week. No arguing about it.

The next question, of course, is how do you know how many dice to roll? After all, just how powerful is that lightning bolt? And if someone hits your hero, just how bad is it going to be?

To answer all that, we've got to set your hero up with a set of statistics that tell us a bit more about who he is. Since he's a make-believe hero, that's the best way to get to know him and to keep track of him, to make sure he's the same kind of character this week as he was last week.

After all, it's only fair.

What You Need to Play

To play *Brave New World*, you only need a few things.

1) This book.
2) A pencil.
3) A fistful of dice.
4) Some players.
5) A wild imagination.

Let's go through these one by one.

This Book

Brave New World is a setting for a roleplaying game, but it's more than that. It's an idea that can take many forms. It can be a comic book, a TV show, a set of action figures, a card game, a miniatures battle game, a movie, a short story, a novel. It could be made into just about any form of entertainment.

Of course, right now we're talking about the roleplaying game, and for that, you need this book.

How to Use this Book

For the most part, you use it just like any other book. You read it from one end to the other. If you're a player though, you should stop reading after Chapter Ten. The rest of the book makes up the Guide's Handbook, which is off limits to players.

If you're the Guide, then you get to read this book cover to cover. Since you're the heroes' eyes and ears into *Brave New World*, we're not holding anything back from you. Well, nothing that would stop you from running a good game, at least.

As a rulebook, *Brave New World*'s not just for reading though. It's also a reference book. When you've got a question about exactly how something

works in the game, you need to be able to find the relevant rules right away. To that end, we've given you a good table of contents in the front of this book. There's also an extensive index in the back.

Brave New Secrets

Brave New World isn't a snapshot frozen in a moment in time. The story behind it all begins centuries, even millennia ago, and it continues to unfold every day. There are some secrets that we're holding close to our collective chest for now, but we've sprinkled clues to some of them throughout this book.

As the *Brave New World* story develops, we'll reveal more and more about what's going on behind the scenes. This will all culminate in a brand-new roleplaying game in which you can explore the tangential ramifications. All we can tell you right now is the title: *Crossroads*.

The Road Goes Ever On

As we've implied, this book you're holding isn't the end of the *Brave New World* story. It's just the beginning.

This rulebook has everything in it that you need to know to play the game, but the story is bigger than we could cram into a single book.

For a good chunk of the rest of the saga, check out *Ravaged Planet*, the *Brave New World* player's guide. Then keep your eye out for more *Brave New World* books and products from Pinnacle Entertainment Group on a regular basis.

Finding Our Products

The best place to find our products is your local game store. Not only should they have our complete line of books and accessories, but they can help you out with any questions you might have about our game, or about games in general. They can also tell you what's going to be coming out soon.

Some stores even have game clubs so they can introduce you to other people interested in playing the kinds of games you like. If you're lucky, we might even have one of our team of Bounty Hunters running a demonstration of *Brave New World* or one of our other games in the store. We're always happy to teach any of our games to anyone bold enough to step up to the gaming table.

If you don't have a game store in your area, you can always contact us directly. Check the front of the book for all the current information.

If you've got access to the internet, stop by **www.peginc.com**. That's where we post regular updates to our games, including new rules, characters, and gadgets, rules corrections, and even the occasional adventure. And it's all absolutely free.

At our website, you can also sign up for mailing lists so you can discuss your favorite games with other fans and get the latest rumors about where we're headed. Plus, there's even a secure online store where you can order your Pinnacle products directly from the source.

Pencils

When you create a hero to play in your *Brave New World* game, you determine a lot of things about him. These range from the color of his hair to how fast he can run circles around gun-toting gangers. When you get all of these things figured out, you write them down on a hero sheet.

There's a sample sheet on page 58 that shows you how to do all this, and there's a blank sheet on page 64 too, that you can photocopy to make blank sheets for your own use. Don't worry about all that right now. We'll get to it all in good time.

We suggest you use a pencil to fill in all the details on the sheet. Some things on the sheet can change from time to time, and if you use a pencil, you can just erase the old details and write in the new ones.

If you're sure your hero's never going to change, then go ahead and use a pen. Just let us tell you one thing: You're wrong.

Your hero's going to get punched, shot at, beat up, and generally kicked around, probably on a regular basis. That's a hero's lot in life.

And when you're done with all of that, hopefully your hero will have learned something. To reflect how he can apply that to new situations, he can improve his abilities in the game, changing himself for the better. See?

The Dice

Let's talk about the dice for a moment.

You know what dice are. They're the little, plastic cubes with pips or numbers on their sides. People use them in casinos and on dining room tables around the world. You've probably got a boatload of them in your house already, stashed inside an old copy of *Monopoly* or *Yatzhee* or any of the rest of those boardgames rotting in a stack in a closet.

Some other roleplaying games use all sorts of strange-looking dice that come in lots of different shapes. *Brave New World* doesn't bother with those. We stick with the old standard: the six-sided cube.

When we say you're going to need a fistful of dice, we're not kidding. The more you have around the better. You can get by with a single die if you have to, but we recommend you have at least 10 dice close at hand.

Dice Codes

Most of the time when the Guide tells you to roll some dice, he says something like, "Roll five dice and add +4 to that." That's just fine, but it's a pain to read something like that in a book every time it comes up.

Instead, we use a code that's pretty much standard for roleplaying games. It works like this.

When we say, "Roll 5d6," we mean, "Roll five six-sided (standard) dice." Simple enough, right? Just count up the sides on one of those cubes, and you'll see we're dead on.

Sometimes you might see, "Roll 5d6+4." That means, "Roll five dice and add +4 to your result." There's really nothing to it.

Reading the Dice

In *Brave New World*, we read the dice in a particular way that you might not be used to. In lots of games, you roll a bunch of dice and add all those results up together to get a final total. Not so in *Brave New World*.

Instead, you roll all the dice and then pick the highest number you get. That's your result.

You might say to yourself that, with that kind of a method of dice reading, a 6 is the highest result you can get. After all, that's the highest you can roll on a single die, right?

It's not so. Dice rolls in *Brave New World* are what we call "open-ended." This means that if you roll a 6 on any of your dice—the highest you can get on a regular, six-sided die—you can pick up that die, roll it again, and add it to what you've already got. If you get another 6, you can roll the die again and keep going until you don't roll another 6.

The best part is that if you get more than one 6 at a time, you can pick up each of those dice and reroll them all. Keep track of each of those open-ended rolls separately. When you're done rolling, the single die with the highest open-ended roll gives you your final result.

Example: *The Guide asks Marty to roll 5d6+4. Marty rolls five dice, and he gets 1, 3, 4, 6, and 6. So far, his highest result is a 6. He picks up the two 6s and rolls them again, getting a 4 and another 6. His highest result is now 12.*

He picks up the 6 and rolls it again, getting a 4. His final highest die number is (6+6+4=) 16. To that he adds the +4, giving him a final total of (16+4=) 20.

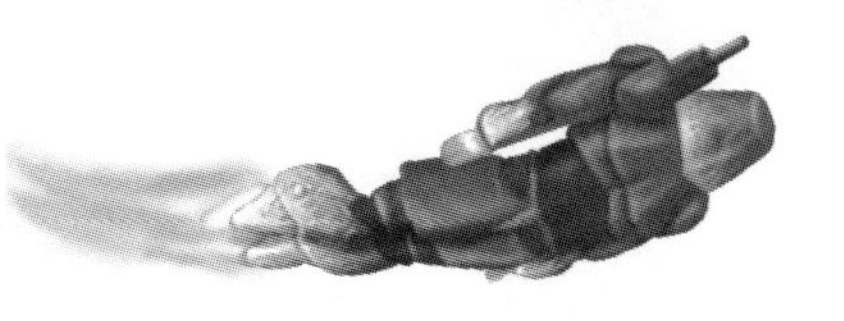

The Players

Roleplaying games are social activities. They're meant to be played with a group of people sitting in a room together, usually around a table. To do that, you've got to fill the game with warm bodies.

You need at least two people to play: the Guide and one player. After that, you can add other people as you like.

Most Guides find it's easiest to work with three to six players. If you're new to roleplaying games, start with a small group and work your way up. Every player demands a certain amount of attention during a game, and it's always easier to juggle fewer people.

Games with more than six players can be more challenging than many Guides care to bother with. If you want to give a bigger group a shot, though, more power to you. Just be sure you know what you're doing, or your group may start shrinking all by itself, as players who don't feel like they're getting enough attention leave.

A Wild Imagination

Roleplaying is also a creative endeavor. It's playtime, pal, and you've got to be ready to open up the box in your head and let all the toys spill out.

If you're a player, you've got to have an idea about what you want your hero to be like and what he wants to do in the game world. What are his dreams and goals? Who does he care about? Who wants him dead?

Coming up with all this stuff requires a healthy imagination, but don't worry too much about it. We've got lots of rules and examples to get you set on the right path to making the coolest *Brave New World* hero around.

Guiding

If you're the Guide, you've bitten off a big chunk, baby. Be sure to chew thoroughly before you swallow.

Guiding can be the most rewarding position in the game, but it's also the most challenging. The players each only have to worry about their own single hero. You've got to handle a cast of thousands.

The upside to this is that you don't have to put as much work into each extra (that's what we call the characters the Guide controls) as the players do into their heroes. If the heroes stop a mugging on the street, you don't really need to know the life history of the mugger and his victim. All you need are a few salient details.

We'll tell you all about this in Chapter Eleven: Guiding the Game, plus we give you a few more ways to make your life easier. We appreciate what you're doing, after all.

The Guide can make or break the game. It's up to you to make sure everyone else is having fun. Preparing for this can suck up a lot of your time, but we're ready to help you out there too. Look for *Power Shield,* the *Brave New World* Guide's kit. It comes complete with a cardboard screen and a 48-page adventure to get your game rolling.

The screen's perfect for hiding all of your Guide-only secrets behind. There are lots of things in the game that the players don't need to know right away. Their heroes will learn about them in the course of playing the game. After all, figuring things out is part of the fun.

The screen's also got all sorts of vital game information printed on it for easy reference. This makes Guiding easier for you, since you don't have to be flipping through this book every time you need to know how much damage a certain weapon does, for instance.

The adventure's not only a great way to launch a *Brave New World* series of adventures. It's also a perfect example of how a game should work. If after reading this book you're still unclear on how to bring an adventure to life, be sure to pick up *Power Shield* too.

Guide as Storyteller

A roleplaying game's got two elements to it, and the Guide has to balance them carefully. It's both "roleplaying" and a "game."

For the roleplaying side of things, the Guide's got to come up with a story that engages the players and makes the game exciting and fun. This can be difficult, and it requires a tremendous amount of imagination. We've got some hints to help you out with this in Chapter Eleven.

Guide as Judge

The Guide doesn't just guide the story along. She also serves as a referee for any questions that come up in the game. Her biggest task here is to judge how difficult it is for the characters to perform actions, setting the Target Numbers for their action rolls.

There's a lot more to it than that though. A roleplaying game is meant to model life—or a strange version of it, at least. There's no way that a set of rules could possibly cover every detail that's going to crop up in the course of the game.

That's where the Guide comes in. It's her job to fill in the gaps as best she can, making decisions on the fly to resolve any kind of situation her player's might present her with.

For this to work, the players must make a tacit agreement to abide by the Guide's judgment. Let's make this absolutely clear:

In matters of the game, the Guide's word is law.

Chapter Two: What It Takes to Be a Hero

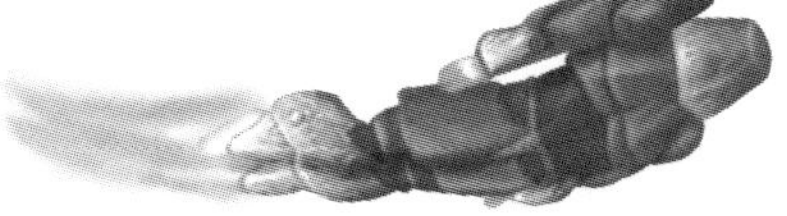

Chapter Two: What It Takes to Be a Hero

Here's where we get down to it: how to make a delta of your own. Of course, if you want to you could just play a reg like a reporter or a street cop, but that's not really the point here.

Brave New World is about having powers that treat the laws of physics like a puppy treats a brand-new pair of shoes. It's about having powers "far beyond those of mortal men" and then dealing with how that makes you different from most everyone else.

It's about power and how it's used. Does it corrupt you, or do you use it responsibly? To struggle with those questions, your hero needs powers.

The Hero Sheet

You might know what kind of hero you want to play. Maybe he's a cop during the day, but at night he wears a mask and bounces bullets off his chest. He fights crime as a Defiant because there are criminals beyond his reach as a cop, and he doesn't want to join Delta Prime and be forced to leave his family.

That's great, but you need to be able to define the hero a bit more solidly. Just how big a bullet can he really bounce of his chest? And how good of a detective is he?

If you were back on the playground, you could just say, "He's the greatest," but that's not much fun for a character, is it? If the hero's the next best thing to God, there aren't going to be a whole lot of challenges for him, and challenge is the heart of adventure.

To help you really pin down who your hero is in terms that mean something in the game, you need to describe him with a set of numbers that rank him against everyone else in the game. Collectively, these vital statistics are called the hero's profile.

Take a look at the hero sheet on the next page for an example of what we're talking about. A lot of the details you can fill in on your own without any help from us: the player's name (that's you, pal), the hero's name, code name, origin story, and so on. Then there's the rest of it.

The Profile

A hero is defined by four different kinds of statistics: traits, skills, quirks, and powers.

Traits

Every character in the game has four basic traits: Smarts, Speed, Spirit, and Strength. These define the hero in broad strokes. They might seem pretty self-explanatory, but let's go over them anyhow.

Smarts tells you how brainy your hero is. This is his ability to learn things quickly, to call on knowledge he's got, and to figure intellectual things out all by himself.

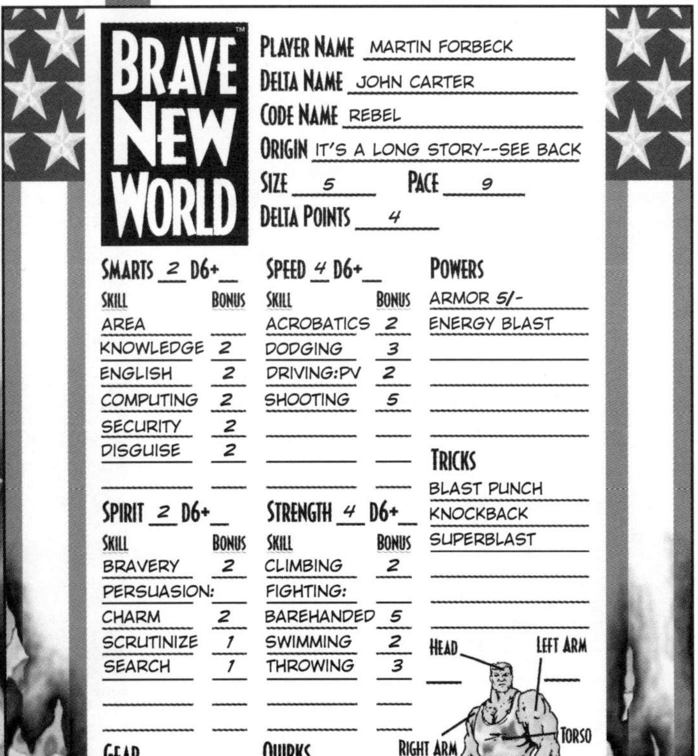

Brave New World™

Player Name MARTIN FORBECK
Delta Name JOHN CARTER
Code Name REBEL
Origin IT'S A LONG STORY--SEE BACK
Size 5 Pace 9
Delta Points 4

Smarts 2 D6+		Speed 4 D6+		Powers
Skill	Bonus	Skill	Bonus	ARMOR 5/-
AREA		ACROBATICS	2	ENERGY BLAST
KNOWLEDGE	2	DODGING	3	
ENGLISH	2	DRIVING:PV	2	
COMPUTING	2	SHOOTING	5	
SECURITY	2			
DISGUISE	2			Tricks
				BLAST PUNCH

Spirit 2 D6+		Strength 4 D6+		
Skill	Bonus	Skill	Bonus	KNOCKBACK
BRAVERY	2	CLIMBING	2	SUPERBLAST
PERSUASION:		FIGHTING:		
CHARM	2	BAREHANDED	5	
SCRUTINIZE	1	SWIMMING	2	
SEARCH	1	THROWING	3	

Gear	Quirks
BINOCULARS	DELTA, SECRET IDENTITY,
CELL PHONE	UNREGISTERED, BEAUTIFUL,
KEVLAR VEST	DESTINED FOR GREATNESS,
HELMET	IMPULSIVE, ALERT, BRAVE,
HARLEY-DAVIDSON	CODE OF HONOR, LOYAL,
	SKEPTICAL

Head
Left Arm
Right Arm
Torso
Right Leg
Left Leg

Speed tells you just how fast your hero is. It also defines how well he can dodge attacks, fire a weapon, and drive a car.

Spirit tells you how together your hero is. This says things about how brave he is and how good he is at influencing other people.

Strength tells you how powerful your hero is, physically speaking. It's his ability to lift things, toss things, and hurt things.

Notice that there are two columns for numbers next to each trait: dice and bonus. Every character has a number in the dice column, but only exceptional heroes get anything listed in the bonus column.

Each trait is defined by a number in the dice column, starting at 1 and going on up. The bigger the number, the better your hero is in that particular trait. When the hero is called upon to use the trait, he rolls that number of dice.

The average number in each trait is 2, and the normal human maximum is 5, but deltas bust through that limit all the time. That means the person on the street has a 2 in each trait, while an Olympic athlete might have a *Strength* or *Speed* of 5.

If the hero's got a number listed in the bonus column, you just add that to the number you get after he rolls his trait dice.

To help you know when we're talking about an actual trait, all trait names are Capitalized and listed in *italics*.

Diceless Traits

There are also two traits that stand apart from the others since you don't roll dice when they come into play. These are *Pace* and *Size*.

Pace tells you how far your hero can move in a round. This is figured by adding the number of the hero's *Speed* dice to any flat *Speed* bonus he's got, plus +5. That's how many inches a figure of the hero can move across a tabletop in a single round. (If you're not using miniatures, a tabletop inch translates to roughly two yards.)

So a hero with a *Speed* of 4 has a *Pace* of (4+5=) 9. Simple.

Size describes how big your hero is relative to other people. The bigger a person is, the easier he is to hit, but the harder he is to hurt. Most people have a *Size* of 5.

Skills

Traits give you an idea of a hero's raw abilities, but abilities aren't worth much if you don't know how to do anything with them. That's where skills come in.

Each trait has a number of different skills listed under it, things like *shooting, language,* and *bravery.* Each skill then has a bonus number listed next to it.

When your hero wants to use a skill, you gather together all the dice for the trait it's under, and roll them. Then you add any trait or skill bonuses to the die roll. That total is your final result.

Each of the skills is described in full in Chapter Four.

Subskills

Some skills are divided into subskills. *Fighting*, for instance, is broken down into *barehanded, blade,* and *club.* Each of these subskills is considered a separate skill. They are not related in any way other than name. The groupings are more for convenience than anything else.

Trait Rolls

Some situations call for a hero to make a raw trait roll. In this case, roll the dice for that trait normally, but don't add any skill bonuses, just the trait bonus.

Unskilled Rolls

If the hero doesn't have the skill he needs for a certain action roll, he can still give it the old college try. He just needs to get an extra success for the action to work. In other words, his first success—assuming he gets one—doesn't even count. It's the second success that gets things going.

Quirks

No one's just a collection of numbers, not even a *Brave New World* hero. Everyone's got something about her that makes her unique. These can be good things or even bad things. Collectively, they're called quirks.

Each of the quirks are described in full in Chapter Five.

Powers

Assuming the hero's a delta, he's got superpowers of some sort. These are listed here. In *Brave New World*, the powers all come in premade packages to make it easier for you to create a balanced hero. See Chapter Eight for these.

Tricks

Tricks are special things your hero knows how to do. She can activate these with extra successes. General tricks anyone can learn are covered in Chapter Seven, while Chapter Eight has some power-specific tricks.

Creating a Hero

Now that you know how a hero sheet works, let's get to slapping a delta together for you.

There are two ways to create your own hero. Going from the simplest to the most challenging, they are:

1) Use an archetype.
2) Make one from scratch.

The Archetypes

On pages 65–74, we've listed a number of typical kinds of heroes you might find in *Brave New World*. These deltas come complete with all the traits, skills, and powers they need, and they're ready to play. All you've got to do is copy their statistics down on a blank hero sheet—you can photocopy the one in this book—and fill in all the missing details like name, origin story, and so on.

If this is your first time playing in a roleplaying game, an archetype is really the way to go. All the work's been done for you.

Go ahead and look over the archetypes and pick one you like. Don't worry about it if you don't understand what all the skills and powers mean. We'll get to that in good time.

To make an archetype your own hero—as opposed to a generic, cookie-cutter character—you still want to spend some time thinking about who your hero is, how he got his powers, and why he's decided to join the Defiance Movement.

Filling in all the empty spaces on the hero sheet is a good start, but you should feel free to add as much more as you like. Use the back of your photocopied sheet and go wild.

Creating Your Hero from Scratch

Making a hero from scratch is more challenging than using an archetype, but it's also more rewarding. If you're not comfortable with taking on such a task quite yet, don't sweat it. Try playing the game with an archetype or a packaged hero first, and then come back here when you're ready to try it all again.

To create a hero from scratch, just follow these simple steps:

1) Assign your hero's traits.
2) Pick your hero's skills.
3) Pick your hero's quirks.
4) Pick your hero's powers.
5) Pick your hero's tricks.
6) Buy your hero's gear.

Assigning Traits

Your hero has four different traits—*Smarts, Speed, Spirit,* and *Strength*—and you need to assign numbers to each of these. You have 12 Trait Points to divide up among these traits.

That's enough for your hero to have 3 points in each trait, just above the average. These are heroes we're talking about, after all, and even without their powers they're a cut above normal.

If you want to, you can put more points into any trait you like, but they've got to come from somewhere else, so your other traits will suffer.

The most points a hero can have in any trait when starting out is 5, and the least he can have is 1. It's possible to improve your traits as time passes in the game, but for now you should focus on the traits that are most important to your hero.

Picking Skills

Each trait has certain skills that are associated with it. For every point you have in that trait, you get 3 Skill Points to purchase skill bonuses with. See Chapter Four for a full list of skills and which traits they each go with. These points must be spent on skills.

Every point you spend on a skill gives you a +1 bonus with that skill. When creating a hero, none of your skills can have a bonus of higher than +5. You can improve this later though.

Picking Quirks

Each quirk has a number listed next to it that's either positive or negative. Positive quirks (like *rich*) cost you that many skill points, while negative quirks (like *poor*) give you extra skill points. When you take a negative quirk, you can add those points to your skills or pick up a positive quirk.

Up to a point, taking negative quirks can add some realism and even heroism to your character. Overcoming these kinds of obstacles can add some meaning to your hero's struggles.

You can't take more than 10 points of negative quirks. It's good to have some quirks to surmount, but overdoing it can turn the game on its ear.

Picking a Power Package

This is where we finally get into the stuff that separates your hero from the people on the street: superpowers.

Superpowers can sometimes be complicated, so we don't just provide you with a list of possible powers and let you mix and match as you like. Instead, we provide you with power packages that knit your hero's powers together into a seamless whole.

Your hero gets to choose a single power package from those listed in Chapter Eight. This package cannot be added to or changed later, so choose carefully.

Picking Tricks

Each hero gets three tricks to start out with. You can choose these from the general list in Chapter Seven or pick ones from your hero's power package in Chapter Eight.

Buying Gear

Unless your hero's *rich* or *poor*, she gets $1,000 to buy gear with. (Otherwise she gets some more or a lot less.) We're talking weapons, armor, cars, and the like here. For a list of available gear, turn to Chapter Nine.

Hero Creation Quick Reference

Creating a Hero

Creating a hero's simple, but to make it easier, we've collected all the information you need on these two pages. See the appropriate chapters for all the details on everything here.

1. Assign Traits

You've got 12 trait points to distribute among four traits: *Smarts, Speed, Spirit,* and *Strength*. You can't start with more than 5 points or less than 1 point in any trait.

Figure your diceless traits here too.

Quirks or powers aside, heroes are *Size* 5.

The hero's *Pace* is his *Speed*+5, in inches.

Again, quirks or powers aside, heroes start with 3 Delta Points.

2. Pick Skills

For each point your hero's got in a trait, he gets 3 points worth of skills under that trait. You can start with up to 5 points in a skill.

Free Skills

Area knowledge: hometown	2
Climbing	1
Language: native	2
Scrutinize	1
Search	1

Recommended Skills

Bravery
Fighting: barehanded
Perception
Persuasion: bluff
Stealth

Smarts Skills

Academia: American culture, comparative literature, history, occult
Artillery
Area knowledge: City, county, state, region, country
Bureaucratics
Computing
Criminology
Demolition
Disguise
Etiquette
Forgery
Gambling
Language: Any language
Medicine
Navigation
Profession: Accounting, administration, architecture, business, clergy, finance, law, engineering
Science: Biology, chemistry, geology, mathematics, physics
Security
Survival: City, desert, forest, mountain
Tactics
Tinkering
Weaponsmith

Speed Skills

Acrobatics
Archery
Boating: Speedboat, sailboat
Dodging
Driving; Personal vehicle, commercial vehicle
Escaping
Flying
Lockpicking: Electronic, mechanical
Martial arts: Barehanded, club, blade
Piloting: Airplane, helicopter
Quick draw
Riding
Sleight of hand
Shooting
Speed-load
Stealth
Trade: Carpenter, electrician, machine operator, mechanic, plumber

Spirit Skills

Arts: Illustrating, music composition, painting, sculpting, writing
Bravery
Faith
Leadership
Mimic
Perception
Performing: Acting, public speaking, music, singing, storytelling
Persuasion: Bluff, charm, interrogation, intimidation, seduction, taunt
Scrounging
Scrutinize
Search
Shadowing
Streetwise
Tracking

Strength Skills

Climbing
Fighting: Barehanded, club, blade
Running
Sport: Baseball, basketball, deltaball, football, hockey, soccer
Swimming
Throwing

3. Pick Quirks

You can choose up to –10 points of negative quirks. You can use these points to buy positive quirks or more skills.

Status Quirks

Delta or reg
Public identity or secret identity
Registered or unregistered

Hero Creation Quick Reference

Positive Quirks

Alert	+3
Ambidextrous	+5
Authority	+1 to +5
Beautiful	+1
Brave	+1
Brawny	+3
Contact	+1 to +5
Dark secret	+1 to +5
Destined for greatness	+5
Double-jointed	+1
Famous	+2
Favor owed	+1
Gear	+1 to +5
Iron jaw	+3
Light sleeper	+1
Lucky	+3
Ordained	+1
Patron	+2 to +5
Photographic memory	+5
Rich	+1 to +5
Self-confident	+2
Sense of direction	+1
Sense of time	+1
Sharp ears	+1
Sharp eyes	+1
Sidekick	+5
Tough	+2
Veteran	±0
Voice	+1
Wise	+3

Negative Quirks

Absentminded	–3
Addiction	–1/–3
Arrogant	–3
Bad habit	–1 to –3
Bigot	–1 to –3
Bloodthirsty	–2
Cautious	–3
Cheap	–2
Clumsy	–3
Code of honor	–3
Coward	–3
Crazy	–1 to –5
Curious	–3
Dark secret	–1 to –5
Death wish	–5
Dependent	–1 to –5
Disabled	–3/–5
Duty	–1 to –5
Enemy	–1 to –5
Frail	–3
Glass jaw	–3
Greedy	–2
Gullible	–2
Heavy sleeper	–1
Hefty	–2/–3
Heroic	–5
Honest	–3
Illness	–1/–3/–5
Illiterate	–3
Impulsive	–3
Loyal	–3
Lusty	–1
Mean	–2
Mute	–3
Obligation	–1/–3
Obvious	–3/–5
Old	–3
Pacifist	–3/–5
Poor	–3
Poor ears	–2/–4
Poor eyes	–1/–3/–5
Savage	–3
Self-righteous	–2
Skeptical	–1
Slow	–2
Slight	–5
Snobby	–1
Softhearted	–1
Stubborn	–2
Stutter	–2
Superstitious	–2
Squeamish	–2
Temper	–2
Ugly	–2
Unlucky	–5
Vengeful	–2
Vow	–1 to –5
Wanted	–5
Young	–1

4. Pick a Power Package

Pick a single power package.

The Packages

Bouncer
Bargainer
Blaster
Flyer
Gadgeteer
Goliath
Gunner
Healer
Scrapper
Speedster

5. Pick Tricks

Each hero then gets three free tricks from either the general list or his power package.

General Tricks

Brilliant idea
Bull's eye
Entangling
Extra damage
Fast learner
First move
Grapple
Knockback
Knockdown
Know the Streets
Make an impression
The natural
New friend
On a roll
Pumped up
Ricochet

Bouncer

Bounce attack
Flip-toss

Bargainer

Jinx
Make it look easy

Blaster

Blast punch
Superblast

Flyer

Burst of speed
Flying dodge

Gadgeteer

Fine tuning
Smack it

Goliath

Rock your world
Superjump

Gunner

Mercy
Pierce armor

Healer

Healing disease
Healing poison

Scrapper

Fast healer
Dirty fighting

Speedster

Afterimages
Burst of speed

6. Select Gear

Unless the hero's *rich* or *poor*, he's got $1,000 to spend on gear. See the lists on pages 188–189 for prices.

BRAVE NEW WORLD™

PLAYER NAME ______________________

DELTA NAME ______________________

CODE NAME ______________________

ORIGIN ______________________

SIZE ________ PACE ________

DELTA POINTS ________

SMARTS ___ D6+__

SKILL	BONUS

SPEED ___ D6+__

SKILL	BONUS

SPIRIT ___ D6+__

SKILL	BONUS

STRENGTH ___ D6+__

SKILL	BONUS

POWERS

TRICKS

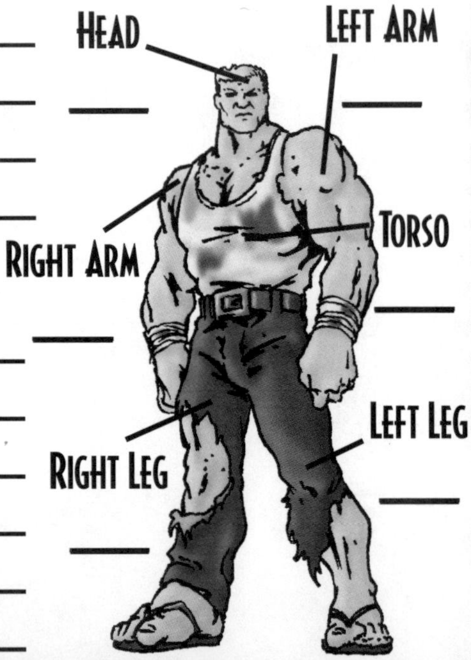

GEAR

QUIRKS

BARGAINER

PROFILE

Smarts: 3d6
Academia: occult 3, area knowledge: Crescent City 2, criminology 4, gambling 2, language: English 2

Speed: 4d6
Driving: personal vehicle 1, escaping 3, lockpicking: mechanical 2, martial arts: barehanded 2, shooting 1, sleight of hand 3

Spirit: 3d6
Bravery 2, perception 2, performing: public speaking 2, persuasion: bluff 1, persuasion: charm 2, scrutinize 1, search 1

Strength: 2d6
Climbing 2, running 1, swimming 2, throwing 2

Size: 5

Pace: 9

Delta Points: 3

Quirks: Arrogant –3, code of honor –3, delta ±0, double-jointed +1, famous +2, heroic –3, unregistered ±0, rich +2, secret identity ±0, self-confident +2, skeptical –1, wise +3

Powers:
Bargaining: Can use totems.

Tricks: Brilliant idea, jinx, make it look easy

Gear: Handheld computer with cell modem, Colt Agent and 20 rounds of ammo, Derringer and four rounds of ammo, one heck of a wardrobe, a mimic totem, a convertible Cadillac (financed) and $2,000.

PERSONALITY

Welcome, my friends. Come in, come in. Whatever it is you're worried about, I'm sure I can help.

I know why you've come to me. You have a problem that only someone with my particular, ahem, talents can resolve.

Of course, I'm right. I always am. You "know a Delta" who wants to join the Defiance? I'm afraid I can't help you there, my friend. I'm not terribly familiar with this organization of which you speak.

Now that you mention it, though, I might know someone who might know someone who can help. If you'll just give me a chance to make a few phone calls, I could possibly put you in touch with her.

Come back after my show tonight. I'll have tickets waiting for you at the will-call window. By then, I should know more. Until then, please be careful.

Quote: Voila!

Blaster

Profile

Smarts: 3d6
Area knowledge: Crescent City 2, computing 2, disguise 1, language: English 2, security 3

Speed: 4d6
Dodging 2, driving: personal vehicle 1, martial arts: barehanded 2, martial arts: blade 1, shooting 4, stealth 2

Spirit: 3d6
Bravery 1, perception 2, persuasion: charm 2, scrutinize 2, search 3, shadowing 1

Strength: 2d6
Climbing 2, running 1, swimming 2, throwing 2

Size: 5

Pace: 9

Delta Points: 3

Quirks: Beautiful +1, curious –3, delta ±0, dependent –2: younger sister, iron jaw +3, rich +3, secret identity ±0, self-confident +2, sharp eyes +1, unregistered ±0, wanted –5

Powers:
Armor: 5/—
Energy Blast

Tricks: Blast punch, the natural, superblast

Gear: Binoculars, cell phone with e-mail capability, collapsible grappling hook, good false ID papers, Chevy Corvette (financed), and $8,000.

Personality

Life as a delta's not all bad. I make a pretty good living at it, after all. There's always someone willing to hire on someone with my unique talents. How many people do you know who can walk the streets of Crescent City unarmed? Who needs bullets when your hands are living guns?

If it wasn't for those Delta Primers, my life would be fine. I can't tell you how many times I've been stiffed by a client who called in the Primers when payment was due. These days, it's cash up front.

I look at helping with the Defiance as a kind of charity work. Everyone's got to do their part, right?

An[illegible]rings down that bastard in the White House, so much the better.

Quote: Everything's negotiable.

BOUNCER

PROFILE

Smarts: 2d6
Area knowledge: Crescent City 2, computing 2, language: English 2, navigation 1, profession: student 2, survival: city 1

Speed: 4d6
Acrobatics 2, dodging 4, driving: personal vehicle 1, martial arts: barehanded 3, stealth 2

Spirit: 4d6
Bravery 2, perception 1, persuasion: charm 3, scrutinize 2, search 2, shadowing 2, streetwise 2

Strength: 2d6+3
Climbing 3, sport: skateboarding 1, swimming 1, throwing 2

Size: 4

Pace: 14

Delta Points: 4

Quirks: Delta ±0, destined for greatness +5, impulsive –3, lucky +3, secret identity ±0, self-confident +2, slight –5, softhearted –1, unregistered ±0, young –1

Powers:

Fast: +5 to *dodge*, *Pace*, and initiative rolls.

Strong: +3 to *Strength*

Tricks: First move, flip-toss, knockback

Gear: BMX bike, skateboard, PC with limited internet connection and loads of computer games, and $50.

PERSONALITY

Hey, look out! Get outta my way, old man!

Sure, you're only 30, but compared to me, you're so far over the hill, I'd need the Hubble to see you. Time to make way for the new generation!

I may not have been a delta for long, but I've already done more for the Defiance than most people twice my age.

Do I hate being a delta? Are you on crack? It's a flat-out blast.

How many people you know who can bounce across the rooftops like me? Hey, if I can do some good for other deltas along the way, well, that's just too fresh for me to mess up.

Plus, I get to wear this way cool mask, and get this: People call me by a codename. It's awesome.

Quote: Try to keep up, old man!

FLYER

PROFILE

Smarts: 2d6
Area knowledge: Crescent City 2, bureaucratics 1, computing 1, etiquette 1, gambling 1, medicine 2, language: English 2
Speed: 5d6
Dodging 3, driving: personal vehicle 1, flying 5, quick draw 1, shooting 3, stealth 2
Spirit: 3d6
Bravery 2, leadership 2, perception 2, persuasion: charm 1, scrutinize 1, search 1, shadowing 2
Strength: 2d6
Climbing 1, fighting: barehanded 2, swimming 2, throwing 2
Size: 5
Pace: 10
Delta Points: 3
Quirks: Beautiful +1, contact +3: a cousin in Delta Prime, dark secret –1: has a cousin in Delta Prime, delta ±0, glass jaw –3, honest –3, pacifist –3, unregistered ±0, secret identity ±0, sense of direction +1, sense of time +1, voice: soft +1
Powers:
Armor: 5/— when flying.
Flying: Can fly at a *Pace* of 50.
Tricks: Bull's eye, extra damage, and flying dodge
Gear: Colt 2000, Kevlar vest, motorcycle helmet, a leather bodysuit, and $50.

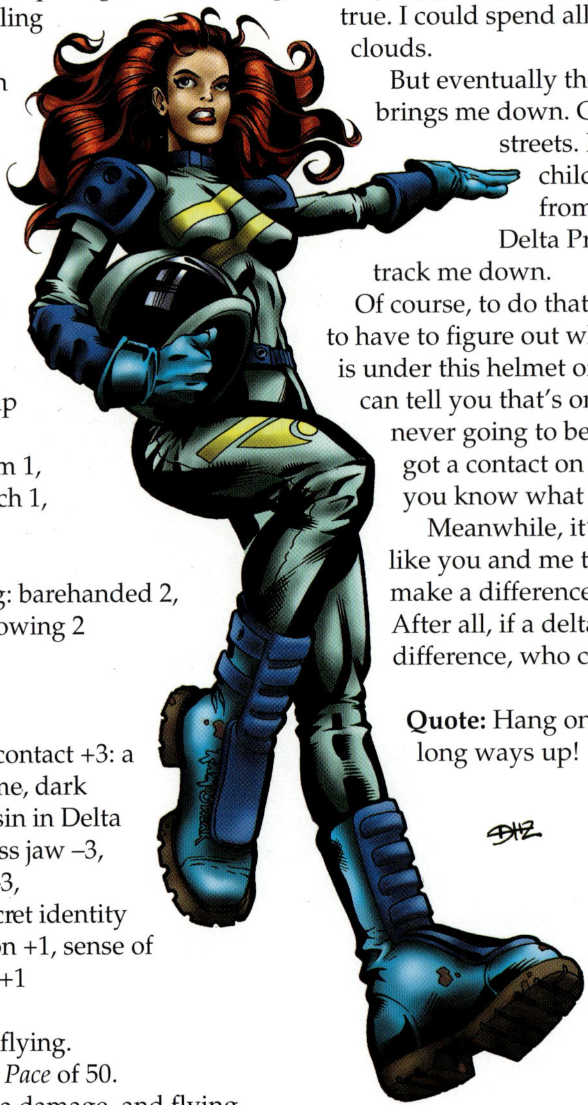

PERSONALITY

Do you have any idea what it's like to fly through the air? Not like a bird, but like a god? Defying gravity is like a dream come true. I could spend all day in the clouds.

But eventually the world always brings me down. Gunfights in the streets. Innocent delta children being taken from their parents. Delta Prime trying to track me down.

Of course, to do that, they're going to have to figure out who's pretty head is under this helmet of mine, and I can tell you that's one thing they're never going to be able to do. I've got a contact on the inside, if you know what I mean.

Meanwhile, it's up to people like you and me to step up and make a difference in our world. After all, if a delta can't make a difference, who can?

Quote: Hang on tight. We're a long ways up!

GADGETEER

PROFILE

Smarts: 4d6
Area knowledge: Crescent City 2, computing 2, language: English 2, navigation 2, profession: engineering 3, science: physics 2, security 3

Speed: 4d6
Dodging 3, driving: personal vehicle 2, flying 3, shooting 3, stealth 1

Spirit: 2d6
Bravery 1, perception 2, persuasion: bluff 1, scrounging 2, scrutinize 1, search 1

Strength: 2d6 (+3 with suit)
Climbing 1, fighting: barehanded 2, fighting: club 2, swimming 1, throwing 1

Size: 5
Pace: 9
Delta Points: 3
Quirks: Absentminded –3, brave +2, clumsy –3, delta ±0, famous +2: under his real name, honest –3, photographic memory +5, secret identity ±0, sharp eyes +1, skeptical –1, unregistered ±0
Powers:
Gadgeteering.
Tricks: Fast learner, first move, smack it
Gear: Power armor (Armor 10/3, fly at *Pace* 40, armed with guns), Colt Agent and 20 rounds of ammo, Jeep Cherokee (financed), tools in his garage, and $300.

PERSONALITY

Careful with that!

That's a prototype I've been working on for months, and I'm not quite finished with it just yet.

Sure, I know what it does. It's for, um— Well, that's not important.

I'm working on my armor right now. A machine this complex needs a lot of care, you know. Hand me that wrench, would you?

I don't really think of myself as a delta. Not really.

I mean, it's not like I'm flying around, blasting people with my fists. Well, okay, that's exactly what I do, but it's not really me, it's the machine. Sometimes it seems like the machine's more of the delta than I am. After all, it's the one with the powers, right?

Still, you've got to admit, I came up with this baby, and man, can I make it sing!

Quote: Now where'd I put that jet pack?

Goliath

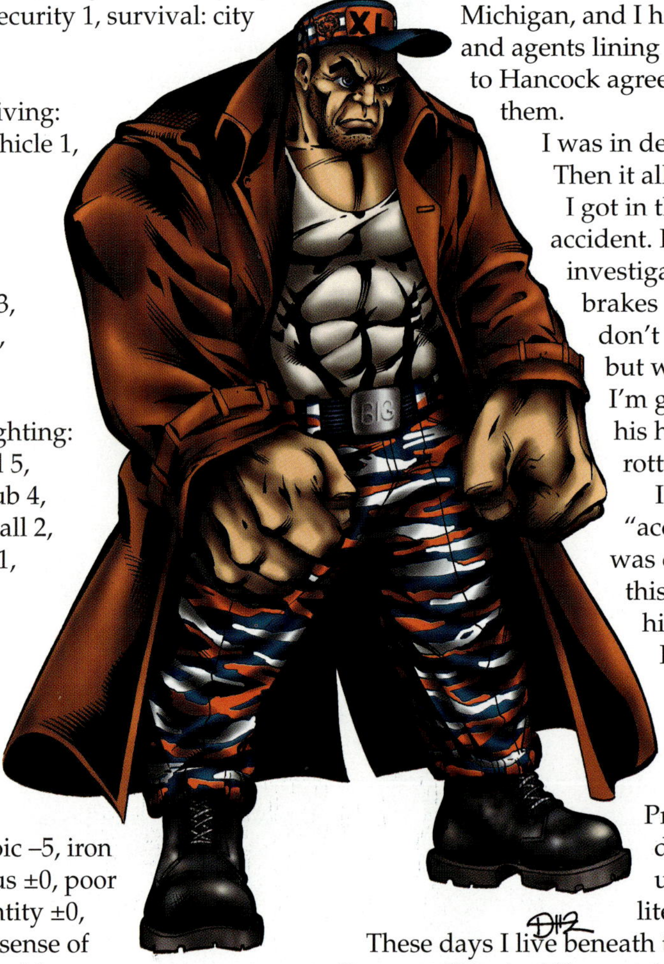

Profile

Smarts: 2d6
Area knowledge: Crescent City 2, area knowledge: Crescent City underground 2, disguise 1, language: English 2, security 1, survival: city 2
Speed: 3d6
Dodging 3, driving: personal vehicle 1, shooting 1, stealth 4
Spirit: 2d6
Bravery 1, perception 3, scrutinize 3, search 1
Strength: 5d6+5
Climbing 2, fighting: barehanded 5, fighting: club 4, sport: football 2, swimming 1, throwing 2
Size: 7
Pace: 8
Delta Points: 3
Quirks: Alert +3, delta ±0, dirt slow ±0: –2 from initiative, heroic –5, iron jaw +3, obvious ±0, poor –3, public identity ±0, registered ±0, sense of direction +1, stubborn –2, ugly ±0, tough +2, voice: hard +1
Powers:
Armor: 10/—.
Big: Add +2 to *Size.*
Powerful: Add +5 to *Strength* rolls.
Tricks: First move, knockback, rock your world
Gear: Brass knuckles, two hunting knives, and $50.

Personality

It's a hard world out there. Trust me, it only takes one slip to fall from grace.

There was a time when I had it all. I was a linebacker for the University of Michigan, and I had pro scouts and agents lining up to get me to Hancock agreements with them.

I was in demand.

Then it all changed.

I got in that car accident. I hear the investigation says my brakes were cut. I don't know who by, but when I find out, I'm going to pop his head like a rotten egg.

I survived the "accident," but I was changed—into this. There's no hiding the fact I'm a delta, and since I didn't really care much for the Delta Primers, I decided to go underground—literally.

These days I live beneath the streets of Crescent City. And I'm not the only one. It's like a whole 'nother city down there.

I still come up sometimes for air and some decent food. Sometimes I even lend people a hand when they need it. They always seem to appreciate it until they get a good look at my face and realize what I've become.

Quote: What are you staring at?

Gunner

Profile

Smarts: 2d6
Area knowledge: Crescent City 2, artillery 1, demolition 1, gambling 2, language: English 2, security 2

Speed: 5d6
Dodging 2, driving: personal vehicle 1, martial arts: barehanded 2, quick draw 2, shooting 5, speed-load 1, stealth 2

Spirit: 2d6
Bravery 1, perception 2, persuasion: intimidation 1, scrutinize 1, search 1, streetwise 2

Strength: 3d6
Climbing 2, sport: basketball 2, swimming 3, throwing 2

Size: 5

Pace: 10

Delta Points: 3

Quirks: Alert +3, ambidextrous +5, code of honor –3, contact +1: Delta Prime, delta ±0, destined for greatness +3, duty –3: help the Defiance, enemy –2: Evil Unlimited, enemy –3: Crescent City mafia, heroic –3, registered ±0, rich +1, secret identity ±0, skeptical –1, tough +2, veteran ±0, wanted ±0: as veteran

Powers:
Crack Shot: Add +5 to *shooting* attacks.
Quick: Add +5 to *Speed* rolls for initiative.
Tricks: Bull's eye, first move, and ricochet

Gear: Barrett M90 with 20 rounds of ammo, twin Colt 2000s with 45 rounds of ammo for each in spare clips, two more spare clips with 15 armor-piercing bullets (AP 10), Kevlar vest, 1976 Dodge conversion van, and $50.

Personality

Yeah, I used to work for Delta Prime. I was one of the bad guys, the people who haul fresh, snotnosed delta kids like you in so the teachers at the academy can get their hooks in you while you're still young and impressionable.

I did a lot of wetwork too. Eventually I just got sick of it, but we don't have time for that story now. If we don't get out of here in the next five minutes, Delta Prime's going to be throwing us a surprise party.

That's one gathering we can both do without.

Trust me, I know.

Quote: Come with me if you want to live free.

Healer

Profile

Smarts: 4d6
Area knowledge: Crescent City 2, bureaucratics 2, etiquette 1, forgery 2, medicine 5, language: English 2, language: Spanish 2
Speed: 2d6
Dodging 1, driving: personal vehicle 1, shooting 2, stealth 2
Spirit: 4d6
Bravery 2, leadership 2, perception 3, persuasion: charm 2, scrounging 2, scrutinize 2, search 1, streetwise 2
Strength: 2d6
Climbing 1, fighting: barehanded 1, fighting: blade 2, swimming 2, throwing 2
Size: 5
Pace: 7
Delta Points: 4
Quirks: Cautious –3, Contact +2: Crescent City Mercy Hospital, curious –3, delta ±0, glass jaw –3, lucky +3, registered ±0, secret identity ±0, self-confident +2, stubborn –2, poor eyes –1: wears contacts
Powers:
Healing: The hero can heal wounds. Add +10 to *medicine* rolls when using the healing power.
Tricks: Healing disease, new friend, on a roll
Gear: Colt Agent with 20 rounds of ammo, Kevlar vest (worn in the field), Chevy Metro (financed), a surgeon's bag, and $250.

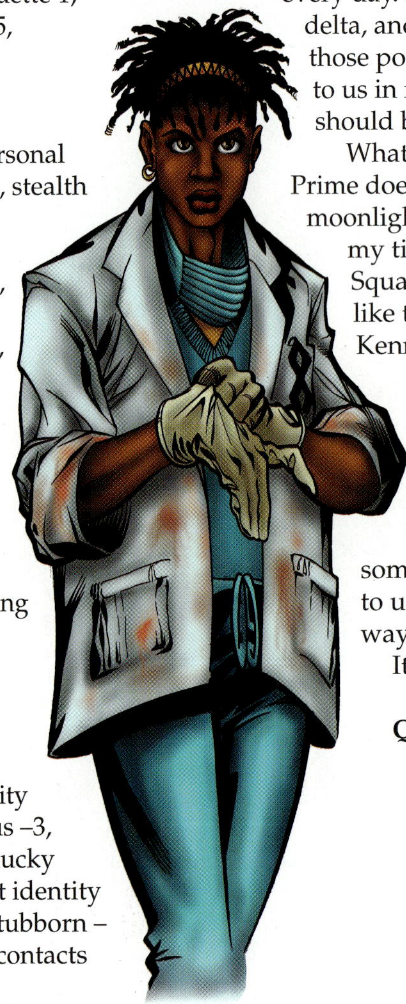

Profile

This is a hard city. I work in the ER at Crescent City Mercy Hospital, and I see it every day. I'm actually a registered delta, and I use my powers to help those poor souls who find their way to us in more pieces than they should be.

What my case worker at Delta Prime doesn't know is that I moonlight with the Defiance. I did my time as a medic in Delta Squadron, and I know what it's like to live as a delta in Kennedy's America.

I don't want anyone else to have to go through that.

Sure, I know we can't change things overnight, but if we keep chipping away at that big rock, someday we're going to be able to use the remnants to pave the way to freedom.

It's just a matter of time.

Quote: Does this hurt?

SCRAPPER

PROFILE

Smarts: 1d6
Area knowledge: Crescent City 2, disguise 1, language: English 2, medicine 1, security 1
Speed: 3d6
Dodging 3, driving: personal vehicle 1, quick draw 1, shooting 2, stealth 2
Spirit: 3d6
Bravery 3, perception 3, persuasion: bluff 1, scrutinize 1, search 1, streetwise 2
Strength: 5d6+3
Climbing 2, fighting: barehanded 5, fighting: club 3, fighting: blade 1, running 1, swimming 2, throwing 2
Size: 4
Pace: 8
Delta Points: 3
Quirks: Alert +3, delta ±0, enemy –2: old gang, impulsive –3, iron jaw +3, public identity ±0, sharp ears +1, sharp eyes +1, slight –5, tough +2, unregistered ±0
Powers:
Armor: 5/—
Healing Factor: Make a healing roll every hour instead of every day.
Strong: Add +3 to *Strength*.
Tricks: Dirty fighting, healing factor, first move
Gear: Nightstick, brass knuckles (hidden under gloves), hunting knife, Colt Agent with 20 rounds of armor-piercing ammo (AP 10), Kevlar vest, and $200.

PERSONALITY

You need some help against the Primers, dude, then I am the man you're looking for. I've busted my knuckles on just about every kind of delta over the years, and I'm always looking for fresh blood, so to speak.

I've never been registered, and I like it that way. Even so, I don't hide behind a mask. Don't believe in them. I mean, would you hide a face like this?

I may be about as subtle as a chainsaw at a church picnic, but I get the job done. Just point me in the right direction and tell me what to do.

Quote: I'm the best there is. Period.

Speedster

Profile

Smarts: 2d6
Area knowledge: Crescent City 2, disguise 2, navigation 2, language: English 2, language: Spanish 2
Speed: 5d6
Dodging 5, driving: personal vehicle 1, martial arts: barehanded 3, quick draw 1, shooting 2, speed-load 1, stealth 2
Spirit: 3d6
Bravery 2, perception 2, persuasion: charm 1, scrutinize 1, search 1, shadowing 2, streetwise 1, tracking 1
Strength: 2d6
Climbing 1, running 3, swimming 2, throwing 1
Size: 5
Pace: 110
Delta Points: 3
Quirks: Alert +3, beautiful +1, brave +2, curious –3, delta ±0, impulsive –3, loyal –3, duty –1: to the barrio, unregistered ±0, secret identity ±0, self-confident +2, sense of direction +1, voice: soft +1
Powers:
Fast Runner: Add +100 to *Pace.*
Lightning Reflexes: Add +5 to *Speed* rolls for initiative and *dodging.*
Tricks: Afterimages, extra damage, know the streets
Gear: Colt 2000 and 45 rounds of ammo in spare clips, 15 rounds of armor-piercing (AP 5) ammo in another clip, nightstick, and $250.

Personality

How can I help you, amigo? You don't look like you're from the barrio.

This is my turf. Actually, there are lots of people fighting over this part of Crescent City, but I was born and raised here. I'll be damned if I'll let them have it.

I want to give this neighborhood back to the pueblo, the good, honest people who scratch out a living here as best they can.

You think Kennedy cares about us? You only see the Primeros down here when they're on a "recruiting drive." Otherwise, they don't bother.

That's okay though. That's what I'm here for.

Quote: Hurry up, slowpoke. ¡Vamanos!

THE FIRST ALPHA: SUPERIOR

Superior at His Awakening in 1944

JFK Gives a Speech in Crescent City

K. SHARPE '98

Chapter Three: The Basic Mechanic

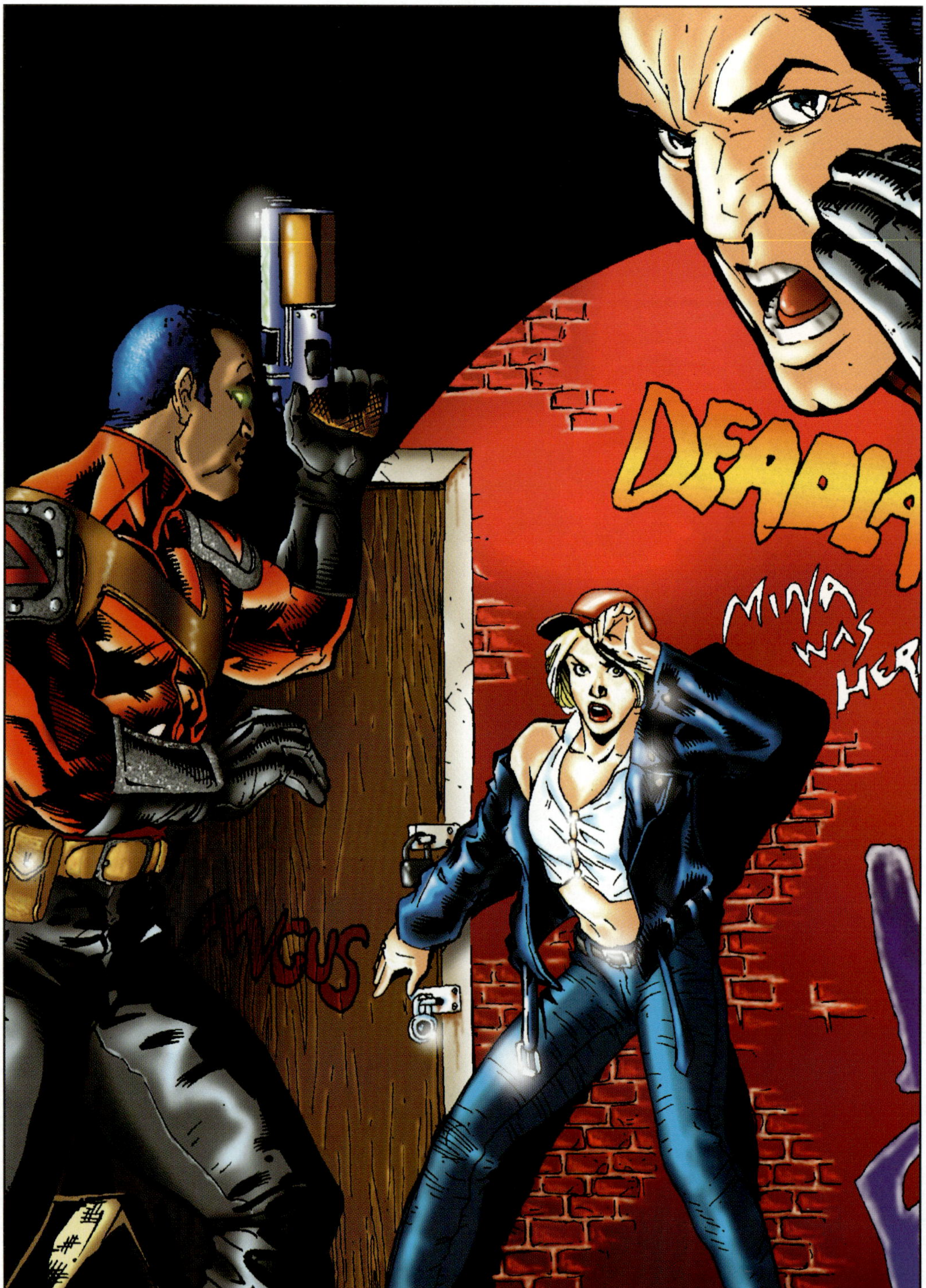

Chapter Three: The Basic Mechanic

Brave New World centers around a single basic game mechanic. When you want your character to do something that might not work, the Guide sets a Target Number (TN) and asks you to roll a certain number of dice.

This is called making an action roll. If your result is equal to or greater than the Target Number, your hero succeeds at whatever she was trying to do. Otherwise, she fails.

Setting the Target Number can take some getting used to, but we make it easy with the following table. Once you've got this down, you've got a handle on most of the game. The table below has some examples.

Target Numbers

Difficulty	Target Number
Easy	5
Challenging	10
Difficult	15
Amazing	20
Incredible	25
Phenomenal	30

Setting a Target Number

Setting a Target Number is simple. The Guide takes a look at thc situation and figures out about how hard it should be for the hero to do what he wants to do. The higher the number, the harder the feat is to accomplish.

If the player wants his hero to do something that's flat-out impossible, the Guide can simply tell him that he's out of luck. Weaklings trying to push over the Empire State Building are going to fail every time, no matter how well they might roll.

Example: *Marty's hero, the Rebel, is chasing a thief across the rooftops of Crescent City. The thief leaps from one building to the next, and Marty wants the Rebel to follow him.*

The Guide thinks about it for a moment and sets the Target Number at 7. There's about 12 feet between the rooftops, and this isn't exactly a nicely groomed running track the Rebel's on.

Marty rolls a number of dice equal to the Rebel's Strength*: 4. They come up 1, 3, 5, and 6. Marty picks up the 6 and rolls it again. He gets a 4, giving him a total of (6+4=) 10.*

The Rebel lands neatly on the other roof and continues after the thief, not even breaking stride.

Extra Successes & Tricks

If you get a really great action roll result, you can rack up more than one success. For every 5 points over the Target Number, you get another success. You can use these successes to do tricks like knock an opponent down or ricochet an attack off a wall.

Many actions have tricks associated with them. For every extra success you get, you can use a trick your hero knows that goes with the action he's using. Better yet, you don't have to choose the trick until after you roll.

To use a general trick (those from Chapter Seven) properly, your hero has to know it. If he doesn't, he can still pull it off, but it takes three extra successes instead of one.

You might have more successes than you know what to do with. Unused successes are wasted, but you can pat yourself on the back for a heck of a roll.

Example: *The Rebel lets loose at a Delta Primer with an energy blast from his fist. The Target Number is 6, and he roll and gets an 11. Since that's 5 more than the Target Number, he got an extra success. The first success slams the blast home into the Primer's chest. Marty uses the extra success to activate Rebel's* knockback *trick, slamming the Primer into a mailbox across the street.*

Opposed Rolls

Sometimes your hero's going to want to do something in direct opposition to someone else. In that case, you don't have to worry about setting Target Numbers. Just have both of the characters roll. The character with the higher result wins.

Example: *The Rebel's somehow got himself in an arm-wrestling match with Savannah's hero, Jackie Savage. Marty rolls the Rebel's* Strength *dice (4), while Savannah rolls Jackie's (3). Marty gets a 5, and Savannah gets a 4. Marty wins, and the Rebel pins Jackie's arm to the table.*

Of course, you can get extra successes with opposed rolls too. All you have to do is beat your opponent's result by 5 or more. Each extra 5 points on the roll counts as another success.

Example: *Jackie and the Rebel go at it again. This time, Marty gets a 4, while Savannah gets a 10. Since Jackie won by (10–4=) 6, she gets two successes. She uses the first one to win the arm-wrestling match. With a grin, Savannah says that Jackie uses the other success to knock the Rebel out of his chair.*

Disasters

Just as a hero can get a really great action roll, he can screw it up too. If a hero makes an action roll and gets 1s on the majority of the dice, something goes wrong. First off, she fails at whatever she's doing, no matter what the result might be. Second, it's up to the Guide to come up with something to put a crimp in the hero's plans.

Example: *Let's go back to the Rebel leaping across the rooftops. Say Marty rolls and gets 1, 1, 1, and 6. He's got a disaster on his hands. He doesn't even need to bother rerolling that 6, since the Rebel's leap automatically fails.*

The Guide thinks about it for a moment, then says, "The Rebel makes a desperate leap, but just as his feet leave the rooftop, he trips. The Rebel's 10 stories up, and it's going to hurt when he hits the ground. A fatal kind of hurt."

Marty looks up at the Guide, his eyes pleading for one last chance. The Guide smiles and says, "There's a clothesline crossing between the buildings at the sixth floor. A quick hero might be able to make a grab for it."

Automatic Successes

Some things are so easy for a hero to do there's no need to roll for them. People cross the street all the time, for instance, so rolling for that's silly.

If the hero's lowest possible action roll is equal to or higher than the Target Number, the hero doesn't have to bother rolling. She can still roll if she wants to—say, if she wants to get some extra successes—but if she does, she opens herself up to the chance of disaster too. Either way, it's the player's choice.

Example: *The Wall wants to pick up a desk. His* Strength *is 5d6+5, so his lowest possible result is a 6. The Guide rules that picking up the desk has a Target Number of 5. This means the Bruiser doesn't have to bother with an action roll, since lifting something like a desk is so easy for him.*

Jargon

There are some new words that we use in *Brave New World* that you might not recognize at first. Just to make things clear, here's what they mean.

Action Roll: When a player wants his hero to do something, this is the roll she makes to see whether or not she succeeds.

Alpha: A particularly powerful kind of delta. Also the first letter of the Greek alphabet.

Defiants: A group of deltas who refuse to register with the government.

Delta: A person with superpowers. Also a Greek letter meaning "change." The term covers all kinds of deltas, even alphas, although there are few alphas these days.

Delta Prime (DP): A bureau of the Department of Justice. The best-known delta group in the US government.

Extra Successes: A bonus for a great action roll. For every 5 points an action roll is higher than the Target Number the player was rolling against, the player gets an extra success.

Extras: The characters controlled by the Guide. These can range from taxi drivers to major villains.

Guide: The players' eyes and ears into the *Brave New World* setting. The person who sets up the game, controls the plot, sets the Target Numbers, and makes rulings in the case of any questions.

Primer: Slang for a member of Delta Prime.

Reg: Regular. A person without any superpowers.

Success: When a die roll meets or beats a target number, the player has a success.

Target Number (TN): The number a player needs to roll equal to or greater than to succeed at an action.

Chapter Four: Getting the Job Done

Chapter Four: Getting the Job Done

By this point, you should know what your hero's *Smarts, Speed, Spirit*, and *Strength* are, as well as all of his diceless traits. Now it's time to pick his skills.

For each point you have in a trait, you get to choose 3 points worth of skills under that trait. You choose skills before you choose a power package. You can't come back here after you've added bonuses to your traits and pick up more skills. The bonuses don't earn you more skill points.

We've listed a lot of skills in this book, but we can't possibly cover everything. If you want your hero to have a skill that's not listed here, just talk it over with your Guide. If she agrees to it, you're all set.

Subskills

Many of the skills listed in this chapter actually describe a broad category of subskills. *Science*, for instance, covers a lot of different kinds of subskills, like *science: biology, science: aeronautics,* and so on.

If you pick a skill with a list of subskills beneath it, you must pick a subskill for your hero. Subskills are handled just like regular skills. They're only grouped together to make them easier to talk about. They're not related in any other way.

Basic Skills

Every hero starts out with a certain number of basic skills for free as shown on the list below. These don't cost anything during hero creation, and they can be added to just like any other skill.

Free Skills

Skill	Skill Level
Area knowledge: hometown	2
Climbing	1
Language: native	2
Scrutinize	1
Search	1

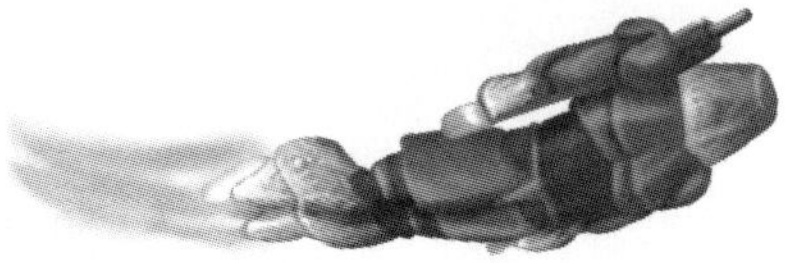

Recommended Skills

There are certain skills that come up so often in the course of a game that every hero is going to want to have at least one point in them. You don't have to pick these skills for your hero, but if you don't, be prepared to suffer the consequences.

Recommended Skills

Bravery
Driving: personal vehicle
Fighting: barehanded
Perception
Persuasion: bluff
Stealth
Swimming

Swapping Skill Points

If you like, you can swap skill points from under one trait and spend them under another on a two-for-one basis. For example, you could take 4 points from under your *Strength* skills and use them to buy 2 points worth of skills under *Speed, Smarts,* or *Spirit.*

Skill Modifiers

It's the Guide's job to set Target Numbers for any action roll, no matter what skill's being used. In general, the number should be Easy (5), but this can be altered up or down by any number of conditions.

Lots of these situations are outlined in each of the skill descriptions on the following pages, but there's one set of modifiers that applies to lots of different skills: lighting. It's just harder to do most things when you can't see what you're doing.

Rather than list these modifiers under each skill, we've collected them here for you. Use common sense when applying these. They often don't affect *Smarts* skills, for instance, and a hero with a flashlight or other light source can ignore a lot of the modifiers.

Lighting Modifiers

Situation	Modifier
Twilight	+2
Night with a full moon	+2
Night with a half moon	+4
Night with no moon (city)	+6
Night with no moon (country)	+8
Total darkness	+10
Blinded	+10

The Skills

The skills your hero can choose are listed here in alphabetical order to make them easy to reference. On the same line as each skill heading, we've listed the trait that's associated with that skill.

Academia (Smarts)

Subskills: *American culture, comparative literature, history, occult.*

The fact is that saving the world isn't always about having a power with which you can blast someone into next week—although that sure doesn't hurt. Sometimes it's more a matter of brains than brawn, and in those cases, it's not what you can do so much as what you know.

Academia covers the kinds of knowledge you pick up out of books or in school. This kind of knowledge rarely has a direct application like a *science* skill would. It mostly deals in matters of information instead.

Acrobatics (Speed)

Ever wanted to bounce off three walls, roll out into a somersault, and cartwheel across a floor, all while pounding the bad guys with your fists? Most folks trying that would start off by bouncing on one wall and then landing ungracefully on their butts.

Not your hero though. With this skill, she can tumble across city streets or over rooftops with the best of them.

You can even use *acrobatics* to halve the damage from a fall. It's up to the Guide to set the Target Number based upon the situation, but as a rule of thumb, the Target Number should be 3 plus +1 for every inch fallen. This means that if your hero falls 10 inches (20 yards), the Target Number would be 13.

Halve the falling damage before the maximum damage cap kicks in.

Archery (Speed)

Bows and arrows may seem pretty primitive, but they have some decent benefits. First, they can be made of wood, plastic, and carbon composites, meaning you can get them past metal detectors without much of a problem.

Second, a bow doesn't make much sound when you fire it, making it great for a sniper. Third, bows don't leave telltale kinds of evidence on the shooter, like powder burns.

The trade-offs, of course, are convenience and speed. It's a lot easier to tote around an automatic pistol than a longbow. Also, a weapon firing on full auto can pop a target full of a fistful of lead in the time you can shoot a single arrow.

A bow has a Quickness of 2. The first action is for loading the bow and drawing the string. The second action is for firing.

Artillery (Smarts)

Most weapons fire in a straight line, but that's not true of mortars, grenade launchers and the like. These things lob their loads up and over obstacles, then explode wherever they hit.

Firing artillery is different than shooting a gun. You've got to figure the height and trajectory, sometimes even calculating in things like high winds. Even then, it often requires a good helping of luck.

Most weapons a hero's going to want to use aren't going to require *artillery* to use, but when the chance to haul out the heavy gear comes out, you want to be prepared.

Area Knowledge (Smarts)

Subskills: *City, county, state, region, country*

This skill tells you how well a hero knows a particular place. The more targeted the place, the more information the hero can get on an *area knowledge* roll.

For instance, if you've got *area knowledge: Wisconsin*, you probably know most of the major cities in the state, as well as what the weather's like there. Your chance of knowing where the best bars in the state's largest city aren't too good though, unless you've got *area knowledge: Milwaukee.*

Every hero starts out with *area knowledge: home town* for free. If you want more, though, it's going to cost you.

Arts (Spirit)

Subskill: *Illustrating, music composition, painting, sculpting, writing*

What's life without art?

Any hero who takes art of some kind as a serious endeavor needs to pick up one of these subskills and then spend some time creating. After completing the work, the artist makes the appropriate *arts* roll to determine the quality of the work. Given time, poor works can be revised, and a new roll can be made.

It's up to the market (in the form of the Guide) to set the cash value of any particular piece, whether it's an impressionist landscape or a column in the *Crescent City Star*. These things tend to bounce up and down with whatever happens to be in vogue in the week in question. Until the artist manages to break through, though, she can plan on putting the "starving" in "artist."

As to whether or not the work is truly art, well, that's for history to decide.

Boating (Speed)

Subskill: *Speedboat, sailboat*

Handling a boat is a lot different than driving a car, and there's an entirely different set of rules on the waterways. With the *boating* skill, you've got all of this down pat.

Speedboat covers speedboats (of course) as well as any other kind of powered watercraft, like a jetski. *Sailboat* works for any kind of boat that uses wind for power.

In general, you don't have to worry about making a *boating* roll to just keep sailing along. It's when things get hectic that you need to think about it.

Here are a few modifiers for common situations. These apply to smaller boats. Bigger boats are affected by conditions differently.

Boating Modifiers

Situation	Modifier
Rough seas (up to three-foot waves)	+2
Stormy seas (over three-foot waves)	+4
Shallow bottom	+4
Calm wind (when sailing)	+4
Raging wind (when sailing)	+4

Bravery (Spirit)

Some people are just more willing to shout into the face of the abyss than others. There are things in *Brave New World* that could scare the pants off a priest. When that kind of situation comes up, you're going to find out what kind of stuff your hero's made of.

If you want your hero to do something insane, the Guide may ask you for a *bravery* roll. See the Bravery Table on page 90 for example Target Numbers. If you succeed, your hero stands tall. If you fail, he's going to hide, take off at full speed, or freeze.

At that point, the hero can't do anything else on his actions (except run, hide, or stand there) until he makes a *bravery* roll at the same Target Number. Once he finally makes the *bravery* roll, he can act normally on his next action.

Bravery Table

Situation	Target Number
Stepping into a fight	5
Running into gunfire	5
Defusing a bomb	10
Driving along the El tracks	10
Spitting on the President	15

Bureaucratics (Smarts)

Sometimes it's who you know, and sometimes it's how well you know how to fill out the paperwork. The American government in *Brave New World* is a mess of shuffled papers and displaced responsibilities. Dealing with just about any government agency only confuses most people, and they have a hard time even knowing how to properly ask for what they need.

A hero with *bureaucratics* knows how to cut through all that red tape to get to what she wants. She knows which forms to fill out, which offices to visit, and what managers to ask for. She knows what she's entitled to, and she knows how to ask for it.

Computing (Smarts)

Even in *Brave New World*, the computer has taken the world by storm. It's an unusual dictatorship, in that Kennedy has done his best to encourage capitalism and innovation, as long as he's in charge at the end of the day. So far, it's worked.

Computing allows a hero to set up and troubleshoot computers and computer networks. It's also used to surf the web for information.

Brave New World's web is a lot more restricted than the one in our world, but it's still a hotbed of rebellious activity. The best-known Defiant spot is www.deltatimes.com, the weekly news site and information clearinghouse for unregistered deltas everywhere.

By its nature, *Delta Times* is a semipublic forum in which people can exchange information and converse with each other. For that reason, it's constantly monitored by Delta Prime. A word to the wise *computing* whiz: Don't post anything here that you don't want the Primers to see.

If the heroes use the web to search for information on something, it's up to the Guide to set the Target Number for each quest depending on what it is the heroes are looking for. The more obscure or particular the information, the harder it is to find.

Even when the heroes do find something on the web, they often can't confirm its accuracy. Government censors spend a lot of time "cleaning" web sites so that most places people would go have biased or only partially true information. Exercising your first amendment rights can land you in jail—or worse.

Climbing (Strength)

Sometimes you need to get from down here to up there, and there's not an elevator in sight. That's when you get back to the basics: climbing.

A hero's *Pace* when climbing is equal to a quarter of his regular *Pace,* rounded down. It's a lot slower to scale the side of a building than it is to dash across a street.

The *Climbing* table gives you an idea about how hard it is to climb various kinds of surfaces. As always, it's up to the Guide to take into account any extra factors and adjust the Target Number accordingly. Good climbing gear can reduce the Target Number by up to –4, for instance.

Climbing

Difficulty	Target Number
Rough, 45° surface	3
Rough, 60° surface	5
Rough, 90° surface	7
60° surface, few handholds	9
90° surface, few handholds	11
Sheer, glassy office building	13

Criminology (Smarts)

No, this isn't where your hero studies how to become a criminal. It's what law enforcement officials use to figure out how a crime was committed and—hopefully—who did it.

With *criminology*, a hero can check for things like fingerprints, powder burns, and other kinds of scientific evidence at a crime scene. He can make a guess at the trajectory of bullets and, with some luck, reconstruct what happened.

If the hero's got access to a lab with the proper facilities, he can determine blood types and even get DNA profiles from pieces of hair, drops of blood, or skin under a victim's fingernails. If he can then tap into the FBI's database, he can search their DNA files for a match. Of course, this all takes time, up to four weeks, even on a rush job.

Demolition (Smarts)

When you're working with things that go boom, you really want to know what you're doing. What's the next occupation of a demolitionist who blew his last assignment? Feeding worms.

This is one skill that most people aren't going to need on a daily basis. Not a lot of people spend their time working with explosives, setting shaped charges, timers, activators, and so on. When you need it though, you really need it.

Demolition is used for disarming bombs as well as making them. Aren't sure if cutting that blue wire shuts the bomb down or sets it off? Time for a *demolition* roll.

Disguise (Smarts)

When your picture's been splashed all over the papers and you've been featured on *America's Most Wanted Deltas*, it's best not to show your face around town at all. Sooner or later, you're going to get stir crazy though, and that's when you need a disguise.

The *disguise* skill is what you use to make yourself look like someone else. If you just want to change your appearance, that's simple enough to do. You make your *disguise* roll to see how well your hero's managed to mask himself. Then, anytime you give someone a reason to be suspicious or just take a good look at your hero, she makes an opposed roll, using her *scrutinize* against your original *disguise* roll.

If you want to try to impersonate an actual person, that's a bit trickier, since you've got to convince people you're really someone in particular. It's extremely difficult to fool a friend of the person your hero's posing as. The closer the friend, the harder he is to fool.

In fact, *disguise* alone isn't often enough, since it only changes how the hero looks. As soon as the imposter opens his mouth, he risks exposure. To complete the illusion, he needs to use the *mimic* skill too.

For some guidelines on this, see the Disguise Modifiers Table. The Guide should feel free to add modifiers of her own as the situation warrants. Apply these modifiers to the suspicious person's *scrutinize* roll.

Disguise Modifiers

Situation	Modifier
The hero's posing as someone well-known	+2
The hero's posing as an acquaintance	+4
The hero's posing as a close friend	+6

Dodging (Speed)

Don't just stand there when someone's shooting at your hero. Get her the hell out of the way!

To do that, your hero needs the *dodge* skill. It's all about figuring out where the bullets—or whatever—are going to be, and then making sure your body's not in the same place when they get there.

Dodging an attack is a big part of combat, so we explain it all in depth in Chapter Six on page 154. Turn there for all the details.

Driving (Speed)

Subskills: *Personal vehicle, commercial vehicle*

Even if your hero's got himself a set of wheels, he's not going anywhere without some driving lessons.

Assuming your hero knows how to drive, he doesn't have to make *driving* checks every round he's on the street. *Driving* rolls are only called for when the hero hits a hazard or wants to do something exceptional, like pull a bootlegger reverse.

A hero with *driving: personal vehicle* can drive most passenger vehicles—cars, motorcycles, pickup trucks, and the like—easily enough. To handle something bigger—like a bus, semi, or limousine—he needs *driving: commercial vehicle*.

Driving can also be used to operate even stranger things, like hovercraft. It's up to the Guide to determine which kinds of vehicles require their own subskills. If the craft sits in the water, try *boating* instead. If it flies, go for *piloting*.

Car chases can crop up a lot in *Brave New World*. See pages 164–165 for how this works.

DRIVING MODIFIERS

Situation	Modifier
Dark	+2
Slick	+2
Icy/oily	+4
Raining	+2
Storming	+4

ESCAPING (SPEED)

What's a villain without a good deathtrap? Smart.

In *Brave New World*, most bad guys don't strap you to a table, point a laser at you and leave, confident that you'll be dead by the time they've brought the world to its collective knees. No, they just shoot you in the head.

Still, there may be times when the villains figure the heroes are more valuable alive than dead. When a hero finds herself tied up in some way, this is the skill she uses to wriggle free from her bonds. It's up to the Guide to set the Target Number, based on how much effort the hero's captor has put into keeping her in one place.

Escaping doesn't allow the hero to pick a lock. That's a different skill. It allows her to figure another way out—if there is one—and then use it.

The table on page 94 gives some sample Target Numbers for common types of bonds.

Escaping Difficulties

Bonds	Target Number
Ropes	5
Handcuffs	9
Straightjacket	13

Etiquette (Smarts)

It's one thing to look good. In a delicate situation, it's almost as important to know how to act.

This skill is more than knowing which one is the salad fork. It tells the hero how to keep from offending people in different situations and how to handle himself in high society. It's vital for diplomats and spies alike.

Faith (Spirit)

Some people believe in a higher power that watches over us all—or ignores us, as the case may be. Whether you call it God, Yahweh, Allah, or the Force, this skill determines how strongly your hero believes in her faith.

Faith is an essential skill for religious people of all stripes: priests, nuns, monks, Covenant ops—whatever. Without it, they're hollow shells of what they once were or could be.

Faith actually helps certain kinds of deltas use their powers. You'll learn more about this as the *Brave New World* saga develops.

Fighting (Strength)

Subskills: *Barehanded, club, blade*

When fancy words fail you, sometimes you've just gotta throw down.

Fighting is what your hero uses to knock the crap out of someone up close and personal. This is the kind of hand-to-hand combat that's all about brute strength. There's no real finesse here, just mayhem.

If your hero's faster rather than brawny, have him try the *martial arts* skill instead. For the most part, it's used just like *fighting*, except it's based on *Speed* instead of *Strength.*

If you want your hero to use a weapon rather than his bare fists, be sure to choose the right subskill. If you want to use something unusual, talk to your Guide about whether or not the weapon falls under a standard subskill. If not, you should come up with a whole new subskill to cover that weapon type.

For all about how to use *fighting*, see pages 153–154.

FLYING (SPEED)

Look, up in the sky!

If your hero has the *flight* power, she can glide through the air with the greatest of ease. That's not going to do her a lot of good when the going gets rough though.

There's nothing to zooming along through open sky, but it's not always just clouds in your way. When there's any kind of obstacle, or if the hero gets attacked in midair, the Guide might ask you to make a *flight* roll.

It's the Guide's job to set the Target Number, based upon the conditions your hero's facing. The base Target Number is usually Easy (5). See the Flying Modifiers Table for some common modifiers.

FLYING MODIFIERS

Situation	Modifier
Rain/snow	+2
Sprinting	+2
Storm/blizzard	+4

FORGERY (SMARTS)

In Kennedy's America, people are required to carry identification papers on themselves at all times. Citizens are subject to random checks by jackbooted thugs either looking for someone in particular or simply abusing their power. Just about the worst thing someone can hear when confronted by a cop is, "Your papers are not in order."

Defiants often don't have their papers in order, particularly if they're on the run. If they've managed to keep their powers a secret, then they're in the clear. Otherwise, their lack of papers can cause them a lot of trouble. Some employers will hire people without papers, but it's a real risk. The jobs are almost always low-paying and menial: washing dishes, picking fruit, detassling corn, and so on.

With the *forgery* skill and the right kind of equipment, the hero can create fake versions of ID papers or just about anything else necessary. Of course, certain things are harder to fake than others. ID documents are tricky, since they revolve around a federal ID card that's got a hologram embedded in it to prevent tampering. That's not to say it can't be altered, just that it takes a skilled hand to pull it off.

Forgery can also be used to fake other people's signatures or to duplicate their handwriting. When the forgery is created, the forger makes a skill roll. From there on after, to see through a forgery, a foe must make an opposed *scrutinize* roll against the *forgery* roll. If the *scrutinize* roll succeeds, the forgery is spotted.

For more complicated forgeries, say of a painting, the hero needs to couple his *forgery* skill with another skill, making successful rolls with both. The lower of the two rolls is used to set the Target Number of an opposing *scrutinize* roll.

In either case, the harder the item is to forge, the more likely it is that someone can identify it as a fake. To represent this, the Guide must set a Target Number for the original *forgery*

roll. If the roll doesn't succeed, the forgery is bad enough that anyone who looks at it closely can spot it automatically.

A hero cannot forge something he's never seen before. In fact, if he doesn't have a version of the original at hand when producing his forgery, he must add +6 to the Target Number.

FORGERIES

Forged Item	Successes Needed
Dollar bill plate	5
ID card	3
ID papers	2
Signature	1
Work of art	3

GAMBLING (SMARTS)

Gambling is a loser's game, but in every game, there's got to be a winner. The trick is making sure that's you.

The fact is that every casino game is stacked in the house's favor. That's where they get the money to put up those titanic hotels in Las Vegas.

In *Brave New World*, gambling's been legalized pretty much everywhere. The feds see it as a way to get a lot of money into their pockets and keep the masses distracted at the same time. The national lottery, for instance, unveils a new, instant millionaire just about every week, holding up hope for even the most downtrodden that they might someday strike it big.

With games that are pure random chance and no real betting strategies—like a lottery—the *gambling* skill isn't worth a whole lot. When the games get a bit more personal, like a friendly poker game or a ruthless round of craps, that's when a seasoned gambler can stack the odds in his favor.

When you've got a group of people gambling against each other, handle it like this. Set a pot for a period of time—an hour usually works nice. Every gambler pitches that amount of money into the pot. Then have everyone make a *gambling* roll.

Total up the number of successes from all of the gamblers, then divide the pot into that many pieces. Each success gets one piece of the pie. Gamblers who fail entirely don't get a thing.

> ***Example:*** *The Rebel, Jackie Savage, and Bear Jackson are playing poker. The stake is $100 each for an hour, making the pot ($100x3=) $300. They each make a* gambling *roll. The Rebel gets one success, Jackie gets two, and Bear gets none. That's a total of three successes, so we divide the pot into three pieces worth ($300÷3=) $100 each. The Rebel gets $100, Jackie gets $200, and the Bear, well, he's out of luck.*

Every gambler knows how to cheat too. It's a good way to give yourself an edge over the other players. If you get caught, it's also a good way to get run out of town—if you're lucky.

There are two ways to cheat: quietly and blatantly. At the start of a round of gambling, each player has the chance to declare that he's going to cheat. Quiet cheating adds +2 to the player's *gambling* roll, while blatant cheating adds +6.

If no one thinks to *scrutinize* the hero, he automatically gets away with it—unless he gets a disaster on his *gambling* roll. In a serious game, though, most people size up the competition right away, so you can count on there being a lot of suspicious players.

The more blatant the cheating, the easier it is to spot. Every point of bonus a player adds to his *gambling* roll also gets added to every opponent's *scrutinize* roll.

Bluffing works in a similar way. When a hero wants to bluff in a game in which bluffing could make a difference (like poker), she makes a *persuasion: bluff* roll. Every success she gets over the highest *scrutinize* roll made against her adds +1 to her *gambling* roll. If no *scrutinize* rolls are made against her, the base Target Number is 5 instead.

If the highest *scrutinize* roll beats the *persuasion: bluff* roll, the bluff can backfire on the hero. For every success the *scrutinize* roll gets over the bluffing hero, take –1 from the hero's *gambling roll.*

Language (Smarts)

Subskills: *Any language*

¿No habla Español? ¡Tiene una problema!

Language is the primary means by which we all communicate with each other. The problem is that we're not always speaking the same language.

Every character starts out with 2 points worth of skill in her native tongue. For most people in *Brave New World*, that's English—the official language of the federal government—but it doesn't have to be.

A hero with 1 point in another language can get along with it, but she talks like a child and is illiterate in the language. At 2 points, the hero's got it down well enough to sound like he scraped through high school, and he can also read and write. The higher the skill, the better the hero's grammar, reading comprehension, and vocabulary.

If there's a question as to how much a hero can understand of a conversation in a foreign tongue, she needs to make an Easy (5) *language* roll. With one success, she gets about half the words right, and she can probably get at least the gist of it all. Each extra success gets her closer to full comprehension. With two extra successes, she puzzles it all out completely.

A disastrous roll means the hero thinks the conversation's about something else entirely.

Leadership (Spirit)

A team without a leader is just a bunch of heroes. It's when they work together that the heroes can really be effective. To do that, they need some kind of coordination. That's where *leadership* comes in.

Before a combat, the hero can use *leadership* to help prevent members of his team from being surprised. (See page 137 for all about this.) When a situation crops up in which the heroes might be surprised, the leader can make a *leadership* roll for the entire group—assuming he's not surprised himself. Then any member of the team can use the leader's *perception* roll result instead of her own, if she likes.

Making a *leadership* roll in combat takes one action, during which your hero barks out orders to the heroes around him. The Target Number is usually Easy (5), but the Guide can change this depending on the circumstances. Shouting out orders in the dark or over a storm can be a lot harder than normal.

For every success on the *leadership* roll, any one friendly hero—including the leader—can give another friendly hero one of his remaining actions.

Lockpicking (Speed)

Subskills: *Electronic, mechanical*

The keyword in Kennedy's America is fear. Keeping people scared is how he gets them to give up their rights. Frightened people use lots of locks.

To get past most, all a hero needs is a successful *lockpicking* roll with the appropriate subskill. Some cunning locks have both electronic and mechanical components, forcing the lockpicker to broaden his skills.

To use the skill, the hero's got to have the right kind of equipment. Mechanical lockpicks are easy to find. Proper tools (like the slim-jim used to open car doors) are illegal, but substitutes (like a coat hanger) work well. When using substitutes, however, the hero needs to get another success.

A hero needs a stethoscope or similar listening device to have a shot at cracking a safe. He can try it with his bare ears, but he needs another success.

Electronic locks are another situation entirely. They require sophisticated equipment which is illegal to have, unless you're a licensed locksmith. Otherwise, you're out of luck. If your hero's a Defiant, though, he's already on the wrong side of the law. What's an illegal equipment charge? Finding the stuff, however, is a Difficult (15) *scrounging* roll.

Lockpicking Difficulties

Type of Lock	Successes Needed
Interior door	1
Desk drawer	1
Front door	2
Padlock	3
Safe	4
Bank vault	5
Improvised lockpicks	+1

Martial Arts (Speed)

Subskills: *Barehanded, club, blade*

There's more to bringing the beat down on someone than just standing toe to toe and pounding each other to a bloody pulp. Sure, that's one way to do it, but why limit your hero to such vulgarities?

There are fighting techniques that rely more on pinpoint accuracy than raw strength. That's where *martial arts* comes in.

If your hero's stronger than he is fast, have him try the *fighting* skill instead of *martial arts*. It's used just like *martial arts*, except it's based on *Strength* rather than *Speed*.

If you want your hero to use a weapon rather than his bare fists, be sure to choose the right subskill. If you want to use something unusual, talk to the Guide about whether or not the strange weapon falls under a standard subskill. If not, you should come up with a whole new subskill to cover that weapon type.

Medicine (Smarts)

Being a delta can be hazardous to your health. In fact, it can be downright lethal. Sooner or later, every hero is going to get into a situation in which she gets hurt, and then she's going to want medical aid—now!

Characters with the *medicine* skill can help other characters piece themselves back together after they've been in a fight. For all about how heroes get wounded and patched back into one piece, see pages 163–164.

A hero with one 1 point of *medicine* knows first aid, but that's about it. A nurse has 2 or more points in *medicine*. A resident has at least 3 points in *medicine*, while an experienced doctor has 4 or more.

Of course, violently inflicted wounds treated at a hospital are immediately reported to the police. A smart hero might have a *contact* or a *patron* with medical skills. Otherwise, getting out of the hospital might be a lot harder than getting in.

Mimic (Spirit)

Rich Little, eat your heart out.

There are times your hero may want to be able to copy the voice and mannerisms of someone else, to *mimic* him. When you're on the run from the law, it's not always safe to be yourself.

Mimic is an opposed roll against an opponent's *scrutinize* skill. At the start of each encounter in which your hero's mimicking someone, make a *mimic* roll. This roll holds for the rest of the encounter, unless the scene changes substantially. The Guide can call for a new *mimic* roll any time she likes.

When the hero first encounters people while mimicking someone, anyone listening to him can make a *scrutinize* roll to see if they realize that the hero is an imposter. People only get to make this roll if they have met the mimicked person or heard him before.

Of course, the better the opponent knows the person being mimicked, the less likely she is to be fooled. For some common modifiers to add to the *scrutinize* roll, see the Mimic Modifiers Table below.

Also, if the hero doesn't look anything like the person he's mimicking, he's going to have a rough time of it—unless that person's known only by his voice. To look more like the person he's posing as, the hero should pick up the *disguise* skill too.

Mimic Modifiers

Situation	Modifier
The hero's posing as someone well-known	+2
The hero's posing as an acquaintance	+4
The hero's posing as a close friend	+6

Navigation (Smarts)

Some people can't find their rear end with both hands, but an experienced navigator can make her way through a thick forest on a dark and stormy night.

This skill helps you figure out where you are, where you want to go, and how to get there from here. With *navigation*, a hero can read a map, figure out which way is north (given any clues at all), and plot a course from one location to another.

In a city the hero knows or has a map of, she can figure out the fastest or easiest way to get from one place to another. She can also give a decent estimate of distances and travel times. *Area knowledge* gives the basic details about an area. *Navigation* tells how to best get around it.

With a successful roll, the hero can find a good route between two points. For every extra success, she can cut the travel time by 5–10%. If the roll is failed, the hero can't come up with a route at all. She can try again only after she comes up with some new information. ("Do you have another map?")

If the hero rolls a disaster, she comes up with a route, but it's entirely wrong. It's up to the Guide as to how much fun he wants to have with this.

Perception (Spirit)

Lots of people wander through life without a clue as to what's going on around them. Others have minds like steel traps.

Heroes with high *perceptions* tend to notice things that escape others, like foes sneaking up on them. It's similar to *scrutinize* in that it helps the hero zero in on salient details, but *perception* is about seeing things. *Scrutinize* is about seeing through them.

Perhaps most importantly, *perception* helps keep the hero from being surprised by someone. In a fight, standing around trying to figure out who's beating the stuffing out of you can be fatal.

Performing (Spirit)

Subskills: *Acting, public speaking, music, singing, storytelling*

Performing covers that broad range of skills people use to entertain others and sometimes even make a living from their abilities.

Some Defiants on the run earn their keep as street performers. For each performance they give, they make an Easy (5) *performing* roll. Each success they get is worth $25.

If the venue isn't one in which you might normally find a street performer (like a park, subway, or city square), the Guide should feel free to raise the Target Number as high as he likes—or have security come and throw the bum out.

Performing skills are not substitutes for other skills. An actor can't use *acting* to bluff his way into a building. That comes under *persuasion: bluff*. Of course, good actors often have great *bluff* skills too.

Persuasion (Spirit)

Subskills: *Bluff, charm, interrogation, intimidation, seduction, taunt*

Hey, look over there! A dune buggy!

Persuasion is the skill you use to deliver that kind of line well enough that people actually turn around to see what you're pointing at. There are lots of ways to get someone to do what you want, whether it's turning around or opening a door. Some people charm their way into a room, while others just face down the bouncer until he walks away. It all depends on the hero's style.

Heroes who concentrate on persuasion prefer words over action. They try to get into fights a lot less often, and for that reason they tend to live a lot longer.

No matter which subskill the hero uses against a target, this isn't just matter of rolling some dice and then making the target do whatever the hero wants. It's all about roleplaying.

Remember before how we talked about needing rules for things like shooting, to help you figure out if you actually hurt someone with an attack. These rules for *persuasion* are pretty much the same thing, except they're for a battle of words.

A *persuasion* must be roleplayed to work. You can't just have your hero walk up to the receptionist and say, "I use my *persuasion: bluff* to talk my way in." You've got to come up with the lie your hero's telling, and then you've got to tell it. The better you pitch it, the more the Guide should reward your efforts.

Of course, most people aren't going to just roll over and let your hero have his way with them. *Persuasion* skills always call for opposed rolls. For every *persuasion* skill, there's a skill to resist it. In most cases, this is *scrutinize* because keeping from being influenced has to do with seeing through the manipulator's efforts. In other cases—most often when the manipulator's trying to scare the target into complying with his wishes—the target resists with *bravery*.

This isn't some kind of Jedi mind trick. It's the ability to convince someone of something by the sheer force of your sincerity. If the listener has direct evidence to the contrary of what you're telling her—or if the effort's just incredibly implausible—it's not going to work. In that case, the Guide should give the listener an appropriate bonus to her roll.

Conversely, if the hero puts a lot of work into the effort, he should be rewarded with a bonus too. Showing up to an office in a UPS uniform, for instance, is a much better way to *bluff* past a door than just walking up in your street clothes and telling the receptionist you're expected.

Of course, each subskill gets its own kind of results. *Bluff* gets the target to believe whatever line of bull the hero's feeding her—up to a point, of course. Even the most gullible people have their limits. *Charm* gets the target to regard the hero as a friend. *Interrogation* forces the target to answer the hero's question. Less scrupulous heroes might actually hurt a target first to get wound modifiers to apply to the target's rolls. (See page 159 for how this works.)

Intimidation spooks the target, hopefully getting her to back down from a confrontation before it turns into a gunfight. *Seduction* causes the target to succumb to the hero's sexual wiles. *Taunt* provokes the target into doing something stupid.

Some persuasion skills can be used against a group of people, like an angry mob. When this happens in the game, the Guide doesn't make a separate resistance roll for each individual in the group. Instead, he chooses a leader of the group, makes one roll for her, and applies the result to the entire bunch. This requires an extra success to work. Sure, it's harder to convince a group of people of something, but if you get the leader on your sheet of music, you've done your job.

The real trick with trying to persuade a mob of anything is getting the people in it to stop and listen. If the hero can't pull off that feat first, no one's going to pay any attention to him anyhow.

See the Resisting Persuasion Table for a quick rundown of which skills work against which *persuasion* subskills. Then check the Persuasion Results Table for how the rolls work out. All modifiers listed on that table are good for the length of the encounter—or as long as the Guide likes.

Resisting Persuasion

Persuasion Subskill	Resistance Skill
Bluff	Scrutinize
Charm	Scrutinize
Interrogation	Bravery
Intimidation	Bravery
Seduction	Scrutinize
Taunt	Scrutinize

Persuasion Results

Successes	Result
Disaster	**Whoops!** The hero automatically fails any other *persuasion* rolls made against the target.
None	**Did You Say Something?** The target is entirely unaffected.
1	**That Makes Sense.** The target adds +4 to the Target Number of any noncombat action rolls made against the hero.
2	**Since You Put It that Way.** The target adds +4 to the Target Number of any noncombat action rolls made against the hero, and she loses her next action.
3	**Whatever You Say!** The target's willing to do whatever the hero wants—as long as it's within reason.

Piloting (Speed)

Subskills: *Airplane, helicopter*

Some deltas can fly all on their own, but most people still need a vehicle to get around in thin air. If you're the person actually operating the airborne craft, you need the *piloting* skill.

Most of the time, flying's easy. You follow the flight plan you submit with the air-traffic controllers, and you move peacefully from Point A to Point B. But that's not always the case. When there's any kind of obstacle, or if the vehicle gets attacked in midair, the Guide might ask you to make a *piloting* roll.

The Guide sets the Target Number based upon the conditions the pilot's facing. The base Target Number is usually Easy (5). See the Piloting Modifiers Table for some common modifiers. Pilots flying a craft with proper instrumentation don't have to worry about lighting modifiers—unless, of course, their craft is for some reason missing that instrumentation.

Piloting Modifiers

Situation	Modifier
Rain/snow	+2
Sprinting	+2
Storm/blizzard	+4

Profession (Smarts)

Subskills: *Accounting, administration, architecture, business, clergy, finance, law, engineering*

There's more to life than dodging Delta Prime all day long. Lots of Defiants have day jobs—or had them before they were flushed out into the Primers' spotlights. Those skill don't just go away once they toss on a mask, and sometimes they can come in handy.

The list of subskills above only scratches the surface of the *profession* skill. There are two different kinds of jobs: professions and trades. (For more on trades, see the *trade* skill.) In general, professions require mostly knowledge, while trades concentrate on work with the hands.

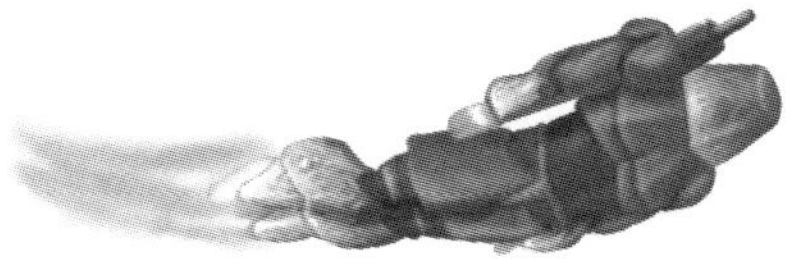

It's up to the Guide as to when a particular subskill might apply to the situation at hand, although the player should bring it up when she thinks it's possible. Most Guides appreciate the heads-up.

Quick Draw (Speed)

When some Primer gets the drop on you, you want to get that gun out of its holster as quick as you can. That's where the *quick draw* skill comes in.

For all about how this works in the game, turn to page 150.

Riding (Speed)

It doesn't come up as often these days as it used to, but sometimes you find yourself out in the middle of nowhere with only a horse to get you moving along. When that happens, you're going to be happy you've got the *riding* skill.

Just like with *boating, driving,* and *piloting,* you don't have to bother making a *riding* roll if the horse (or whatever) is just trotting gently along. It's when things get hectic that you've got to worry.

When applying wound-effect modifiers (see page 159), be sure to apply modifiers for both the rider and the mount.

Running (Strength)

Anybody can sprint across a street. It's when you're going for the distance that you need to know what you're doing.

Running long distances is all about endurance. Every 10 minutes the hero runs, he needs to make an Easy (5) *running* check. For each additional 10 minutes the hero runs, add +1 to the Target Number.

If the hero fails the roll, he's stunned and has to sit down to recover. This takes one quarter of the time he ran, after which he can continue on. Don't roll for the recovery. It happens automatically once the time has expired.

Science (Smarts)

Subskills: *Biology, chemistry, geology, mathematics, physics*

This skill covers all sorts of purely scientific endeavors, the kinds of things that only researchers at universities and large corporations usually bother themselves about. Heroes who like to think of themselves on the cutting edge of the new frontiers in science need to have some points in this skill.

Science skills don't come up in every game, but when you need them, you really need them. If the heroes don't have these skills, they might want to get to know an extra who does and might be willing to lend them a hand.

Scrounging (Spirit)

You don't have to have everything you might need with you at all times, but you'd better know where to find it. In the Defiant game, there are some things you're just not going to be able to find at the local S-Mart.

A hero with the *scrounging* skill knows where to get just about anything she might need. Of course, that doesn't mean the product's always going to be in stock. It's up to the Guide to set the Target Number, based upon how rare the item in question is. Don't bother rolling for something anyone could find in a local store.

A failed *scrounging* roll means the hero couldn't find what she was looking for. Her sources are dried up. She can try again tomorrow.

On a successful *scrounging* roll, the hero scores. For each extra success, she either finds more of what she's looking for, or she finds it at a better price.

The Guide is well within his rights to say that some things just can't be scrounged no matter how well a player may roll. Nuclear payloads, for instance, aren't on the market at any price.

Well, at least as far as the heroes know.

Scrutinize (Spirit)

Some people are like an open book, while others are as stonefaced as a cliff. With the *scrutinize* skill, you can read them all.

Scrutinize is what you use to see if someone is being honest with your hero. It's also a measure of how skeptical your hero is, how savvy he is in sizing up the people he meets. In these cases, this is an opposed roll against the person the hero's interacting with. See the description of the *persuasion* skill for how this works in the game.

Scrutinize can also be used to evaluate a person based upon looks and manners. Does that doctor seem nervous? Is that woman hiding something? This an opposed roll against the opponent's *persuasion: bluff*.

Search (Spirit)

Some people can't find the chair they're sitting on, but a hero with a high *search* skill can spot a diamond in the rough.

Searching is about finding things, whether they've been hidden intentionally or not. With objects like evidence at a crime scene, the Guide figures the Target Number by how well-hidden the thing is.

Search is also used to find people who are trying to not be found. When a hero is hiding in a place in which she's entirely concealed, looking for her is a *search* roll. When the hero's potentially in sight, this should be a *perception* roll instead.

A *search* roll can turn up things like muddy footprints, but to really follow someone requires the *tracking* skill. (See page 111.)

Security (Smarts)

In Kennedy's America, the citizens worry a lot about security. There are locks on everything from purses to palatial mansions. The more valuable something is, the more elaborate its security system, up to and including remote cameras, electric fences, razorwire, motion detectors, and the like.

A hero with the *security* skill knows how to set up security systems that can withstand determined attacks by the worst of the criminal element. Better yet—for most Defiants—she also knows how to disable them.

Of course, knowing how to disable a security device is not always the same as actually doing it. That's why *lockpicking* is a separate skill listed under *Speed*. It involves some manual expertise.

On the other hand, doing some things is simply a matter of knowledge. Hot-wiring a car, for instance, is simple once you know how.

Sleight of Hand (Speed)

Even in a world in which deltas can run rings around the regs, the hand's faster than the eye. Okay, it's faster than most eyes.

With *sleight of hand*, the hero can pull something out of his pocket or sleeve

without anyone noticing. This can come in handy when the hero wants to cheat at cards, whip out a holdout gun, or just pull a quarter from behind a kid's ear.

It can also be used to steal things. With this skill, the hero can palm something or even pick someone's pocket.

If someone's actively watching the hero—or is getting her pocket picked—the hero needs to make an opposed *sleight of hand* roll against the foe's *perception* skill.

Sleight of hand can also be used like the *quick draw* skill (see page 105) when the hero's got a small gun (Derringer) or small knife.

Shadowing (Spirit)

Sometimes a hero wants to stick to someone like a shadow, following her for as long as he can. That's where *shadowing* comes in.

Shadowing is an opposed skill that's rolled against the *perception* of the person being followed. If the shadower loses, he's spotted by the person he's following. Otherwise, the shadowed person moves along, blissfully ignorant of the fact she's got someone on her tail.

Once the shadowed person figures out she's being tailed, it's up to her to come up with a way to lose the shadower. That's got nothing to do with *shadowing* as such, and everything to do with *stealth* (see page 109). The person being shadowed has to get the tail to lose sight of her for a moment, and then she sneaks away—if she's lucky.

Shooting (Speed)

If you don't know how to fire a weapon properly, you're more of a danger to yourself than any foe. Even if you manage to get the gun pointed in the right direction, chances are you couldn't hit water if you fell out of a boat. All you're going to do is make a lot of noise.

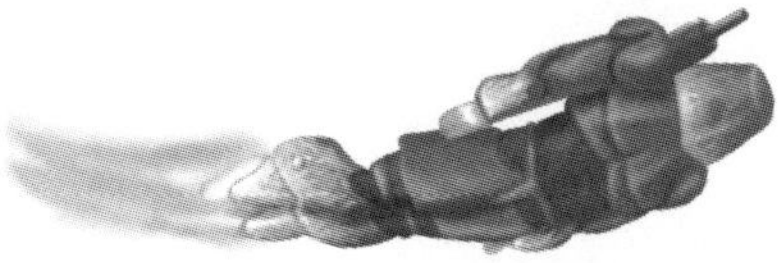

On the other hand, if your hero has a high *shooting* skill, he could knock the spots off a ladybug at 100 yards.

In a nation in which guns are so prevalent, using them comes up a lot. Most citizens have at least 1 point of *shooting*, and many have more.

Shooting covers not only firing a gun but also using just about any other kind of weapon that fires projectiles in a straight line—except bows or artillery.

This skill is also used by heroes that can fire energy blasts. After all, just because a hero has the power doesn't mean she knows how to use it properly.

For all about how *shooting* works, see Chapter Six.

Speed-Load (Speed)

What's the worst sound you can hear in a gunfight? Click.

If your hero gets into a lot of gunfights (as Defiants tend to do), eventually he's going to empty a gun. If he's still got enemies standing, he's going to want to reload right away.

With the *speed-load* skill, the hero can pop bullets back into his weapon fast enough to get himself right back into the action. For all about how this works, see page 151.

Sport (Strength)

Subskills: *Baseball, basketball, deltaball football, hockey, soccer*

Hey, life's not all about running from the law. Sometimes you get a chance to take a break and play a game, something athletic maybe. Lots of deltas are pretty athletic, and some of them even make a living playing their favorite sport.

A hero with a *sport* skill can play the game at a high level. For one, she knows the rules backward and forward. Second, anytime she needs to do something in the game, like dribble a ball or make a shot, she gets to add her *sport* skill to the roll. If she's lucky and highly skilled, she might even be able to make a living at it—and a good-paying one at that.

Stealth (Speed)

Some deltas like running around in bright costumes. This makes them a target instead of innocent bystanders, and if they're wearing a mask, it also hides their true identity.

Others think it's better not to be spotted at all. That's where *stealth* comes in.

Stealth allows the hero to hide—even in plain sight—within reason.

The key part to that sentence is "within reason." If you try toting a sniper rifle through the grocery store as you shop, people are going to notice. Try sneaking around from shadow to shadow instead.

Stealth is an opposed roll. The hero who's sneaking around makes a roll for her current conditions, and that lasts until the conditions change—someone turns a light on in the room, she moves, someone walks into where she's hiding, and so on.

If the hero's in plain sight (or could be seen by someone with sharp eyes), then someone trying to spot her must make a *perception* roll. If she's actually hidden behind something—entirely out of sight—then the hunter must make a *search* roll instead.

The Guide should feel free to add to the hider or the hunter's rolls as much as the situation calls for. Poor lighting conditions, for instance, would favor the hider, while a night scope would help the hunter.

Streetwise (Spirit)

Life on the street has an etiquette all its own. It's about how you walk, how you talk, how you carry yourself. A yuppie from one of Crescent City's skyscraper palaces can get eaten alive if he wanders into the wrong part of town.

With *streetwise*, your hero knows how to handle himself on the street. Not only can he duck into an alley without looking like an easy mark for a mugging, he also knows where to find people who might know things.

With a good *streetwise* roll, your hero can put his ear to the concrete (so to speak) and find out what the proverbial word on the street is about any current topic. Sometimes there's nothing out there to find out. It all depends on how likely it is that word about whatever the hero's asking after has filtered down to street level—which is the Guide's call.

Asking about high-security matters involving Delta Prime is silly. That information is tightly controlled, and anyone who knows anything about it is going to be tight-lipped as can be. If you want to hear something about the gang that pulled that jewelry heist last week, though, you've got a much better chance.

It's up to the Guide to set the Target Number for a *streetwise* roll. The higher the hero's roll, the more information can be revealed. If the roll comes in under the Target Number though, the hero comes up empty.

Survival (Smarts)

Subskills: *City, desert, forest, mountain*

Life in the city is easy—if you've got money. You run out of food, you go to a restaurant. You need a place to sleep, you find a hotel.

When you're out of your element though, it's a whole other matter. Heroes with the *survival* skill can forage in the kind of places covered by their chosen subskill, for both food and shelter.

Each success on the skill roll is worth food and shelter for one person for one

day. Extra successes can be used to extend how long those essentials hold out, or they can be used to help other people.

SWIMMING (STRENGTH)

When your hero finds herself in a "sink or swim" situation, she better hope she's had swimming lessons. Without the *swimming* skill, she's liable to sink like a rock in the deep, blue sea.

A hero with the *swimming* skill can keep herself afloat and even move along in the water at a decent clip. A swimmer's *Pace* in the water is equal to her *Strength*. For more about how to keep your hero from drowning see page 161.

TACTICS (SMARTS)

Knowing how to handle yourself in a fight or being able to direct a team of heroes against a common foe is all a matter of tactics. Brilliant tacticians can actually use a smaller force to defeat a bigger and stronger foe. It's all about using your forces to their best effect, as well as knowing your opponent's weaknesses and being able to use your surroundings to your best advantage.

This is a skill that should usually be roleplayed. The player can't just roll some dice and force the Guide to tell him what to have his hero do. Nothing in life comes that easy.

Instead, it should be used to help evaluate a plan that the heroes come up with. With a successful roll, the hero should be able to spot holes in the plan, which the team can then do its level best to plug.

The better the roll, the more holes the hero spots. With this kind of feedback, the hero should hopefully be able to come up with a better, more solid plan.

THROWING (STRENGTH)

Whether the hero's tossing knives or chunks of concrete, this is the skill she needs. With the *throwing* skill, the hero

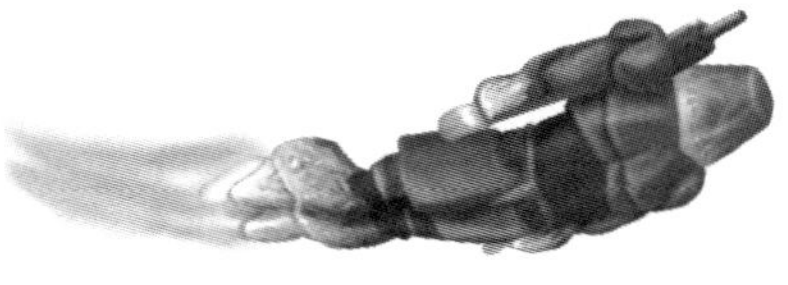

can hurl whatever she can pick up at the foes of her choice.

For more about how to use this in the game, see pages 151–152.

Tinkering (Smarts)

This is the skill gadgeteers use to maintain their equipment. See page 179 for more about how this works.

Tracking (Smarts)

Sometimes you just have to be able to follow someone's trail, even after they've long gone. That's where *tracking* comes in.

This skill's a lot more useful outside of a city. It's nearly impossible to track someone down a busy boulevard. Most shoes don't leave much of an impression on concrete, and the constant traffic obliterates most signs of passage almost instantly. There are times, however, when *tracking* can come in really handy.

This skill can also be used to hide a hero's tracks. When a hero wants to do this, the player makes a *tracking* roll. After that, anyone who tries to follow the hero's tracks must beat the original roll—or at least a 5—with an opposed *tracking* roll of her own.

The base Target Number to track a person not covering his tracks is Easy (5). There are a number of common situations that can modify this Target Number, and these are listed on the Tracking Modifiers Table. It's up to the Guide to come up with any other modifiers the situation warrants.

When tracking someone, the tracker should roll every 100 yards or so, but the Guide can change this interval to fit the situation. It could be once a mile over long distances, or even more. The Guide is also perfectly within her rights to declare a trail simply untrackable.

Tracking Modifiers

Situation	Modifier
High traffic area	+5
Precipitation after tracks were made	+5
Precipitation before tracks were made	–5
Tracking only one or two people	+5
Tracking over water or concrete	+10

Trade (Speed)

Subskills: *Carpenter, electrician, machine operator, mechanic, plumber*

Not every delta got her powers at an early age. Some awakened later in life, and most of them had jobs beforehand. Those skills don't just go away when the hero pulls on that uniform or mask.

There are a lot more *trade* subskills than we could possibly list here. There are two different kinds of jobs: professions and trades. (For more on professions, see the *profession* skill.) In general, trades are jobs that require the hero to work with his hands, while professions involve sitting behind a desk.

Whenever the player thinks a *trade* skill might come into play, she should bring it up. As always, though, it's the Guide's call as to what actually works.

Weaponsmith (Smarts)

Most deltas can't just shoot beams out of their hands or eyes or whatever. Instead, they rely on things like guns, blades, clubs, and the like to stack the odds in their favor.

A hero with the *weaponsmith* skill can repair standard weapons and even build custom weapons if he likes. He can also make his own ammunition if need be.

Chapter Five: The Well-Rounded Hero

Chapter Five: The Well-Rounded Hero

A character's not just a collection of traits and skills. Just like in real life, there are things about most heroes that can't be pinned down so simply. To help fill in some of these gaps, we use quirks.

Quirks are things that make your hero different from the rest of the crowd. Maybe he's rich, he might have a family who depends on him, or possibly he's afraid of the dark.

Quirks can be good or bad, so we have positive quirks and negative quirks. This chapter's full of descriptions of all sorts of quirks and how they work in the game.

If the quirk's positive, there's a positive number after it, and that's how many skill points it costs to add that quirk to your hero.

If the quirk's negative, there's a negative number after it. That's how many points you get back for saddling your hero with that trouble.

You can only have up to 10 points worth of negative quirks. We're creating heroes here, not basket cases.

Roleplaying Quirks

A lot of the quirks describe your hero's personality and how you should roleplay it. Sometimes, though, a player may want a hero to do something against one of her quirks. In that case, the Guide has two choices.

First, the Guide can simply say that the hero has no choice. She has to live by her quirk. She already got the points for it, after all, and now it's time to pay the piper.

Second, if the Guide's in a generous mood, he can give the hero a chance to work against her nature. To do this, the hero needs to make a Challenging (10) *Spirit* roll. The Guide should feel free to modify the Target Number to reflect the situation.

Either way, if a hero is consistently working against her quirks, she needs to reconsider having them at all. Characters in *Brave New World* are capable of change as they progress in the game. To learn more about this, see pages 193–194.

THE QUIRKS

The heading over the description of each quirk lists the name of the quirk and the number of points the quirk costs or gets for your hero.

Positive quirks cost points, while negative quirks get them back for you.

STATUS QUIRKS

There are certain special status quirks that a hero must take. These don't cost anything. It's more like checking a box saying that your hero's either this or that.

Of course, either way, your hero has to live with the consequences.

DELTA OR REG ±0

A delta is a person who's developed superhuman powers. In game terms, the hero can't pick a power package unless she's a delta.

We pretty much assume that you're playing a delta, but that doesn't have to be true. If you like, you can stick with your hero being a reg instead. Most regs don't get hunted down by Delta Prime just for being who they are, after all, so it's not so bad.

For all about the power packages deltas can have, see Chapter Eight.

PUBLIC IDENTITY OR SECRET IDENTITY ±0

Your hero's identity as a delta is either public or secret.

With a public ID, your hero doesn't have to worry about living a double life. The downside, of course, is that anyone who's got a gripe against the hero can find out all about him. This makes it a lot easier to track the hero down. Worse yet, it makes it pretty darn simple to find the hero's friends and family and threaten them instead.

If your hero has a secret identity, you're theoretically safe from the Primers and your enemies. However, she's got to wear a mask and hassle with people trying to figure out who she is.

An *unregistered* delta with a *public identity* must take the *wanted* quirk.

REGISTERED OR UNREGISTERED ±0

If your hero's registered, then at some point in the past, she complied with the Delta Registration Act. All of her information is now on file with the US government, most notably Delta Prime. This means that she likely served with either Delta Squadron or Delta Prime or spent some time at the Delta Academy. In fact, maybe she's still there—at least officially.

The problem with all of this is that the hero's DNA and power profile are on file with Delta Prime. This means that anytime the hero's involved with something the federal government or Delta Prime investigates, there's a good chance they'll be able to identify the hero's involvement. Of course, if someone with the same power profile does something and the hero doesn't have an alibi, the hero might come under suspicion too.

On the other hand, if your hero doesn't want to Hancock that dotted line on the bottom of the DRA, hey, she knows the score: You register within seven days of gaining your powers, or you go to jail. Well, those seven days are long gone, and your hero doesn't exactly have writer's cramp from filling out forms.

Being unregistered does have its advantages. When your hero's involved in something and her face isn't seen, the Primers usually pin her activities on a delta they know about.

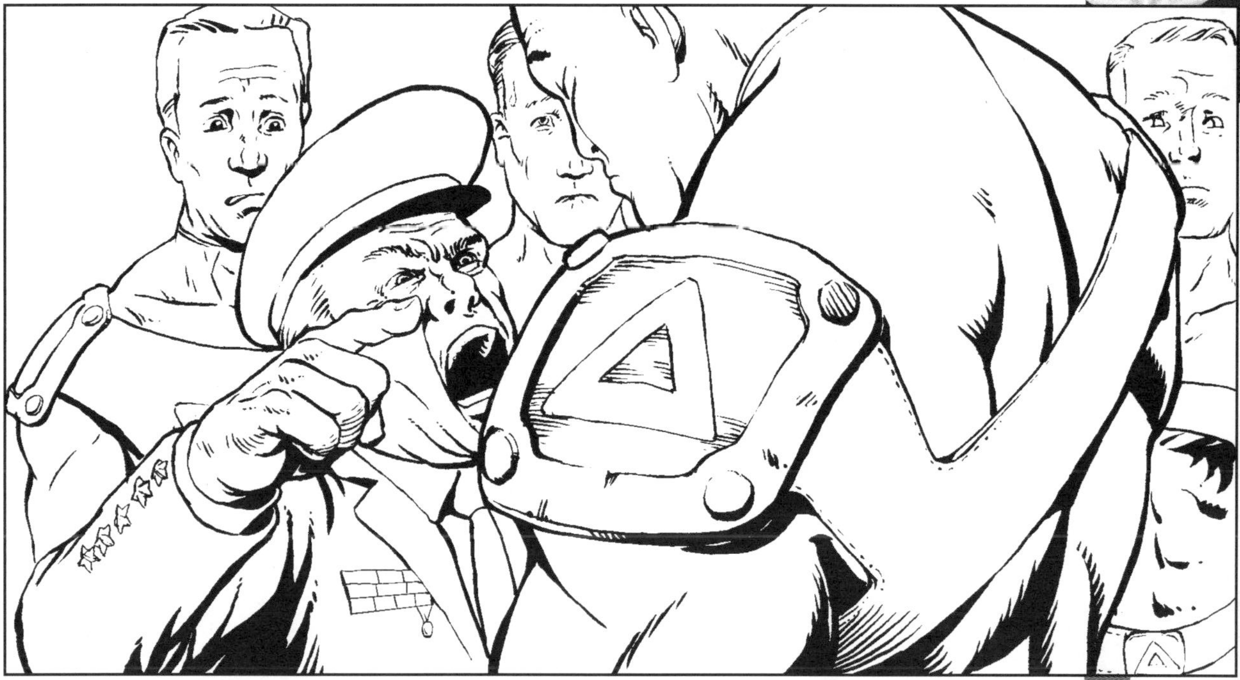

Standard Quirks

Here are the regular—positive and negative—quirks your hero can have.

Absentminded -3

When you've got a lot on your mind, other—usually less important—details fall to the wayside. After all, when you're struggling to crack a Delta Prime code, knowing where you left your keys doesn't seem all that important—until you have to drive over to a friend's house to tell her what you've learned.

The hero can hyperfocus on something, but just about everything else gets ignored. In the game, this means the hero has to add +3 to the Target Number of any *perception* roll for anything he's not currently focused on. For this reason, *absentminded* heroes tend to get surprised in combat a lot, unless they go around looking for trouble. They also often lose things or forget details that are important.

Any time the hero needs to remember a salient detail—like where he parked his car or what that raving lunatic's address was—the Guide can have him make a Challenging (10) *Spirit* roll. If the hero fails the roll, he can't recall that detail, even if the player does.

Addiction -1/-3

If you just can't live without it, it's an addiction, no matter if you're talking about drugs, alcohol, tobacco, sex, or Oreo cookies. We're not going to get into the physical effects—both good and bad—of satisfying your hero's habit. That depends too much on what it is that's got its hooks in her. If you want, you should talk to your Guide about exploring the gory details.

The *addiction* quirk is more concerned with what happens to your hero when she can't get your habit off. Not having what you need is, at the least, distracting. At the worst, it can ruin your whole day.

There are two different levels of addiction: mild and severe.

A mild *addiction* means the hero's got a jones for something mildly harmful, like tobacco. Alternatively, she might only have a slight need for something potentially more harmful.

With a severe *addiction*, the hero's got a true need that just can't be denied.

After denying his habit for 24 hours, the mild addict has to add +3 to the Target Number of any *Smarts* rolls. In the case of a severe *addiction*, the modifier rolls up to +5. At the Guide's discretion, this can get worse with time.

ALERT +3

Your hero's the sharpest knife in the drawer. He's got a mind like a steel trap, and little gets past him.

Your hero gets to add +2 to his *perception* and *search* rolls.

AMBIDEXTROUS +5

Left-handed, right-handed, who cares? You're both-handed!

The hero is a real switch-hitter. This can come in handy in a lot of situations, but most heroes use it so they can double their attacks more effectively. (See Chapter Six for more on this.)

ARROGANT –3

Just because you've got powers "beyond those of mortal men," it doesn't mean you're any better than the next person. But you don't believe that.

Your hero is pretty full of herself, and it shows. Add +2 to the Target Number of any friendly-style *persuasion* attempts. This quirk doesn't hurt aggressive kinds of *persuasion*, and in fact it might help in some cases. After all, if your hero thinks he's the toughest kid on the block, maybe there's a good reason.

AUTHORITY +1 TO +5

Whether you deserve it or not, you've got the authority to get people to ask "How high?" when you tell them to jump. Maybe you have a badge, or maybe you're a ranking officer in the military, but you can usually get people to listen to you because of the power you represent.

The more authority the hero has, the more the quirk costs. See the Authority Costs Table for suggestions. Of course, with the benefits come responsibility. Any hero with the *authority* quirk must take the *duty* quirk too.

Authority's only as effective as those around the hero let it be. A Defiant may not listen to a beat cop, but he should respect the cop's authority to arrest him or call in reinforcements.

AUTHORITY COSTS

Hero's Occupation	Cost
Beat cop	1
Detective	2
Military sergeant	2
FBI agent	3
Delta Primer	3
Military officer	3
Police chief	4
Police commissioner	5
Military general	5

BAD HABIT -1 TO -3

Do you know someone who does something that just annoys the heck out of you? Maybe it's the way they spin dice or don't look at you when they're talking to you or often don't bother bathing. Reactions to this kind of thing range from slightly bothering the viewer to making her want to vomit.

The value of the quirk depends entirely on how revolting it is and how often it comes up. Get together with your Guide to set the exact number.

No matter what the number is, that's the modifier that characters get to add to their opposing rolls whenever the hero engages in his habit and tries a friendly *persuasion* roll. At important moments when the hero's habit might come up, the hero must make a Challenging (10) *Spirit* roll or give in to the habit.

BEAUTIFUL +1

Not only does your hero have amazing powers, she's good-looking to boot. As you might guess, this can come in handy.

The hero can add +2 to any *persuasion* rolls in which her looks might come into play.

BIGOT -1 TO -3

The fact is there are some people the character just can't stand. This might be because of their race, sexual orientation, gender, or the kind of clothes they like to wear. Even if the character wouldn't do something to actively hurt them, he wouldn't piss on them if they were on fire.

The character doesn't like a particular group of people, and he stays away from them whenever possible. Anytime the character can't avoid a member of the group he's bigoted against, he feels the need to insult and provoke them whenever the chance presents itself.

The value of the quirk depends entirely on how often the character runs into those he's intolerant of and how violently he reacts to the situation when he does.

This quirk isn't recommended for heroes. Bluntly put, being a bigot isn't heroic. However, the quirk is certainly going to come up in extras all the time. Lots of people are bigoted against deltas, for instance. There are even some deltas prejudiced against deltas. Just ask some of the people in Delta Prime.

BLOODTHIRSTY -2

In a fight, your hero sees red—blood red. She's got a real "take no prisoners" attitude, something which potential prisoners tend to object to.

Whenever someone surrenders to your hero during a fight in which she's involved, she has to make a Challenging (10) *Spirit* roll to actually stop beating the poor bastard to a bloody pulp. Even if she manages to control herself, once the prisoner has outlived any usefulness, she thinks that finishing the job is a good idea.

Brave +1

When others are running with their tails between their legs, your hero stands tall—even when running might be best.

The hero adds +2 to all *bravery* rolls. On the other hand, whenever the player thinks the hero should run instead of fight—and he's made any necessary *bravery* roll—he needs to make a *Spirit* roll.

Sure, discretion's the better part of valor, but that never occurs to your hero when he's in the thick of it.

Brawny +3

When your hero walks into a room, people take notice. It's not because he's so handsome or ugly. It's just that he takes up most of the room.

The hero must have a *Strength* of at least 4 to take this quirk.

A *brawny* hero has a *Size* of 6.

Your hero can't be both *brawny* and *slight* or *hefty*.

Cautious -3

Your hero never leaps in where angels fear to tread. Oh, she might eventually work her way in there, but she's going to make sure she checks out the situation thoroughly first.

This is the opposite of the *impulsive* quirk. Anytime your hero might just jump right into something, she decides she needs to make a plan beforehand, which may include gathering more information. She can only overcome this urge with a *Spirit* roll.

This is a negative quirk because it tends to annoy more action-oriented heroes, but the upside is it could save your hero's life.

Cheap -2

Your hero never spends a dime when he could spend a nickel. He has to always buy the cheapest gear available. If the opportunity to dicker over the price comes up, he haggles over it forever.

The hero often finds cheap gear for 25% off. This can save your hero some pennies, but cheap gear isn't always that reliable. Every time cheap gear is damaged in any way, roll 1d6, open-ended. On a 10 or more, the gear breaks.

Clumsy -3

Sometimes your hero has trouble walking a straight line, and we're not just talking about after a state trooper asks her to step out of the car.

Every time your hero makes an unskilled *Speed* roll, add +2 to the Target Number. Skilled rolls are unaffected, since the hero has taken the time to practice those specific things.

Code of Honor -3

Your hero believes in the concept of a fair fight. He refuses to kill needlessly or in cold blood, and he never ambushes a foe or attacks from behind.

In short, he's one of the good guys.

Unfortunately, not everyone plays by the same rules, which puts your hero at a distinct disadvantage. Still, most people appreciate the honor your hero stands for, and if they know about his *code of honor*, he can add +2 to any friendly *persuasion* rolls against people who might be swayed by such things.

Contact +1 to +5

Heroes don't grow up in a vacuum. They interact with all sorts of people. Some of them become hated foes. Others are valued friends.

When the hero's got a friend that's in a position to do him some good on a regular basis, that's a *contact*. The quirk's value is determined by how powerful the friend is and how often the hero can count on her.

Having a friend in the police department who might help you if it didn't put him at risk is worth about 2 points. Being a close, personal friend of President Kennedy is easily worth 5.

There are lots of ways to define this quirk, so sit down with your Guide and hash out the details before you go assigning a point cost.

Coward -3

Your hero would rather flee than fight.

The hero avoids combat or any other kind of obvious danger whenever possible. He cannot have the *bravery* skill and this quirk.

Most people don't care much for cowards. If a person the hero is trying to use a *persuasion* skill on someone who knows the color of the hero's belly (canary yellow!), the coward must take –2 from his own roll.

Crazy -1 to -5

You don't have to be crazy to join the Defiance, but it sure doesn't hurt.

Your hero has some kind of mental illness. The value of the quirk is based upon how crippling the illness is and how often it comes up in play. If the hero's got a horrible phobia of polar bears and he lives in Florida, it's not going to come up often enough to be worth more than 1 point. If he's afraid to go outside, that's worth 5 points for sure.

There are far too many ways for your hero to be loco for us to go into them all here. Beyond just phobias, there's schizophrenia, depression, delusions, obsessions, compulsions, and all sorts of deviancies.

Be sure to sit down with your Guide and work out all the details on this quirk before you take it for your hero.

Curious -3

Your hero may not follow around a man in a yellow hat, but she has a real monkey on her back when it comes to not knowing about something.

Your hero is horribly curious. She cannot resist a mystery, and she tenaciously works at a question until she comes up with the answer. Unfortunately, she also often lets her curiosity drag her into putting her nose in where it doesn't always belong.

This curiosity overwhelms the hero's good sense from time to time, and she's forever scrambling out of the situations it draws her into.

Dark Secret ±1 to ±5

In *Brave New World*, it seems that everyone's got something he'd rather other people didn't know about it. This can range from who your hero took to the prom to the number of interns he's "inducted."

Dark secret is an unusual quirk, since it can be positive or negative. If your hero has a *dark secret*, then it's a negative quirk. If he knows about someone else's dirty laundry, then it's positive.

The point value of a *dark secret* is determined by how awful the secret is and how likely it is that anyone's ever going to be able to bring it into the light.

A *dark secret* could be both positive and negative. For instance, your hero might have a shameful incident in his past that he'd like to keep quiet. If there was someone else involved, though, he's got that dirt on them too. When that happens, be sure to split out the two sides of the secret and count them as two separate quirks.

A *secret identity* is not a *dark secret*. That's its own kind of quirk.

Death Wish -5

Your hero's got a personal invitation to the afterlife from Death himself, and he's looking to cash in on it early.

Maybe your hero's got a bad case of survivor's guilt. Maybe he's contracted a fatal disease and doesn't want to die in bed. Maybe he's just got nothing left to live for. Either way, life's become tiresome to him, and he's looking to check out at the next opportunity.

Still, he's not the kind to do himself in—directly. Instead, he takes greater and greater risks, tossing himself fearlessly into dangerous situations of all kinds.

You need to be careful with a hero with a *death wish*. Unless he somehow manages to lose the quirk, he's sure to someday get his wish.

Dependent -1 to -5

People are counting on your hero. We're not just talking about the faceless masses. We mean loved ones who aren't as capable as your hero and always seem to be getting themselves in trouble.

The value of this quirk depends entirely on how often the hero needs to take care of the dependent. A grandmotherly aunt who fusses over the hero whenever he's home is probably worth 3 points. A kid sister who's always insisting on tagging along or getting into trouble on her own is worth 5 points.

When you take the *dependent* quirk, you need to sit down with your Guide and figure out just who this person is and how much she affects your hero's life. You and the Guide can even create the *dependent* from scratch, just like she was a hero. If the character's a delta, she can't be a *dependent*, although she could be a *sidekick*.

Never forget, though, that this character is an extra. The dependent is controlled entirely by the Guide.

DESTINED FOR GREATNESS +5

The hero seems to be fated for bigger things, so the little things just can't drag him down.

When your hero is *destined for greatness* he can't be killed by just any crook on the street. No, he's got to go out in a blaze of glory, and only at the hands of a properly dangerous villain.

The hero can't be killed by a minor extra, only a major one. When a lesser character has done enough damage to kill the hero, the hero instead falls into a coma. It's up to the Guide to determine which extras are powerful enough to put an end to this hero.

DISABLED -3/-5

One of the hero's limbs is either lame or permanently useless, either from an injury or birth defect.

If the hero's limb is only lame, then he has to add +3 to the Target Number to do anything with that limb. If one of the hero's legs is affected, then his *Pace* drops by a quarter of his normal rate.

If the hero's limb is entirely useless or even missing, then he can't do anything with that limb at all. If one of the hero's legs is affected, his *Pace* drops to one quarter of his normal rate.

Of course, if both legs are useless or missing, the hero's *Pace* is reduced to nothing.

There are ways to get around the effects of being crippled, but they aren't always as reliable or convenient as the hero might wish. These things range from crutches and wheelchairs all the way up to artificial limbs or power armor that a delta might invent for himself.

Unless the hero develops some way to almost entirely and permanently alleviate the problem, he still gets the points for the quirk, but if the Guide likes, she can lower the number of points the quirk's worth.

Double-Jointed +1

The hero's body is double-jointed. Besides making for great party tricks, this allows the hero to slip out of bonds more easily.

Add +2 to the hero's *escaping* rolls.

Duty −1 to −5

The hero has an obligation to someone or something that she cannot ignore. This can range from a promise to check in on a friend's kid from time to time (–1) to serving in the Secret Service (–5).

The more demanding the duty, the more points it's worth. Be sure to sit down with the Guide to figure out how much your hero's *duty* is worth.

Enemy −1 to −5

Somewhere out there, there's someone who's got something he wants to tear out of your hero's chest. For whatever reason, this *enemy* is ready to spend some time hunting your hero down, maybe even to the ends of the earth—or beyond.

The more powerful and determined the enemy, the more points the quirk is worth. For instance, a punk who shows up to hassle your hero every fourth or fifth game session is worth 1 point, while a high-ranking, bloodthirsty Delta Prime officer who's made it his life's mission to hunt you down is worth 5 points.

An enemy has to be a distinct person or group. A faceless organization like Delta Prime just doesn't do. Most Defiants think of Delta Prime as an enemy, but in fact, they're just *wanted*.

Famous +2

Everyone on the street recognizes your hero—or his mask at least.

Fame is a double-edged sword. While it makes it a lot harder to get around without being spotted, it can actually work in the hero's favor. It all really depends on what the hero's famous for. If the hero's famous for something bad, add +2 to all hostile *persuasion* rolls. If the hero's well-known as a good person, then add +2 to all friendly *persuasion* rolls.

Of course, whether or not what the hero's famous for is something bad is often up to the observer. A hero who's *famous* for being a Defiant, for instance, might be a hero to other Defiants, while the regs likely see him as a menace.

If the hero has a *secret identity*, you need to decide which identity is the famous one. If it's both, be sure to take the quirk twice.

FAVOR OWED +1

At some time in the past, your hero did someone a favor. When it's time to call it in, the hero knows he can count on the favor being repaid.

This quirk's only worth 1 point because once the favor's called in, it's gone. The point does not revert to the hero, so he should be sure to use it wisely.

When setting up this quirk, the player needs to come up with who it is that owes the hero the favor, and why. As always, the Guide has the final call on approving whatever the player comes up with.

FRAIL –3

Your hero starts whining whenever he gets a paper cut.

Anytime the hero takes a wound, add +1 to the wound-effect modifier. When the hero is totally healthy, this quirk has no effect, but the moment he's wounded, it hurts like hell.

GEAR +1 TO +5

Sometimes it's not who you are so much as what you have.

The hero has some kind of belonging that is either extremely expensive or just difficult to find. The more costly or rare the item is, the higher the quirk's value. Each point of *gear* is worth roughly $50,000 or more. Keep in mind that *gear* explains how a hero has something he might not normally be able to afford. It's not a means for him to go on a shopping spree. For that, see *rich* on pages 129–130. Either way, the gear doesn't cost the hero a single nickel, just points.

If the piece of *gear* designated by the hero's quirk is somehow lost or destroyed, the points don't revert to the hero. However, since the hero had the connections to lay hands on the gear at one point, it's presumed he could do so again, although it might take a while.

The costlier the quirk, the harder it is to replace the gear. Doing so could be the basis for several adventures.

GLASS JAW –3

Your hero might be built like a brick house, but one good punch and he folds like a house of cards.

Whenever your hero has to make a stun check, add +2 to the Target Number.

GREEDY –2

At the end of the day, your hero knows what it's all about: money.

It doesn't have to be cold, hard cash. Jewels, precious metals, and easily convertible stocks and bonds will do. Either way, the hero's not willing to let anything or anyone stand in the way of him getting more of the long green stuff.

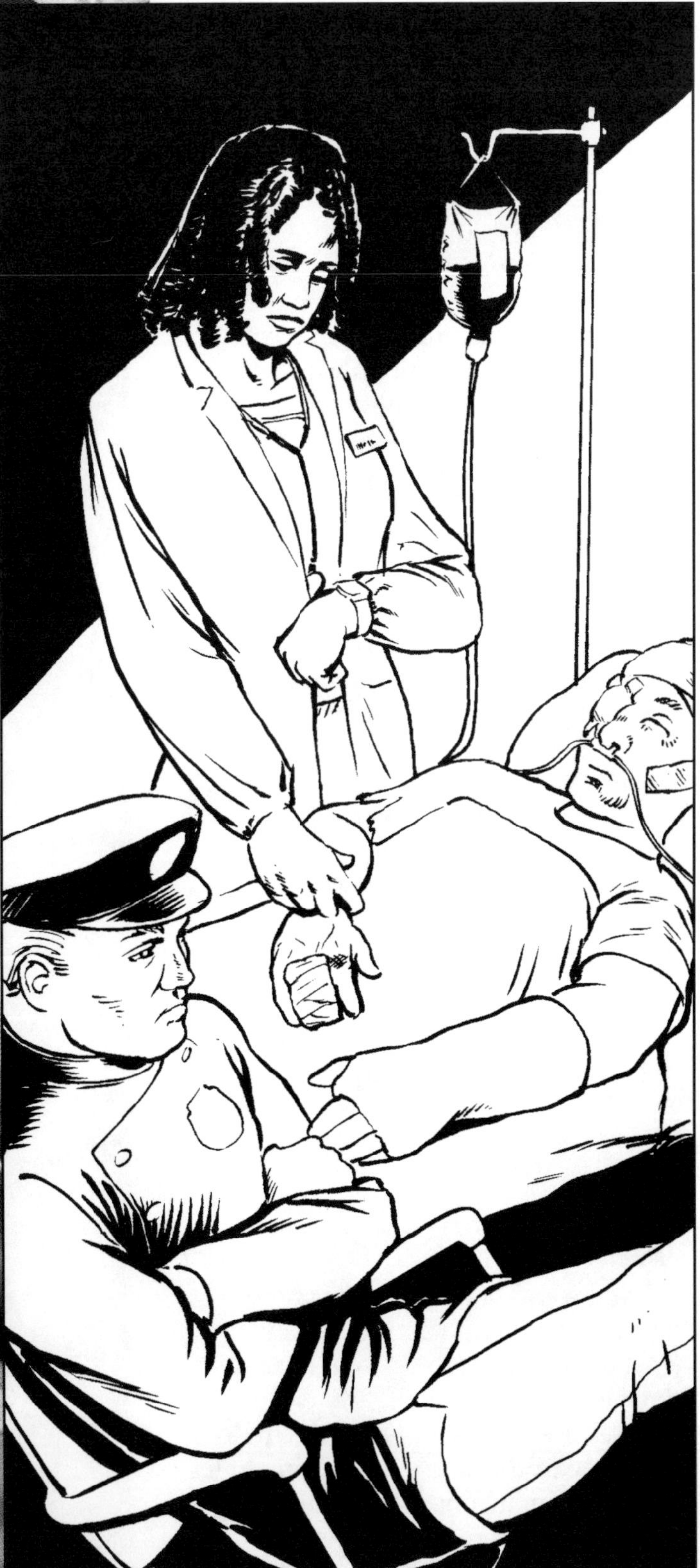

Gullible -2

Did you know they took the word "gullible" out of the dictionary? Go check. We'll wait right here.

If you fell for that, you know what your hero's like. She believes anything she's told, read, or seen on TV.

Anytime your hero tries to resist a friendly *persuasion* attempt, her opponent gets to add +2 to his roll. Simply put, she's easily led.

Heavy Sleeper -1

It takes three alarm clocks and a wakeup call to get your hero going in the morning.

When checking to see if a noise or disturbance rouses your hero from sleep (usually an Easy (5) *perception* roll), add +2 to the Target Number.

Hefty -2/-3

Your hero shops at the "Big and Tall" stores, and it's not because he's tall.

There are two levels to being *hefty*. A *slightly hefty* hero has a *Size* of 6 and has his *Pace* reduced by –2. A *really hefty* hero has a *Size* of 7, and his *Pace* is reduced by –4. Your hero can't be both *hefty* and *slight* or *brawny*.

Heroic -5

Your hero's, well, a hero. She can't turn the other way when she sees someone in need. Sure, she can gripe about it all she wants, but at the end of the day, she knows she's going to lend a hand, even if it puts her life or freedom at risk.

Even if your hero didn't have any powers, she'd be out there on the front lines, ready to lend a hand. As it is, she feels obligated to use her powers for the greater good, even if doing so risks exposing herself as a delta.

Honest -3

Your hero can't ever have a career in politics. He just flat out can't tell a lie.

Oh, sure, he can give it a try, but he's stinking awful at it. Anytime the hero tells a lie, the listener gets to make a *scrutinize* roll, even if she's not suspicious. Worse yet, she gets to add +2 to that roll.

A hero with this quirk cannot take the *persuasion: bluff* skill.

The upside to this is that the hero can add +2 to his friendly *persuasion* rolls when talking to someone who's aware of his reputation for honesty.

Illness -1/-3/-5

Your hero's sick, and in a way that's not going to get better. In fact, she's tried just about every cure, including the paranormal variety, and they've all failed. It looks like she's pretty much stuck with it.

Just because she's got an *illness*, though, doesn't mean she's done living. At the start of each game session, have the hero make a *Strength* roll against the Target Number listed on the Illness Table. If it's failed, add the listed modifier to all of the hero's actions for the entire session. If the hero rolls a disaster, her *illness* becomes worse, and she moves one step further down the table.

If the hero gets an extra success on her roll against an *illness* that's gotten worse before, she can move one step back up the table. Until that happens, though, she's stuck with the worse level, and she gets no extra points for it. Either way, she can never get better than her regular *illness* level.

If a hero gets a disaster with a *fatal illness*, she is doomed to die at the end of the session. She'd better do her best to make those last hours count.

A *minor illness* is one that causes the hero some discomfort, but she can usually soldier on through it with only some small difficulties. Examples include bad allergies, mild asthma, recurrent hives, or a cough the hero just can't kick.

Severe illnesses cause the hero a lot of discomfort, enough to give her pause when she wants to try something difficult. These include severe asthma, gout, kidney stones, and the like. It can also include the early stages of a *fatal disease*.

A *fatal illness* is one that's eventually going to kill the hero, like AIDS, cancer, and so on. The hero's in the final stages of the disease and could go at any time. Be careful when taking this one, or you might end up creating a new hero soon.

Illness

Type	Target Number	Modifier
Minor	5	+1
Severe	7	+3
Fatal	9	+5

Illiterate -3

Even in Kennedy's America, society places a lot of emphasis on being able to read. After all, if your hero can't read, how can he know that his papers aren't in order?

Of course, illiteracy is no excuse. The hero might claim that he didn't know about the Delta Registration Act because he couldn't read the posters splashed all over the place, but that kind of reasoning's not going to hold water.

An illiterate hero can't read even the most basic words of any language. Additionally, the highest level the hero can have in any *language* skill is 1.

Impulsive -3

Your hero's the kind to rush in where wise men fear to tread. She doesn't care for thinking things over too much, and she wholeheartedly believes that she can come up with something better than anyone else's well-laid plans by simply thinking on her feet.

To reflect this, any time the hero stops to make a plan, she must make a Challenging (10) *Spirit* roll. If she fails it, she gets impatient and immediately leaps into a "plan" of her own, whether it's a good one or not.

Guides should watch out for heroes with this quirk. They tend to not only put themselves in danger but everyone around them as well.

Iron Jaw +3

People have been known to shatter their knuckles on your hero's head. When they do, he's more likely to grin at them than anything else.

Whenever your hero has to make a stun check, take –2 from the Target Number.

Light Sleeper +1

Your hero sleeps with one eye open. (That's a figure of speech, you know, not some funky kind of power.)

When checking to see if a noise or disturbance rouses your hero from sleep (usually an Easy (5) *perception* roll), take –2 from the roll's Target Number.

Loyal -3

Your hero takes her friendships seriously. She's willing to lay her life on the line to keep them safe. It takes a *Spirit* roll to turn from a friend in need.

A person who feels loyal to a larger organization has a *duty* instead.

Lucky +3

The world treats your hero like she's Irish and every day's St. Patrick's feast.

Each game session, the hero gets one extra Delta Point (see page 193) to spend. This spare Delta Point is special because—in addition to being useful in all the normal ways—it can be spent to turn around a disastrous roll.

When this is done, don't bother rolling another die. Instead, it's up to the Guide to figure out what happens. Ideally, the hero should be on the brink of disaster and then have things turn entirely around for her. It's the equivalent of stepping into a cowpie and somehow coming out smelling like roses.

Lusty -1

Whenever possible, your hero's on the prowl. He's looking for Ms. Right—or at least Ms. Right Now.

A *lusty* man is known as a womanizer. A *lusty* woman is known by less-kind terms. Being *lusty* can affect the way people treat your hero. If they like the fact the hero's *lusty*, add +2 to friendly *persuasion* rolls the hero makes. If, on the other hand, they have a prudish take on the hero's hormone-laden hobby, take –2 from the hero's rolls.

Mean -2

People who don't know your hero well don't tend to like her. Those that do, they like her even less.

Your hero's a coldhearted bastard who wouldn't spit on someone if he was on fire. For this reason, she has to take –2 from friendly *persuasion* rolls. On the upside, she gets to add +2 to hostile *persuasion* rolls against people who know her reputation.

Mute -3

For some reason or another, your hero is physically unable to speak. Maybe he's got *poor ears*, or perhaps its something else.

The hero can use sign language or other, less-efficient ways of communicating, like pointing or writing, but he can't say a word.

Obligation -1/-3

Somebody did your hero a favor once, and someday he's going to call it in.

For –1 points, this is the opposite of *favor owed*. It's a onetime thing, but once it's over and done with, the hero still gets to keep the negative points.

For –3 points, the *obligation* is ongoing. Maybe someone saved the hero's life way back when, and one favor's just not enough payback. This shouldn't come up in every adventure, but it should always hang over the hero's head.

It's up to the hero and the Guide to figure out exactly what the *obligation* is. The Guide can then call the favor in whenever she likes, and it's up to the hero to answer. It takes a Challenging (10) *Spirit* roll to refuse. That, and a bad attitude about paying back what you owe.

Obvious -3/-5

You can't pick out most deltas by just looking at them, but that's not true of your hero. Maybe he's 10 feet tall and made of blue rocks, or possibly he's sprouted wings. Either way, it's almost impossible for him to deny being a delta, and when you're unregistered that makes life on the run sheer hell.

If the *obvious* part of the hero's deltahood can be easily concealed, then the quirk's only worth –3 points. If it's impossible to cover up, the quirk's worth –5 points.

An *obvious* hero can still have a *secret identity*. He just takes pains to conceal his real name.

OLD –3

Lots of deltas find about their powers in the springtime of their lives. Your hero, she's more of the autumnal kind.

No matter what your hero's actual age, she feels old and acts old. She likes to talk about the old days, back when deltas weren't such a problem and Kennedy was actually elected.

Take –1 from your hero's *Speed* dice.

ORDAINED +1

Not only is your hero the pious type, he's got the papers to prove it. Your hero has been *ordained* as an official member of his chosen religion's clergy. This might be as simple as answering an ad in the back of *Rolling Stone* magazine, but in most cases it involves a serious ceremony and—after that—serious responsibilities.

Sit down with your Guide and figure out which religion your hero belongs to and what position she holds in it. If it's a position of any power, your hero should also have a *duty* to other members of his religion.

PACIFIST –3/–5

It's not that your hero can't kill, it's just that she refuses to.

For whatever idealistic or moral reasons, your hero has vowed to never willingly do mortal harm to another human being. Of course, ideals don't always work so cleanly in the real world.

There are two levels to *pacifist*. If the hero refuses to kill unless it's absolutely necessary, say in clear-cut cases of self-defense, then the quirk's worth –3 points. If the hero refuses to kill under any circumstances, the quirk's worth –5 points.

PATRON +2 TO +5

We don't all get where we're going on our own. Some of us have a little help.

Your hero has someone powerful watching over him. This could be a rich relative or an old friend in Delta Prime. Whatever the case, when the chips are down, this is someone the hero can call on regularly.

The *patron*'s power and the frequency with which she can be relied on to help out determine the quirk's cost. Be sure to meet with your Guide to figure out just who the patron is and how reliable she's going to be.

PHOTOGRAPHIC MEMORY +5

The hero can recall just about anything she's ever seen, read, heard about, or done. She's a walking encyclopedia, and she's ready to prove it.

Of course, just because the hero's got this ability doesn't mean the player does. If the hero ever needs to remember something that the Guide talked about in the context of the game, all you have to do is make an Easy (5) *Smarts* roll. If you succeed, the Guide then must tell you whatever it is that the hero's forgotten.

This is not a way to get more information out of the Guide than has already been given. It's just a way to make sure that what the Guide's told you in the past jibes with what you remember having heard. It's especially handy if you're lazy about taking notes in the course of a game.

Additionally, the hero can add +1 to any *Smarts*-based skill roll. This bonus does not apply to raw *Smarts* rolls, just skills.

Your hero cannot have this quirk and *absentminded* at the same time.

Poor -3

Most of the time, your hero hasn't got two thin dimes to rub together, and when he does, he spends them before he can stop himself.

Poor isn't just a starting point for your hero, it's a way of life. Money runs through his fingers like water, and even if he manages to get his hands on a large sum, he just can't hold on to it.

Most heroes start with $1,000 to buy gear with. Your hero has $100, and he's got little in the way of prospects for getting more or ever obtaining credit.

Poor Ears -2/-4

What's that you say? Speak up!

Your hero is either hard of hearing or completely deaf. If he's just hard of hearing, add +3 to the Target Number of any *perception* rolls that have to do with hearing. That's the –2-point version of the quirk.

If the hero's deaf (–4 points), he automatically fails *perception* rolls that have to do with hearing.

A hero who's only hard of hearing can use a hearing aid to correct the problem. However, having a hearing aid isn't the same as having good ears. The hero still has to add +1 to the Target Number of hearing-based *perception* rolls, and he always runs the risk of losing or damaging his hearing aid.

Poor Eyes -1/-3/-5

The hero has some kind of problem with his eyesight. This can range from a mild astigmatism to total blindness.

An entirely correctable vision problem is only worth –1 point. The hero can see normally, but she must wear glasses or contact lenses. These can be lost or damaged, especially in combat, so the hero has to be careful. If the hero loses her corrective lenses, she must add +3 to the Target Number of all *perception* rolls that have to do with seeing something.

At –3 points, the vision difficulty isn't correctable. The hero always has to add +3 to vision-based *perception* Target Numbers.

At –5 points, the hero is entirely blind. She automatically fails such rolls.

Rich +1 to +5

The hero's loaded, and there just doesn't seem to be any end to it.

A *rich* hero not only starts better off than other heroes, he's got access to more money as well. Most people start off with $1,000 to purchase gear with, and they can expect to make about $20,000 a year. A *rich* hero stands to rake in a whole lot more.

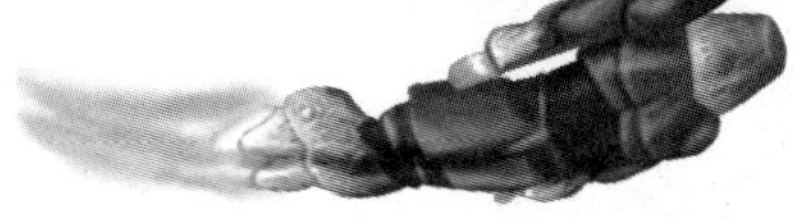

See the Rich Table for exactly how much more a *rich* hero can expect to have to start out with and make.

Of course, few players are going to want to keep track of every dime they spend. Most people get enough of that kind of thing in real life. The yearly salaries are only benchmarks to give you an idea of how much cash the hero has coming in regularly.

Rich

Quirk Value	Starting Money	Yearly Salary
1	$4,000	$40,000
2	$7,500	$75,000
3	$12,500	$125,000
4	$25,000	$250,000
5	$50,000	$500,000

Savage –3

Sure, we're all animals under the thin veneer of civilization we wear, but that veneer is thinner for some.

The hero doesn't care much for manners or other "civilized" ways, but he usually suppresses his animalistic urges when in polite—or even not-so-polite—society. Whenever he's in a stressful situation, however, he needs to make an Easy (5) *Spirit* roll or turn savage.

In combat, the hero must make this roll at the start of the first round of the fight and immediately after taking a wound. If the hero fails the roll, he immediately charges into close combat with any enemy nearby. He cannot use ranged weapons of any kind while in this state, except as a club.

Add a flat bonus of +3 to the hero's *Strength* while he's in this *savage* state. At the same time, take –3 from any *Smarts* rolls he might have to make.

Self-Confident +2

This is one hero who knows who she is. She's a real skeptic who believes in herself first and everything else second.

Anytime someone tries to make a *persuasion* roll against this hero, whether friendly or hostile, she gets to add +2 to her roll to resist.

Self-Righteous –2

The hero is holier than thou—and anyone else in the room too.

The hero has the annoying habit of not only having true convictions in the correctness of her beliefs, she's also happy to broadcast it to the world given the slightest chance. When dealing with someone who doesn't agree with her, take –2 from any friendly *persuasion* attempts.

Of course, when the hero's got a friendly audience, she's at the top of her game. In that case, add +2 to any friendly *persuasion* attempts.

Sense of Direction +1

The hero can always roughly tell which direction is north, and from there he can figure out the rest. This works even if the hero doesn't have any outward clues.

Sense of Time +1

The hero always knows roughly what time it is, give or take 15 minutes. If she needs a more precise guess, a Challenging (10) *Spirit* roll narrows it down to plus or minus two minutes.

Sharp Ears +1

Your hero's the kind who can pick out a single voice in a room and home in on it like a tiger on fresh prey. His keen ear allows him to add +2 to any *perception* rolls involving hearing.

Sharp Eyes +1

Eagles pine for eyesight as razor-sharp as your hero's. She adds +2 to any *perception* rolls involving vision.

Sidekick +5

It never hurts to have an extra set of eyes watching your back.

Your hero's got a younger partner he mentors in the delta game. This is a great way for rookies to learn about handling their burgeoning powers. They've got the ability, but they need the experience an older hand can offer. In exchange, they lend the veterans some much-needed muscle.

A sidekick is an extra who's agreed to hang out with your hero and help out whenever he agrees to let her. In exchange, the hero promises to teach the sidekick what she needs to know to survive in Kennedy's America.

You might pick up a sidekick in the course of the game, but if you want your hero to start out with a junior friend, then he's got to take this quirk.

First, give your Guide a brief description of the sidekick. Include who she is, what her powers are, and how she met your hero. From there, it's up to the Guide to actually create the sidekick's profile and record her statistics on a hero sheet.

Unless your hero makes an effort to shake a sidekick, she's almost always around. Even then, the sidekick does her level best to figure out where the hero's going and then tags along, hidden in the shadows.

A sidekick is not a second hero for the player to control. The Guide is entirely in charge of her. Sure, the hero can make suggestions about what the sidekick should do or even give orders, but the Guide chooses whether or not the sidekick listens.

As part of having the sidekick, the hero automatically takes a *vow* to do his best to protect the sidekick at all costs. This *vow* doesn't have an actual value of its own. It's figured into the cost of the *sidekick* quirk.

SKEPTICAL -1

Even in a world in which people walk around with all sorts of strange powers, your hero is always apt to accept answers that jibe with the laws of reality as she understands them. This can sometimes get in the way of her taking the proper precautions, but it does have one upside. Anytime someone tries to make a *persuasion* roll to convince the hero of something that she doesn't have personal proof of, the hero gets to add +2 to her opposing roll.

SLOW -2

Crosstown traffic moves faster than your hero.

Take –2 off your hero's *Pace.*

SLIGHT -5

Not every delta's a bruiser. "Slight" is a polite way of saying your hero's skinny, short, or just petite. This might make her harder to hit, but it also means that when she's hit, she takes it hard.

Take –1 from your hero's *Size.*

SNOBBY -1

Your hero's nearly cross-eyed from looking down his nose so often. Even before he got his delta powers, he was pretty sure he was better than anyone else. Now he knows it.

Anytime the hero tries a friendly *persuasion* roll, take –1 from his roll. Most people just don't like being talked down to.

SOFTHEARTED -1

There's nothing like a good sob story to get your hero's waterworks flowing—or his wallet open. The hero's not exactly *gullible*. That's something else entirely. He just finds it hard to turn down someone in need. He's the kind of guy who's always got spare change for the asking, and he's forever donating time or money to one cause or another.

This is a good trait. It just makes it easier for people to take advantage of your hero, whether they're truly needful or not. The hero must make a Challenging (10) *Spirit* roll to ignore someone in need.

STUBBORN -2

As your hero likes to say, "It's my way or the highway!"

Once your hero gets an idea in her head, she has a hard time letting it go. Unless she gets conclusive proof that she's wrong, she stands by her beliefs, come hell or high water. Even if someone presents her with entirely convincing evidence that she's incorrect, she only grudgingly admits it, and she keeps looking for ways to prove herself right. Otherwise, it takes a Challenging (10) *Spirit* roll for her to change her mind.

STUTTER -2

Oh, d-d-dear.

Your hero's got a bad stutter. In most cases, this is nothing much to worry about. It does take –1 from his friendly *persuasion* rolls, as people sometimes find it difficult to hold a conversation with him.

In stressful situations, though, the hero has to make a Challenging (10) *Spirit* roll to be able to communicate verbally. If he gets an extra success on the roll, he's actually so distracted by the enormity of what's happening around him that he momentarily forgets he's got a stutter at all, and he can speak normally.

SUPERSTITIOUS -2

Black cats, broken mirrors, and sidewalk cracks all give your hero fits. She lives by old wives' sayings and other even less-scientific sources of knowledge. The hero must make a Challenging (10) *Spirit* roll to ignore a "bad luck" superstition or suffer a –1 penalty to all rolls until the object of superstition is gone.

SQUEAMISH -2

Your hero's not afraid of a fight, but man, the sight of blood does him some harm.

Anytime your hero looks (whether on purpose or not) at something most people might think of as gross, he has to make a Challenging (10) *bravery* roll. If he fails it, he either faints, vomits, freezes, or runs screaming into the night. It's up to the Guide exactly what happens and what might set the hero's tender nature on edge.

TEMPER -2

The hero has a short fuse that's easily lit. When people are messing with him, it takes everything he has (in the form of a Challenging (10) *Spirit* roll) to not react.

When the hero lets loose with his temper, he doesn't get any special benefits. He's just stuck his foot in it, and now it's up to him to get out of it.

TOUGH +2

Your hero chews lightbulbs for breakfast.

Pain just doesn't seem to bother your hero as much as it does other people. Whenever she's suffering from a wound-effect modifier that adds to her Target Numbers, take –1 from that modifier.

For instance, with three wounds in her torso, your hero would normally add +3 to the Target Number of any actions, reflecting the suffering she's going through. (See Chapter Six for more on how this works.) Since she's *tough,* though, she only adds +2.

Some quirks you can take more than once. Unfortunately, that's not the case with this one.

UGLY -2

Your hero's face couldn't really stop a speeding bullet, but it could sure make the bullet regret going the way it did.

There's no other way to say it: Your hero is butt-ugly. In friendly *persuasion* rolls, he must take –2 from his result. On the other hand, he might get to add +2 to hostile *persuasion* rolls, at the Guide's option.

Unlucky -5

If it seems like the world's out to get your hero, you just might be right.

When making an action roll for your hero, you need one less 1 than normal to trigger a disaster. For example, if you're rolling five dice, you normally needs three 1s for a disastrous roll. Because your hero's *unlucky*, you only needs to roll two 1s to ruin her day.

It's possible for a hero to be both *lucky* and *unlucky*. Some people's fortunes just seem to run in streaks that way.

Vengeful -2

Your hero holds onto a grudge like a long-lost love. It's not going anywhere until he's done with it—and that's never going to happen.

When someone does your hero wrong, he's not the forgive and forget type. More like the revenge and remember. Whenever possible, he goes to great pains to even the score, at least in his own mind.

Veteran ±0

The hero's seen a lot of action in his time. He's learned from it, but it's left its mark on him too.

This quirk doesn't cost anything because it's a wash. When you select it, your hero gets an extra 5 points to spend on skills, quirks, or tricks. The only problem is he has to take an extra –5 points of *enemies*, plus he's *wanted*, for which he gets no points. You don't wander around that long and not attract the attention of Delta Prime.

None of these points count against the 10-point limit for negative quirks. After all, they're all built into the *veteran* quirk, which doesn't cost your hero a thing—at least on paper.

Voice +1

Your hero's got a voice that can either open doors or get them slammed in his face.

There are two kinds of *voices*: hard and soft. A *soft voice* adds +2 to friendly *persuasion* rolls when used, and a *hard voice* adds +2 to hostile *persuasion* rolls when used. The hero doesn't necessarily use the *voice* all the time, only when he needs to. Otherwise, it tends to lose its effect.

A hero can have both kinds of voices, and he can pull either of them out whenever he likes. He just can't use them both at the same time.

Vow -1 to -5

Your hero's sworn an oath to uphold some kind of ideal that's important to him. This can range from a priestly *vow* of celibacy or poverty to a *vow* to uphold the tenets and duties of public office—a rarely kept vow in *Brave New World*.

The more intrusive the *vow* is in the hero's life, the more it's worth. You should come up with the *vow* and then talk about it with your Guide. It's up to the Guide to set the exact value of the *vow*.

Wanted -5

When you're on the wrong side of the law, you're always watching over your shoulder.

To take the *wanted* quirk, your hero doesn't have to actually commit a crime. She's just got to be suspected of committing one—like being an unregistered delta—whether she actually did it or not. On the other hand, being a criminal doesn't necessarily mean the hero's *wanted*, especially if she's got a clean record.

With Kennedy's nationwide CrimeNet database, the record of anyone that's arrested for anything can be pulled up in a matter of seconds. Any law officer in the country can haul the hero in for any known crimes, even if they were committed in another state—even if the wrong is only unpaid parking tickets. And then he's got to sit there until someone makes bail for him—assuming the judge even sets a bail.

This means that the hero can't ever approach the police for help. As soon as she does, they're likely going to run a check on her, figure out who she is, and then slap the cuffs on her.

An unregistered delta with a public identity must take the *wanted* quirk.

Wise +3

There's a little voice inside your hero's head that stops him when he's about to do something stupid. Some call that wisdom. Others worry about you hearing little voices.

When your hero's about to do something unbelievably stupid, the Guide can ask you to make a Challenging (10) *Spirit* roll. If you fail it, your hero continues on with his course of action. If you succeed, your hero can take a moment to reconsider and then alter his plans to something less foolish.

It's up to the Guide to give you a last chance before something blows up in your hero's face. If she forgets, well, you should have played the hero a bit wiser, right?

Young -1

If your Defiant gets captured, he's headed for the Delta Academy instead of Delta Squadron or Delta Prime. They don't take children in the army—yet.

Because of your hero's age, many people don't take him seriously, and there are some things he can't legally do: drive, have a drink, enter an R-rated movie alone, and so on. Take –2 from any *persuasion* rolls.

Chapter Six: The Big Throwdown

Chapter Six: The Big Throwdown

No matter how much your hero might try to prevent it, eventually he's going to get into a fight. It's a violent world, after all, and the heroes deal with violent people.

Here's what to do when that happens.

Surprise

Most of the time, your hero's not going to stand toe-to-toe with a foe. Each character in the fight's going to do whatever he can to get the odds in his favor, and that often involves things like laying an ambush.

If there's a chance that a character might be surprised by another, his player needs to make a *perception* roll. It's up to the Guide to set the difficulty. It should be Easy (5) if the hero is expecting trouble, but it can go up to Difficult (15) or higher if the ambusher's really set the trap well or the hero's just plain clueless—or both.

If a hero fails the roll, he's surprised and can't do any actions that round.

The Combat Round

Most of the time you're playing *Brave New World*, you don't need to watch the clock too closely. You just assume the rest of the world keeps spinning along with little chance of you being interfered with.

That's different in a fight.

When the fists start flying, there's a lot to handle. To do that, there are some rules you've got to keep in mind. The first has to do with keeping track of what's happening in the fight.

When the fight starts, anyone in the area who might have any kind of effect on the fight "enters combat." From that point until the fight's over, the Guide breaks the game down into rounds of five seconds each.

In the course of a "round," each combatant gets a chance to take one or more actions. Once the round's over, the Guide checks to see if the fight's still going on. If it is, combat enters another round. You keep this up until the Guide declares the fight over.

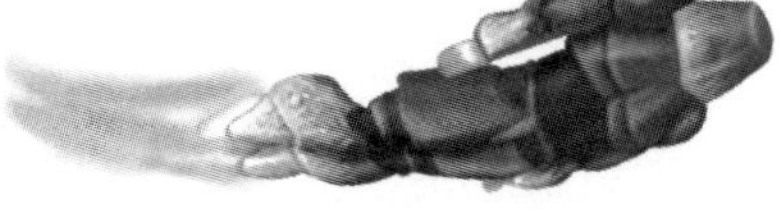

The Order of Combat

It's kind of a contradiction in terms, since most fights are anything but orderly. In a roleplaying game, though, you need a way to keep track of all the action that's going on. You do that by setting up the order of combat each round.

This is the easy part. To start out with, every hero gets one action per round, but he has a chance of getting more. To figure out how many more, every player must make an Easy (5) *Speed* roll for his hero. We call this an "initiative" roll. For every success a hero gets, he can perform one additional action during this round, up to his *Speed*.

The most actions a reg can have during a round is 5, but that limit doesn't hold for deltas.

The combatant with the highest result gets to go first, then the person with the next highest result, and so on, until every combatant that has an action has had a chance to go. If a character doesn't have an action left, just skip over her. She's done for this round.

If there's a tie, the combatant with the highest *Speed* trait goes first. If that's tied too, then the actions of the tied combatants all take place simultaneously.

Once every character in the fight's had a chance to take an action—if he's got one—start over again with the combatant who had the highest *Speed* roll. Make sure you skip over any combatant who've already used all of their actions.

Keep going around like this until everybody's used up all their actions. Then the round's over, and it's time to start another one.

Example: *The Rebel's got a* Speed *of 4d6, so Marty rolls five dice. He gets 1, 3, 5, and 6. He rerolls the 6 and gets 5. This gives him a total of (6+5=) 11. That's two successes, or two extra actions. He adds this to his free action for three total actions.*

The thug he's facing off against rolls his Speed *of 2d6 and gets 2 and 4. The 4 gets no successes, but the thug still has his one free action.*

Since the Rebel got the higher roll, he goes first. Then the thug gets an action. Then we start over with the Rebel again. After that, since the thug doesn't have any more actions left, we skip him this time around and let the Rebel use his final action, ending the round there.

Actions

The fact is that some tasks take longer than others. Cocking and firing a shotgun takes a lot longer than squeezing the trigger of an automatic pistol for instance. To help you with this, we break tasks down into three categories: simple, short, and long.

Simple Tasks (Zero Actions)

A simple task is something that requires little or no concentration and can be done at the same time as something else. This includes things like moving, talking, or making an opposed roll when your hero's the defender.

None of these require an action to do, but your hero can't just do them at any time. With the exception of defending himself, he's got to wait for his turn to come around, and then he can perform a simple task at the same time as he tries something more difficult, if he likes.

A hero can perform as many simple tasks at a time as he likes. Of course, this can quickly get ridiculous. It's up to the Guide to step in if that happens.

Short Tasks (One Action)

Most things a hero's going to want to do during combat are short tasks. These are things like cocking a weapon, firing a gun, throwing a punch, or using a power. These all take a single action to complete.

A short task takes up the entire action. A hero can do a simple task and a short task at the same time, but she can't do two or more simple tasks or long tasks at once.

Long Tasks (Two or More Actions)

Long tasks are those that take more time to pull off. Certain powers have to be charged up for an action or two before they can be used, for instance. When you start a long task, you tell the Guide what your hero's doing, and the Guide tells you how many actions it's going to take.

When your hero's spent the required number of actions on the task, the task is complete. If you need to make an action roll for this action, you roll the dice at the end of the last action spent.

Classifying Tasks

It's up to the Guide to figure out how many actions a task requires, using the guidelines given here. If she really has no idea, she should just roll a single die and tell the player the task requires that many actions.

Holding an Action

Sometimes you don't want your hero to just go charging into the fray. Savvy heroes often take a step back to let events unfold before they make a move. When that happens, you want your hero to hold his action instead of using it.

If you want to do this, when your hero's turn comes around, just tell the Guide you're holding your action. The rest of the round progresses normally.

You can hold an action until your next turn to use an action comes around or the fight ends. When your next turn comes up, you lose your held action, but you can just hold your next action too if you like.

Using a Held Action

If you've got a held action, you can use it any time you like. All you've got to do is tell the Guide what you're doing.

If you want to interrupt another character's action, then you've got a bit of a problem. The other character's not likely going to just roll over and let you have your way. You've got to fight for it.

When this happens (you've got two or more characters trying to do something at once), they each have to make a *Speed* roll. The character with the highest result gets to go first. If there's a tie, the actions are resolved simultaneously, with both taking effect at once.

Showing the Fight

Although most of the action in *Brave New World* happens in the collective imaginations of the Guide and the players, when the heroes get into a fight, that arena is often not as precise as you might want. Instead, the players are going to want to know exactly where their heroes are in respect to their foes.

The best way to do all of this is to show the players what's happening by putting miniature figures on a map of the area they're in. You can sketch the map out on a piece of paper if you like, but there's a better way.

Lots of good gaming stores sell vinyl mapsheets you can draw on with erasable markers. These come printed with a grid on them to make it easy to gauge ranges between combatants. Alternatively, you can pick up a whiteboard from an office-supply store and use dry-erase markers to draw out your map.

Once you've got the map drawn, you need to have something to show where the heroes and their foes are on the map. In a pinch, you can use dice or bottlecaps, but these really suffer from a lack of coolness. The best things going are metal miniatures.

Pinnacle sells a line of lead-free pewter metal miniatures. These represent a number of different kinds of characters from *Brave New World*, and they're perfect for breaking out whenever a fight starts. They paint up nice too, and they can really help make the battle seem a lot more concrete.

The miniatures come in a 30mm scale, which makes an inch on the map roughly equal to two yards. Keep that in mind when drawing your map, and you shouldn't have any problems.

Moving

Each round, a hero can move up to one inch (two yards) for every die and bonus point of *Speed* he's got, plus +5. This number is the hero's *Pace*.

> ***Example:*** *The Rebel's* Speed *is 4d6. He can move up to (4+5=) 9 inches—18 yards—in a round.*

Heroes often have several actions during a round, and they can break their movement up among these actions as they like. They can even move, take an action, and then move some more on the same action.

Any movement not used up during a round is lost. It cannot be carried over from round to round.

> ***Example:*** *The Rebel's got a* Pace *of 9, and he's got two actions this round. He can move nine inches on his first action and none on his second. Or he can stand still on his first action and move nine inches on his second action. Or he can move five inches on his first action and four on his second. Or he can break it up any other way he likes.*

Moving on a Held Action

A hero can move normally on a held action, as long as he's got *Pace* left to use during that round. If he's already used up all of his *Pace*, he can't move, although he can still act.

Sprinting

If a hero wants to, she can put her head down and push every ounce of speed out of herself for an action. This is a short task, which means the hero can't do anything else while she's sprinting.

A sprinter gets an extra inch of movement (two yards) on each action she sprints. If she's got lots of actions during a round, she can keep sprinting on each of them, racking up lots of extra movement.

At the end of a round in which a hero sprints, she must make an Easy (5) *Strength* roll. If she fails it, she becomes

stunned. For each round the hero sprints in a row, the Target Number goes up by +1 until the hero either stops sprinting or is stunned.

See pages 159–160 for more about being stunned and recovering from it.

Getting Down—and Back Up Again

A hero can lie prone with no movement penalty. If the hero is off his feet for some reason, whether on purpose or because she was knocked down, it takes 4 inches worth of movement to stand up.

If your hero doesn't have that much movement left, she can't get up. If your hero somehow has less than 4 inches of movement in an entire turn, she can instead use all of her movement for the turn to get up.

While on the ground, a hero can crawl at up to a quarter of her *Pace.* Also, take –4 from any *dodge* rolls.

Leaping

A hero can jump forward up to a half-inch for each point of *Strength* he's got.

Lifting and Moving

The fact is it's hard to haul tail when you're loaded down with a lot of gear. The more you're carrying with you, the slower you're going to move.

To reflect that, check the following tables. The Size Table gives the relative weights for things or creatures at each *Size*. As you can see from the table, *Size* is hardly an exact measurement, although it works just fine in most cases. If something's weight stands between two *Sizes*, you should usually go with the closer number, although it's the Guide's call in the end.

The Carrying Table shows how much a hero can carry and how fast he can move with it. A hero can carry an amount of weight with a total *Size* up to his *Strength*+2. The Guide should feel free to alter these guidelines if the weight being carried is particularly bulky or just hard to handle.

Size

Size	Typical Weight	Examples
1	Up to 5 pounds	Cat, bowling ball
2	20 pounds	Young child
3	50 pounds	Average dog
4	100 pounds	Small person
5	150 pounds	Average person
6	250 pounds	Big person
7	400 pounds	Huge person
8	650 pounds	Sumo wrestler, gorilla
9	1000 pounds	Bear, horse
10	1750 pounds	Small car
11	2500 pounds	Large car
12	2 tons	
13	3 tons	
14	5 tons	Elephant
15	8 tons	
16	13 tons	
17	20 tons	
18	30 tons	
19	50 tons	
20	80 tons	
21	130 tons	Blue whale
22	200 tons	
23	300 tons	

Carrying

Size of Items Carried	Pace
Up to *Strength*	Normal
Strength+1	50%
Strength+2	0%
Strength+3 or more	—

Attacking

There are two basic kinds of attacks: ranged combat and close combat.

Ranged combat attacks are things like gunshots, energy blasts, and the like—basically anything your hero has to fire at a foe.

Close combat attacks include smacking someone with a club or whaling on him with your fists.

Let's start with ranged combat attacks.

Ranged Combat Attacks

When words fail, people get to fighting, and more often than not, they resort to something they can shoot people with.

Shooting

Shooting a target is really simple. It's an action that uses your hero's *shooting* skill. The base Target Number is 5.

The Target Number can be modified by a lot of things, which we'll get to in a bit. The only thing you really need to know right now is that if your action roll meets or beats the Target Number, your attack hits.

Line of Sight

With a ranged attack, the first thing you've got to figure out is whether or not your hero can see the target he wants to shoot at.

This is one really good reason to use miniatures in your game. If you've got the figures set out on the table, all the Guide has to do is get down, get herself a miniature's eye view of the action, and make the call. Otherwise, it's a lot of guesswork.

If the attacker can see his target, then he can fire at it. Otherwise, he's out of luck.

Figuring out the line of sight can get tricky. In all cases, it's up to the Guide to use common sense to work it out.

RANGED WEAPONS

Just like with characters, each weapon has a profile that tells you exactly how it works in the game. Let's take a look at one example. For the rest of the list, see page 188.

WEAPON TYPE

This is the kind of weapon we're talking about.

ACTION

This is the means by which the weapon works. "Auto" means the gun's an automatic.

AMMO

This is the kind of ammunition the weapon takes. This is usually listed by caliber (like .45) or in millimeters (mm).

SHOTS

Every weapon only holds a certain number of bullets, charges, or whatever. This number tells you how many shots you can fire with the weapon before it has to be reloaded or recharged.

QUICKNESS

Every weapon has a Quickness score that tells you how many actions it takes to use it in combat. This number's based on how unwieldy the weapon is. It takes a bit longer to draw a bead with a rifle than with a pistol, for instance.

RATE OF FIRE

A gun can fire a number of bullets up to its Rate of Fire on each action. Any weapon with a Rate of Fire of more than 1 is treated as an automatic. This has more to do with what it's like to fire a lot of shots with the gun at once than it does with the gun's action.

RANGE INCREMENT

The farther away a target is, the harder it is to hit. Some weapons, like rifles, are meant to be used against targets at further distances, so it's easier to hit a distant target with these than with a pistol. We boil this down into the weapon's Range Increment.

When your hero's shooting at someone, measure the range between the figures in inches. Then you divide the range by the weapon's Range Increment, round down, and add that number to the shot's Target Number. This is known as the "range modifier."

> ***Example:*** *A policeman fires her revolver at the Rebel. The regular Target Number for a ranged attack is Easy (5). The range between them is 12 inches. The Range Increment is 5, so the range modifier is (12÷5=2.2) 2. The Target Number for the shot is 7.*

DAMAGE

When the shot hits the target, it does a certain amount of damage, as listed under this entry. You read the damage dice just like you do for an action roll.

SAMPLE WEAPON

Weapon Type	Action	Ammo	Shots	Quickness	Rate of Fire	Range Increment	Damage	Cost
Colt 2000	Auto	9mm	15	1	1	5	5d6+5	$600

Ranged Attack Modifiers

Okay, you know all about weapons, how to fire them, and how range affects the shot, but that's not all there is to it. A fight is a chaotic thing, and there's a lot more going on in it than just pointing a gun and pulling the trigger.

Certain situations happen often enough that we've assigned standard modifiers to them. A lot of stranger things can happen too, and in those cases it's up to the Guide to assign modifiers as he sees fit.

Each of the modifiers listed on the table below are added to the attack roll's Target Number.

Ranged Attack Modifiers

Situation	Modifier
Shooter is moving on foot	+4
Shooter is in a moving vehicle	+2
Target's *Size*	Varies
Target is hidden	+6
Lighting:	
Twilight	+2
Night with a full moon	+2
Night with a half moon	+4
Night with no moon (city)	+6
Night with no moon (country)	+8
Total darkness	+10
Blinded	+10

Shooter is Moving on Foot

If the shooter moves at all during this action, she has to add +4 to her Target Number. Remember, she can't shoot and sprint at the same time.

Shooter is in a Moving Vehicle

Even a luxury car with the sweetest shocks bumps around a bit. If the shooter's in a moving vehicle, she has to add +2 to the Target Number.

Size

It's a lot easier to hit a bigger target than a smaller one. Add +1 to the Target Number for every point of *Size* the target has over 5. Or take –1 from the Target Number for every point of *Size* the target has under 5.

Target is Hidden

This is the exception to the line of sight rule. If the target's entirely hidden behind something, your hero can still fire at him. All he's got to do is guess where the target really is and then hope his attack can penetrate whatever the target's hiding behind.

The standard modifier for this is +6, but the Guide can move this up or down as she sees fit. This should depend on the relative size of whatever the target's hiding behind.

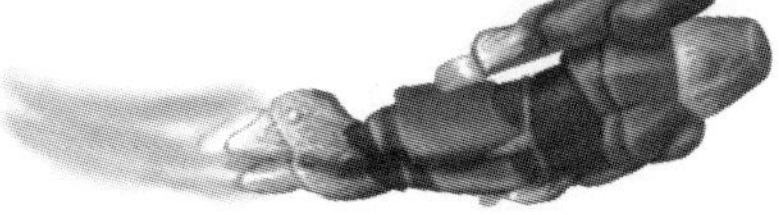

LIGHTING

The harder it is to see something, the harder it is to hit it with a ranged attack. The Guide should figure out what the available light is and then apply these modifiers.

Other light sources like flashlights can affect these modifiers too. If the target's carrying a light source the attacker can see, for instance, then none of the modifiers should apply.

DIFFERENT WEAPON TYPES

The regular rules work fine for things like shooting revolvers or firing energy blasts. Not all ranged attacks fit those models well though.

FIRING A BURST

With many weapons and some powers, you squeeze the trigger and fire a burst of bullets. To keep things simple, don't roll for each bullet. First, figure out how many bullets you want to fire. You can fire from one bullet up to the weapon's Rate of Fire.

Then you just make a standard *shooting* roll, adding an extra die for each bullet you're firing past the first. For each success you get on the roll, a bullet finds its mark. These successes can't also be used for tricks.

The attacker can aim (see page 150 for how to use this maneuver) before letting loose a burst of automatic fire.

The attacker can also make a called shot with an automatic burst, but only the first shot hits in the called location. The rest are rolled for randomly.

A double-barreled shotgun is a bit of a special case. It's got a Rate of Fire of 2 because both barrels can be fired at once. We treat this like an automatic weapon for purposes of the rules.

MULTIPLE TARGETS

Sometimes when you're tossing that much lead in the air, you get the urge to share the wealth.

To hit more than one target with a burst, do this. Pick your primary target and roll the dice for the burst. Once you know how many bullets have hit, assign as many of them as you like to your primary target. (She's got to take at least one.)

Then choose another target within one inch, and assign as many of the leftover bullets as you like to him. You can keep doing this—as long as each new target is within one inch of the last—until you run out of hits.

If you want to switch to a new target that's more than an inch away from the last, you can, but you have to waste one remaining hit for each extra inch away the next target is.

You must assign each of the bullets to a potential target before you make your attack roll.

SHOTGUNS

Unlike regular guns, shotguns don't fire a single bullet. Instead, they fire shells which let loose a barrage of tiny, metal balls.

Shotguns are great for close-in fighting, but the barrage tends to spread out as it travels away from the shooter, so they're not so great at longer ranges.

SHOTGUN DAMAGE

Range	Damage
Point blank	5d6+15
1–5 inches	5d6+10
5–10 inches	5d6+5
10–15 inches	5d6

Shotgun Slugs

Shotguns usually fire shells—packs of metal pellets—but they can also be loaded with a different kind of ammunition called a slug. A slug is a huge chunk of lead, and when it smacks into a target, it's time to call for a medic—or a hearse.

When firing a slug, add +4 to the Target Number, due to the poor way such a hunk of metal slides through the air. However, a shotgun slug always does 5d6+15 damage, no matter the range.

Double Your Fun

With a double-barreled shotgun, a hero can let loose with both barrels at once. You make a single attack roll and hit-location roll for both barrels, but you roll damage for each barrel separately. The attacks are considered simultaneous, so you should treat both barrels as if they were firing at armor in the same condition, no matter how battered it is by either attack.

Explosives

Explosives are listed with a Blast Radius, say 5 inches. That means that anything within 5 inches of the explosive when it goes off takes full damage.

There are two other rings around the primary Blast Radius, each of which is as wide as the Blast Radius. The damage in the secondary Blast Radius is half the regular damage total, while people in the tertiary Blast Radius take only a quarter of the standard damage. If the Blast Radius is 5 inches, the secondary ring is from 5–10 inches away, and the tertiary is from 10–15 inches away.

If a target is actually on a Blast Radius line, the target takes the worse of the two possible damage totals.

When figuring damage from an explosion, just roll once, then apply it to everyone affected by the blast. Explosions deal massive damage. See page 160 for how this works.

__Example:__ A Primer fires a grenade at the Rebel. The grenade has a Blast Radius of 5 inches, so anything up to 5 inches from the target takes full damage. People 5 to 10 inches away takes half the damage, and anyone 10 to 15 inches away takes a quarter of the damage. If the rolled damage was 22 points, those in the primary radius take all 22 points, those in the secondary radius take (22 ÷ 2=) 11 points, and tertiary targets take (22 ÷ 4= 5.5=) 5.

Deviation

When you miss with area-affect attacks—things like grenades, rockets, and the like— you need to check for deviation. After all, even if you miss the target, the attack is going to hit somewhere.

That is, unless you roll a disaster. In that case, the attack goes off between your hero's feet.

Direction

First you need to know which direction the attack went from the targeted point—not from the attacker. Unless the roll was disastrous, we assume it got going in the right direction at least.

Place a marker down where the attack was meant to hit. Then roll 1d6. (This die roll isn't open-ended, so don't reroll if you get a 6.) Double the result and read it just like you would off a clock's face centered on the target, with the 12 o'clock position pointing away from the attacker. That's the direction in which the attack deviates from the target.

__Example:__ A Primer fires a grenade at Jackie Savage, who's 15 inches away, but misses. Checking for direction, he rolls 1d6 and gets a 6. Doubling that, he gets (6 x 2=) 12, meaning the grenade heads off in the 12 o'clock direction, directly away from the Primer.

DISTANCE

Next, you need to figure out how far from the targeted point the attack went. Roll 1d6 for every full 10 inches between the attacker and the targeted point. If the range is less than 10 inches, just roll 1d6 instead. This roll is open-ended like normal.

Either way, the attack deviates that many inches along the direction you rolled. If the attack deviated backward (to the 4, 6, or 8 o'clock positions), the attack can't deviate any further than half the original range.

> ***Example:*** *Checking for distance, the Primer rolls 1d6. He gets a 6, then rerolls it and gets a 1 for a total of (6 + 1=) 7. The grenade travels 7 inches over Jackie's head.*

TWO-HANDED WEAPONS

It only takes one good hand to fire a pistol, but most longer weapons (rifles, shotguns, machine-guns—even axes or chainsaws) require two. Any time a hero uses a two-handed weapon in one hand, add +3 to the Target Number. Also, if the hero's in close combat, he loses the weapon's Defensive Bonus.

BYSTANDERS

One of the things you're going to see a lot of in *Brave New World* is collateral damage. Lots of deltas can kill a reg without breaking a sweat, and many can even do so accidentally. After all, if your hero's standing on a crowded street and he lets loose with a barrage of energy blasts, there's a good chance he's going to harm some innocents along with his foes.

If your hero's in a situation where stray shots don't have a chance of hitting anyone, don't worry about them. In a congested city—or a big fight—the issue is going to come up. This is especially true if the attacker's firing a burst. Remember, any bullets that go into the burst that don't come up as hits are stray bullets.

STRAY BULLETS

If a shot misses, look along the line of sight between the attacker and the target, continuing the line past the target. Anyone within a half inch (one yard) of that line could be hit by the shot, no matter if she's friend or foe.

Starting with the possible victim closest to the attacker, roll 1d6. On a 1, the attack hits that bystander. If a potential target isn't hit, keep checking on down the line until someone is hit or you run out of bystanders.

The spray from a shotgun shell is a lot more likely to injure an innocent. For these attacks, roll 1d6 like normal. A bystander is hit on a 1 or 2.

HUMAN SHIELDS

If a bystander's directly between the attacker and the target—say the defender's using someone else as a bullet catcher—and the attack hits, it's a bit simpler. All you've got to do is figure out if the attack hits a location on the target that's covered by the shield by making a roll on the Hit Location Table. (We'll get to that in just a bit, on page 154.) If so, the shield's hit instead.

When this happens, the Guide should be able to figure out what part of the shield was covering the target's "hit" location. If it's not absolutely clear, just make another roll on the Hit Location Table.

Ranged Combat Maneuvers

There are some things a hero can do to stack the odds in his favor.

Aiming

The regular ranged attack rules assume that the attacker's in the middle of a fight. That's not always the case though, and if your hero wants to take the time to set up a good shot for herself, more power to her. You can even aim before firing a burst.

Aiming is a short task, so it requires one action. For every action the hero spends aiming at a target, take –2 from the Target Number. The maximum modifier for aiming is –6, so after your hero's aimed for three actions, she's not doing herself any more good.

The attack must be made right after an aiming action for the aiming to have any effect. You can hold the shot as long as the Guide lets you, but you can't aim for three actions, sprint to a different position, then fire. Well, you can, but then you lose out on any modifiers for aiming.

Called Shots

Where you hit a target can be just as important as if you hit it. Attacks that hit the head are particularly nasty, and more than one hero has tried to blast an attacker's gun out of his hands instead of hurting him directly.

When your hero wants to shoot at a particular part of the target's body instead of just firing away, that's called "making a called shot."

The smaller the body part is, the harder it is to hit it. See the following table for examples. The Guide should use these to figure out proper modifiers for anything else that might come up.

Called-Shot Modifiers

Location	Modifier
Torso	+2
Leg or arm	+4
Head	+6
Weapon	+6

Disarming

To disarm a foe, the hero must first make a called shot to the weapon, which adds +6 to the Target Number. If the weapon's hit, the foe must make a Challenging (10) *Strength* roll or drop the weapon.

Hipshooting

Sometimes when that Primer's bearing down on you, you don't have the time to properly point a gun at a target. You can always try shooting from the hip.

When hipshooting, you fire a weapon with a Quickness of more than 1 in a single action. You just have to add weapon's Quickness to the Target Number to account for the hasty shot. Hipshooting a weapon with a Quickness of 2, for example, would add +2 to the Target Number.

You can't aim while hipshooting, although you can try a called shot if you're feeling lucky.

Quick Draw

Drawing a weapon takes a full action. With the *quick draw* skill, you can draw your weapon and fire it—or do whatever else might happen to come to mind—in the same action. This is an Easy (5) roll.

If you blow the *quick draw* roll, you still draw the gun, but and you can't fire on that action.

Reloading

If you keep blasting away with a weapon, you're going to end up with an empty gun. Then it's time to reload.

How long it takes a hero to entirely reload a weapon depends on what kind of weapon you're talking about. See the Reloading Times Table for all the details. Each weapon's action is listed on the Ranged Weapons Table on page 188.

Reloading Times

Weapon Action	Actions to Reload
Automatic	2
Bolt	3
Drawn	1
Revolver	3
Shotgun	2
Pump	3

Speed-Loading

Fumbling around with all that ammo can prove a fatal delay in a firefight. A hero with the *speed-load* skill can pop a clip back in and keep firing without missing a beat.

When you want your hero to slap the ammo back in faster, make an Easy (5) *speed-load* roll. For each success you get, it takes the hero one less action to reload her weapon. If this reduces the number of actions needed to 0 or less, the hero can actually fire the weapon on that same action.

Firing with the Off-Hand

Unless your hero's *ambidextrous*, he favors one hand over the other in most things. Firing a gun with the offhand is a bit tougher. Whenever he tries this, add +4 to the attack's Target Number.

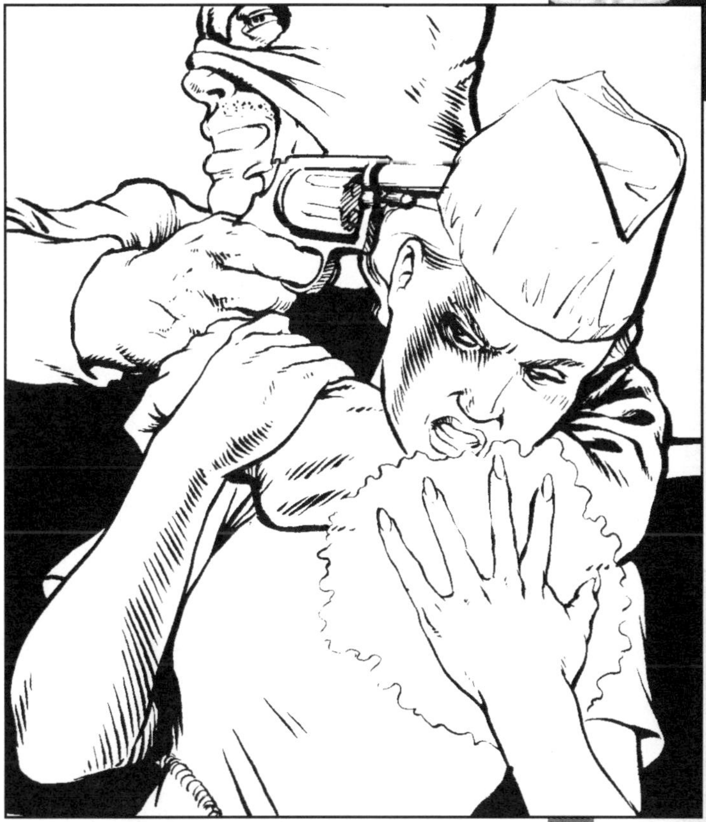

Using Two Weapons

Most folks have seen enough John Woo movies to think that waltzing around with a gun in each fist is the way to go. Sure, it looks cool, but there's a reason most folks don't bother.

When a hero fires two guns at once, add +4 to the Target Number of each attack. This is in addition to the +4 penalty for the off-hand's attack.

Thrown Weapons

There's another way to hurt someone from a distance: throw something at him. The worst most regs can do is throw something like a dart or a grenade. Some deltas can toss around bowling balls like they were skipping stones off the Chicago Bay. Either way, the game treats these things the same.

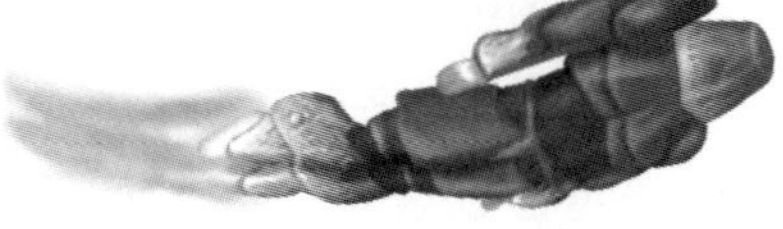

Throwing something at a target is just like shooting at him. You figure in all of the same modifiers, even the Range Increment, to set the Target Number. When you roll the dice, though, you use your hero's *throwing* skill instead of his *shooting* skill.

Ranges

The maximum distance a hero can throw most small things is 10 times his *Strength* in inches. This rule works well for things with a *Size* of 1, but the Guide should adjust this top range for heavier things. A hero can throw larger things, but not as far. Divide the hero's regular top range by the object's *Size* to get the new top range, rounding down.

If the hero tries to throw an object with a *Size* equal to his *Strength*, the farthest he can throw it is his *Strength* in inches. If its *Size* is 1 more than his *Strength,* the maximum is half his *Strength* in inches. If it's 2 more, he can only throw it a quarter of his *Strength.*

> ***Example:*** *The Rebel has a* Strength *of 4d6. He can throw a* Size *1 object up to (4 x 10=) 40 inches (80 yards). If he wants to throw a* Size *5 woman to safety from the top of a burning building, the furthest he could toss her is 2 inches (4 yards).*

Range Increments

The Range Increment for a thrown weapon is equal to the thrower's *Speed* dice, plus any bonuses. It doesn't matter what the *Size* of the thrown object is.

> ***Example:*** *The Rebel's got a* Speed *of 4d6. His Range Increment when throwing is 4.*

Close Combat Attacks

As powerful as they are, deltas often resort to their fists.

The hero has to be within reach of his foe to make a close attack. With most weapons, this is usually less than 1 inch, but it can be more if the hero's got a longer weapon. If the hero's attacking with her fists, she has to be touching her opponent (or at least close enough to reach him).

Once the foe's within the attacker's reach, the attacker makes a *fighting* or *fighting weapon* roll. The base Target Number is Easy (5), but you add the defender's *fighting* bonus to that. If the defender's using a fighting weapon, add his *fighting weapon* bonus instead.

> ***Example:*** *The Rebel takes a swing at the Primer who's been hassling him. The Primer's* fighting: barehanded *skill is 3, so the attack's Target Number is 8. The Rebel's* Strength *is 4d6, and his* fighting: barehanded *skill is 5, so he rolls 4d6+5. His final result is 12, which hits.*

Defensive Bonuses

Some close combat weapons are useful for blocking attacks too. We describe this parrying ability with a Defensive Bonus statistic.

In a fight, if the defender's weapon has a Defensive Bonus, add that to the attack's Target Number, along with the defender's *fighting weapon* skill.

> ***Example:*** *The Rebel punches at another Primer who's brandishing a huge knife. The Primer's* fighting: blade *skill is 3 and the weapon's Defensive Bonus is +1. That makes the Target Number 9.*

Close Combat Maneuvers

Just because your hero's decided to work with his fists doesn't mean he's not as tricky as a goon with a gun. Here are some things you can do to give your hero an edge. And remember: There's no such thing as a fair fight.

Most times, for close combat attacks, a hero's going to use a *fighting* or a *martial arts* skill. These are essentially the same skills, just based on different traits. Pick whichever your hero is better with, and dive on in!

Charging

A hero who moves directly into a close combat attack from a distance can add +1 to his damage roll for every full 5 inches he moved, up to a maximum of +10. The weapon or fist or whatever takes just the damage bonus as damage itself, so be careful with this. Most weapons can take three wounds before being destroyed.

For instance, if your hero charges 10 inches and punches a foe, he gets a +2 bonus to his damage, but he takes 2 points of damage to his fist. Since this is under his *Size*, he's fine, but if he's moving faster, he could hurt himself.

Disarming

To disarm a foe, the hero must first make a called shot to the weapon, which adds +6 to the Target Number. If the hero then wins an opposed *Strength* roll, he's grabbed the weapon away from his foe.

Rushing an Attack

Close combat weapons have a Quickness statistic, just like ranged weapons. In much the same way you can hipshoot a gun, you can rush an attack with a close combat weapon too.

A hero can make an attack with a high-Quickness weapon in a single action, but doing so adds the Quickness to the Target Number.

Off-Hand Attacks

Sometimes you can't always punch someone else with your favorite fist. Unless you're just as good with both hands, it's not so easy.

Your hero can use her offhand for a close combat attack, but unless your hero is *ambidextrous,* you have to add +4 to the attack's Target Number.

Two-Fisted Brawling

A hero can make two close-combat attacks in a single action, but this adds +4 to the Target Number of each attack. If the hero's not *ambidextrous*, the offhand penalty still applies. This means you need to add a total of +4 to the attack with the good hand and +8 to the offhand attack.

Dodging

Your hero doesn't have to just stand there and take it while someone's shooting at him or trying to punch him out. Smart heroes who can't take it as well as they can dish it out do what they can to get the hell out of the way.

When an attack is declared against your hero, you can declare that he'd like to dodge it. You must do so before the attack roll is made.

To dodge, the hero has to give up his next action in the round. If he's holding an action, he has to give that action up instead. The dodge only works against this one attack.

If the hero doesn't have any actions left in the round, he's out of luck. He's just stuck without a way to dodge.

If the hero does have an action to use, just tell the Guide you'd like the hero to dodge. Then roll your hero's *dodge* skill. Instead of adding any attack modifiers to a Target Number of 5, the attacker uses your result—or the original Target Number of 5 if that's higher—at the base Target Number.

When dodging, your hero can use any movement he's got left for the round, but you must resolve the attack before moving the hero.

> ***Example:*** *A Primer shoots at the Rebel with a pistol from at 12 inches, so the range modifier is +2. The Rebel decides to dodge the attack, so he surrenders the action he was holding. The Rebel's* Speed *is 4d6, and his* dodge *is 3. He rolls and gets a 14. The Target Number for the Primer's attack is now (14+2=) 16. The Primer rolls and gets a 10, so the shot misses.*

Hit Locations

Once an attack hits an opponent, you've got to figure out where the attack hit her. For that, all you've got to do is roll on the Hit Location Table. This roll is *not* open-ended. Just roll the die once, and check the table.

This table assumes the target's human—or at least human-shaped. If that's not the case, it's up to the Guide to modify the standard table to fit.

Hit Location

1d6	Location
1	Leg*
2–4	Torso
5	Arm*
6	Head

* If you get a hit in the arm or leg, roll again. On an odd number, the left limb is hit. On an even number, it's the right.

Cover

In a ranged combat, most people don't just stand facing each other and keep blasting away until one or the other falls. Instead, they scramble like hell to find whatever advantage they can, using anything good and solid they can find—cars, mailboxes, lampposts, and so on—for cover.

The real question is: How much good does the cover do?

If you've got a target behind cover, you handle the attack just like normal, right up to and including rolling for the hit location. Then, if the attack supposedly hits a body part that's behind cover, it goes into the cover instead of the target.

The cover then acts like armor. At the Guide's discretion, he can simply rule the cover is hard enough to deflect the attack. See pages 156–158 for details.

> ***Example:*** *The Rebel's firing an energy blast at a Primer who's shooting at him from behind a car. The Rebel can only see the Primer's head, arms, and torso, but he lets loose at his pursuer anyhow. The attack hits, but he gets a 1 on the hit-location roll, which would be a hit to the Primer's leg. Since the leg is behind cover, the Rebel's shot smashes into the car instead of the Primer, leaving the Primer unhurt.*

Prone Targets

In a fight, some people like to throw themselves on the ground to make a smaller target for attackers far away. This is called "going prone." A prone target is assumed to have cover for everything but his head and arms—unless someone sneaks up behind him, of course.

Damage

Now you know how to have your hero attack a target, hit it, and figure out where she hit it. It's time to see what happens to the target.

Damage dice are rolled just like skill dice. They're open-ended, and you pick your highest roll, adding in any modifiers.

Damage rolls do differ in one way. No matter how badly you roll, you can't have a disastrous damage roll.

Ranged Weapon Damage

Every weapon's profile has an entry for Damage. When your hero hits with an attack with a weapon, roll the listed dice for his weapon, then add the bonus. That's how much damage the attack does.

Example: A thief shoots the Rebel in the arm. She's firing a Colt 2000, so the damage is 5d6+5. She rolls and gets 1, 2, 3, 4, and 4 on the dice. She adds the weapon's damage bonus to that to get (4+5=) 9 points of damage.

Bare-Handed Damage

Sometimes your hero just wades in with his fists. When he hits with a *fighting* attack, just roll his *Strength*. That's your total damage.

***Example:** The Rebel takes a swing at the punk that just shot him. He hits, so he rolls his* Strength, *4d6. He rolls 1, 2, 4, and 5. His highest die is 5, so the attack does 5 points of damage.*

Close Combat Weapon Damage

There are times when a fist just isn't going to do the trick. If your hero's using a club, knife, or any other kind of close combat weapon, it's got a "Damage" entry in its profile too. Most times, the entry reads "*Strength+*" a bonus. This means you roll your *Strength* and add the bonus to it to figure the damage done.

***Example:** The Rebel decides his punches aren't doing enough damage, so he picks up the leg of a broken chair and goes to work. He smacks the punk in her right arm. The Guide rules the chair leg is a small club, so it does* Strength+1 *damage. The Rebel rolls his* Strength *and gets 2, 4, 5, and 6. He rerolls the 6 and gets 2, making his* Strength *roll (6+2=) 8. He adds the weapon's bonus to get a total damage of (8+1=) 9.*

Head Shots

Hits to the head do a bit more damage than normal. For hits to the head, add two extra dice to your damage roll.

***Example:** The thief shoots the Rebel again, this time getting a shot to the head. She adds two damage dice to her damage roll, so instead of rolling 5d6+5, she rolls 7d6+5.*

Size

Now that you've got the amount of damage done figured out, you've got to determine how badly the target is wounded. Take the damage points and divide them by the target's *Size*. (For most people, this is 5.) Leave off any remainders. That's how many wounds the target takes to that hit location.

***Example:** When the Rebel clubbed the thief, he did 9 points of damage. That means he did (9÷5=1.8=) 1 wound to him.*

Armor

All armor is described by two numbers separated by a slash like this: 10/3. The first tells how much damage the armor can deflect from a single attack. You just subtract the value from the amount of damage done. This happens before dividing the damage by the defender's *Size*.

The number after the slash tells how many wounds the armor can absorb once the attack gets through the deflective value. If the armor can absorb damage, split up the wounds between the armor and the wearer evenly, up to the armor's absorbing ability. If there is an odd number of wounds to be applied, the wearer takes the extra one.

Once the armor takes all the wounds it can in a location, the wearer takes any extra wounds. Also, the armor no longer even gives any deflective benefits in this hit location.

> ***Example:*** *An Armorgeddon trooper's armor is rated Armor 10/3. This means it deflects up to 10 points of damage from any attack and can then absorb up to three wounds in each hit location. Once the armor takes three or more wounds in a location, it's useless against any further attacks against that location.*
>
> *The trooper takes an energy blast to his left leg. It does 26 points of damage. The armor deflects 10 points of damage, reducing it to (26–10=) 16 points. Since the trooper is* Size *5, the attack does (16÷5=3.2=) 3 wounds. The armor takes one wound, and the trooper takes two.*

If the number after the slash is a dash, like 10/—, that means that the armor has no absorbing ability. On the other hand, it also never wears out.

Layered Armor

Some heroes may want to stick as much armor as they can between themselves and the bullets flying around their heads, but it quickly just gets too bulky. A hero can only wear one layer of armor, not including any protection her own skin may give her.

If a hero with armored skin is wearing armor, use the higher deflective value. If both the armor and the skin have an absorbing value, the hero still takes every other wound, but the worn armor starts taking wounds first. The skin only takes wounds in a hit location after the worn armor there has been destroyed.

Shields

Most shields cover the hero's shield arm and torso, unless she's hunkered down behind it. They only protect against attacks from the front.

If the hero's wearing armor or has armored skin, only use the highest deflective value. The shield takes wounds first, then any armor the hero's wearing, then the hero's skin.

Improvised Armor

Some heroes will try anything to stop a bullet. It's up to the Guide to give the impromptu cover an *armor* value. Here are some guidelines.

Improvised Armor Values

Material	Armor Value
Steel, plate	10/3
Steel, thick	20/5
Wood, thin	5/1
Wood, solid	10/2

Battering It Down

Sometimes a hero's wants to go through something. For this, just use the Improvised Armor Values Table. When the thing's taken three times its absorbing value, it's destroyed.

Armor-Piercing Ammo

Each kind of AP ammo has a number that shows how much of an armor's deflection it ignores. For instance, AP 5 ammo ignores 5 points of deflection.

> ***Example:*** *A thief fires an AP 5 bullet at an Armorgeddon trooper. It hits the Armor 10/3. Only (10–5=) 5 points of the damage are deflected.*

Wounds

A character can only take up to his *Strength* in wounds in each hit location before it becomes useless. If the hero's head or torso is made useless, she's been knocked out. Don't forget to mark the wounds on the hero's sheet.

> ***Example:*** *The thief has a* Strength *of 3d6. This means she can take up to 3 wounds in each hit location. The Rebel's blow hit her in the right arm, so she can still take (3–1=) 2 more wounds there before her arm is made useless.*

Useless Limbs

When an arm's been made useless, it can't be used for anything. (That's why they call it "useless," smart guy.)

A hero with a useless leg has her *Pace* cut in half (rounded down). If both her legs are useless, she can crawl along at a half inch each round.

Death and Dismemberment

When a character's hit location takes double her *Strength*, it's been pulped. This is really bad news.

In the case of a limb, being pulped means it's been shattered or severed. If the hero doesn't get medical attention of some sort real soon, he might even bleed to death.

At the end of every round after the hero's limb has been pulped, he must make an Easy (5) *Strength* roll. If he fails three of these in a row, he bleeds to death. Anyone—even the injured hero—can stop the bleeding with an Easy (5) *medicine* roll.

If the victim's torso or head is pulped, he's flat-out dead. Start making the funeral arrangements.

Pulling a Punch

The problem here is that some deltas can kill a foe with a single punch without really even trying to. It's impossible to change how much damage you do with a gun, but in close combat, you can pull a punch, hurting the target a bit less.

When you want your hero to pull a punch, just have him hold back as many of his *Strength* dice as he likes, up to but not including his last die. He only rolls the remaining dice. Bruisers with a *Strength* bonus can use all, part, or none of their bonus too, as they like.

Even when a hero pulls a punch, he can still cause some serious damage, since the dice roll is open-ended. Hey, if someone wants to run his face into your fist, you can only do so much.

When you want your hero to pull a punch, you have to announce this to the Guide before you roll the attack dice.

> ***Example:*** *The Wall has a* Strength *of 5d6+5 He wants to pull a punch, so he decides to roll only one die and use only +3 of his* Strength *bonus. This makes his damage roll for the punch 1d6+3.*

Wound-Effect Modifiers

There's a lot more to being wounded than standing up or falling down. When you're hurt, it really slows you down.

When a hero's wounded, take the highest of all her wound levels and add that to the Target Number of any action roll she has to make.

If the hero's making an opposed roll, add the modifiers to her opponent's roll instead.

Wound-effect modifiers don't affect damage rolls unless there's a trait roll involved as part of the damage. Then the modifiers only affect the trait roll, not the weapon's bonus.

> ***Example:*** *The thief who the Rebel banged up before now has one wound to her torso and two in her right arm. She has to add +2 to the Target Number of any action roll—until she's healed.*

Stun

There's more to a wound than just aches and bruises. When someone clobbers you, it often knocks the wind out of you too.

Every time your hero takes a wound, you need to make a stun check. This is an Easy (5) *Strength* check. Don't forget

to add the wound-effect modifier to this Target Number, and take this wound into account when you do.

If a hero has a pulped limb, he has to make a stun check every round.

> ***Example:*** *The Rebel whacks the thief for two wounds in her right arm. She had one wound in her torso, which made her wound-effect modifier +1, but with the new wound, it's now +2. That means she needs to make a* Strength *check against a Target Number of 7.*

STUNNERS

Some weapons, like tasers or cattle prods, are meant to stun rather than kill. Their Damage is listed as "Stun (#)." The number in parentheses is the Target Number the victim must roll to avoid being stunned. The weapon does no actual damage.

RECOVERY

A stunned hero can't really do much of anything, including defend himself against an attack. Don't add the hero's close combat skills to the Target Number of a close combat attack against him, and he can't dodge either. Keep rolling to see how many actions the hero gets each round, but the only thing he can do on these actions is try to recover from being stunned.

Don't forget those wound-effect modifiers for each roll!

The victim needs to make another *Strength* check to recover. This is rolled against the same Target Number that he failed the stun check on—unless the hero's wounds are somehow healed or he takes more damage, in which case you should recalculate the wound-effect modifiers.

If a victim rolls a disastrous stun or recovery check, he's immediately knocked out. He stays out for 1d6 hours, or until he gets some medical attention. (It's an Easy (5) *medicine* roll to wake the victim back up.)

MASSIVE DAMAGE

Certain kinds of damage don't target a certain body part. They can hurt you all over. We call this "massive damage." Massive damage is caused by fire, falling, and explosions.

For massive damage, roll the attack normally, but skip the hit location roll. Figure out how many wounds the victim takes, then apply that result to every hit location.

Don't worry about extra damage for wounds taken to the head. Most massive damage attacks don't have the kind of penetrating power needed for the extra damage bonus. Besides, the victim's got enough problems.

Most piecemeal armor isn't much good for deflecting massive damage. The exceptions are full suits of armor and the *armor* power. With these, you can deduct the armor's deflective value once from the total damage. If this is the kind of damage that armor might do some good against, apply the armor's absorbing effects normally.

> ***Example:*** *The Rebel falls from a three-story building. He takes 24 points of damage. As a blaster, his skin is* armor *5, so he only takes 19 points of damage, which comes to (19÷5=3.8=) 3 wounds in every hit location. He's wearing Kevlar on his torso (Armor 10/—), which absorbs nothing, and a helmet on his head (Armor 10/3), which absorbs 1 wound.*

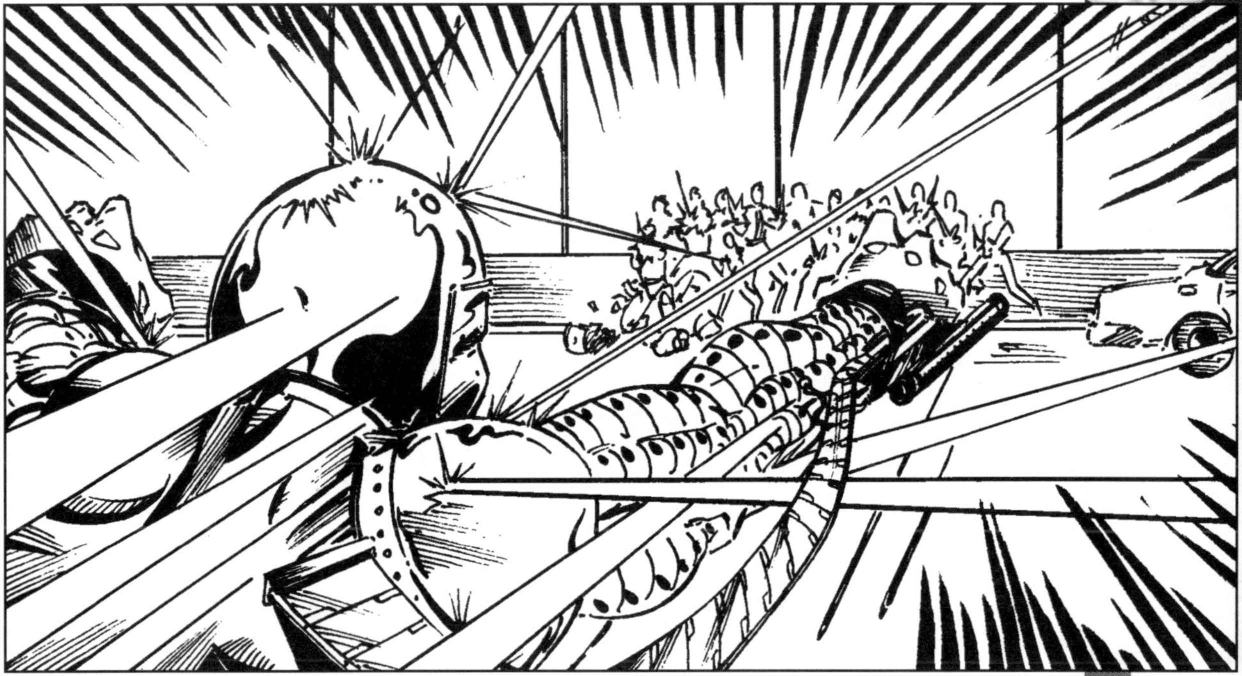

Other Ways to Get Hurt

There are plenty of ways for a hero to meet her doom beyond getting shot or beat to death. Let's cover a few of the more common here.

Drowning and Suffocating

Unless a hero's got the ability to breath water, sucking down a few gallons of wet stuff into her lungs can really ruin her day. The same goes for a chestful of vacuum or smoke.

Most heroes are fine for holding their breath for a minute—about 12 rounds. At the end of every round after that in which a hero is deprived of air, he must make an Easy (5) *Strength* or *swimming* roll. If he makes it, he's fine. If he fails, he takes a wound to his torso.

For every consecutive round after the first that the hero's rolls this check, add +1 to the Target Number. Once the hero's knocked out, he automatically fails the rolls until he dies.

This system assumes the hero's in combat. Otherwise, it's the Guide's call as to how long without air is too long before the *Strength* or *swimming* rolls begin.

Shrapnel

Explosions are often awful enough, but sometimes people wrap them in all sorts of metal before setting them off. When the thing explodes, it blasts out shards of metal known as shrapnel. If the explosive has shrapnel, each person in the first Blast Radius is hit by 1d6 pieces of flying metal. (This is an open-ended roll.) In the second Blast Radius, that reduces to 1d6–2 pieces, and in the third Blast Radius, it's only 1d6–4 pieces.

The damage the shrapnel does is listed in the weapon's description. For many homemade bombs and the like, it's 3d6+3 each. This damage is handled normally and is in addition to any massive damage from the boom.

Falling

With all the flying heroes and the kind who like jumping from rooftops, someone's going to take a fall. If no one catches her, he's going to land in a painful way.

Assuming the hero lands on something hard, he takes 1d6+3 points of massive damage for every two inches (four yards) he falls—that's roughly equal to a single story of a building—up to a maximum of 20d6+60.

Landing in water cuts the damage in half. With a Challenging (10) *Speed* roll, the hero hitting a decent body of water can make a clean dive and cut the damage to a quarter instead. Be sure to halve the damage before the maximum damage cap comes in. It's still possible to take 20d6+100 damage from a fall in the water. All the hero's got to do is fall two or four times as far.

Of course, if the water's shallow enough, the hero might smack into the bottom, hurting himself again. That's the Guide's call.

Improvised Weapons

Sometimes your hero's not going to have a weapon handy, and he's going to just pick up and use whatever's nearby. When he does this, it's up to the Guide to figure out how much damage the weapon does.

The damage for most thrown or close combat weapons is based on the thrower's *Strength*, plus a bonus. The bonus is based upon how heavy or sharp the weapon is. A thrown hunting knife, for instance, has a damage of *Strength*+3, while a beer bottle would likely have a damage of *Strength*+1. See page 189 for examples of different kinds of damages.

For large, blunt weapons—or if the hero leaps onto someone from above—simply add the object's *Size* to the *Strength* roll. If the object's *Size is* 4 or more higher than the victim's, the attack does massive damage.

When it comes to Defensive Bonuses, use the weapons on page 189 as a guide. The longer and nastier they are, the higher the bonus.

Improvised weapons often break. Roll 1d6 when the weapon hits something. On a 6, it breaks. The Guide should adjust this for fragile weapons.

Smoke and Fire

Heroes are always jumping into burning buildings to save people. When that happens, they're in as much danger as the people they're hoping to help.

The first danger in a fire is from smoke inhalation. For how to handle this, check out the **Drowning and Suffocating** rules.

After that, the poor hero's got to worry about bursting into flames. It's up to the Guide as to how likely this is, depending entirely on the situation at hand.

A small fire, one that's limited to a single hit location, does 1d6+5 damage at the end of each round the hero's on fire. Larger fires do massive damage to the tune of 3d6+5 points.

Most fires can be put out by doing the trusty, old "stop, drop, and roll"—assuming, of course, that the hero's not rolling around in something that's burning too. Pulling this maneuver off requires an Easy (5) *Speed* roll.

That's fine for normal fires, but there are things like napalm that stick to the victim and burn tenaciously. Putting out stuff like this requires a Difficult (15) *Speed* roll.

Healing

Now that we've told you all about how to get new holes torn in your hero, it's time to talk about how to patch him up.

Waking Up

A hero who's been knocked out is in serious trouble. At the start of every round after the hero's been knocked out, have him make an Easy (5) *Strength* roll. If he makes it, he's conscious and unstunned for that round.

Even so, he's still badly hurt. The only thing he's good for is crawling or staggering along on crutches or a friendly shoulder. In fact, he must still make the Easy (5) *Strength* roll every round to stay awake.

The hero's stuck in this state until he manages to heal enough so that he has less wounds remaining in the useless hit location than his *Strength*. Medical attention is usually called for.

> **Example:** *The Rebel's got a* Strength *of 4d6, and he's taken five wounds to his torso. This means that he's pretty much useless until he heals two wounds. At that point, he's only got three wounds in his torso. Since that's less than his* Strength, *he can move around normally—not forgetting the wound-effect modifiers, of course.*

See the Doctor

The first place most people go when they're hurt is to a doctor, often in an emergency room. Of course, if you're an unregistered delta, this can cause you all sorts of problems.

All that aside, doctors can only do so much to patch a person up. Most of the work has to be done by the victim's own body. Still, doctors do what they can. As long as the hero receives medical attention within the first hour after injury, a physician can make a *medicine* roll to help.

The doctor works on each body area separately. The Target Number for each roll is Easy (5) for an injured area that's not been made useless. If the area's been made useless, the Target Number goes up to Challenging (10). A success eliminates a single wound in the damaged location.

Pulped limbs cannot be healed by normal means. They're pretty much gone. The wound itself still has to heal though, and the hero still suffers from the wound-effect modifier until that happens.

On the Mend

Healing is pretty straightforward. At the end of every day in which a hero gets full bedrest, she makes a healing roll. This is a Challenging (10) *Strength* roll. Each success the hero gets on the roll heals one wound in every wounded hit location at once.

Wound-effect modifiers aren't applied to healing rolls. This is already figured into the healing roll.

> ***Example:*** *The Rebel's taken two wounds to his left arm, five to his torso, and one to his head. He makes his healing roll and gets a 10. This is one success, so he heals one wound in each hurt location. Now he's got one wound in his left arm, four in his torso, and his head is entirely healed. At this rate, he'll be up and around in no time.*

On the Road

Even in Kennedy's America, most people—especially those who live outside a large city—have a car. There's a list of common types of vehicles on page 189. Of course, a list doesn't tell you how these things work in a game—especially in combat.

Move Now!

In a combat round, vehicles move first, before anyone else. The fastest vehicle moves first, then the next, on down to the slowest. These moves don't use up any driver's action.

After that, the heroes take their actions normally. There's one notable exception to this sequence. If a hero wants to, she can always use up her next action *dodging* an oncoming vehicle.

The Need for Speed

A vehicle can't just hit its top speed from a standing start in one round, and it can't turn on a dime. To account for these things, we break the vehicle's *Pace* into four stages: dead stop (not moving), up to quarter *Pace*, up to half *Pace*, and up to full *Pace.*

A vehicle can accelerate +1 *Pace* stage in a single round. It can decelerate –2 *Pace* stages. If your hero's driving, you decide what she's going to do before you move the vehicle at the start of the round.

The vehicle must move enough inches for its *Pace* to fall within its *Pace* stage. If it can't move that far, the driver must make a Challenging (10) *driving* roll to bring the car down to an acceptable *Pace* stage. If this is failed, the driver crashes the car into whatever was keeping him from going fast enough.

Turning

A vehicle can make one 45° turn during its move with no problem. Each turn after the first requires both the driver's next action and a *driving* roll. The Target Number for this roll is listed in the vehicle's profile under *Turn.* Once the driver runs out of actions for the turn, he can no longer make turns.

Each turn after the second gets more difficult, adding another +2 to the Target Number each time. A hero can try a turn of 90° if he likes, but it adds another +3 to the Target Number.

The vehicle's current *Pace* affects how well it can turn, as listed on the Driving Modifiers Table. Just apply the listed modifiers to the Target Number. Of course, the Guide can always come up with any other modifiers the situation might call for.

If the *driving* roll is failed, the vehicle moves straight ahead, and no more turns can be tried that round. On a disastrous roll, the car crashes and might even flip.

Driving Modifiers

Condition	Modifier
Quarter *Pace*	–4
Half *Pace*	±0
Full *Pace*	+2
Each turn after the second	+2
90° turn	+3
180° turn	+6

Drive-Bys

A hero riding in a vehicle can make an attack *during* the vehicle's move if he's got a held action. Using the vehicle to ram another vehicle or run someone down counts as an attack.

If the hero doesn't have a held action when the car's moving, he can't make an attack, even with the vehicle. He's just plain out of luck.

Similarly, a hero with a held action can attack a vehicle at any point during its move. This allows a hero to take a swipe or a shot at a speeding vehicle as it zooms by.

Heroes don't have to attack with a held action. They can take the opportunity to move, shine their shoes, or whatever they like. It's really up to them.

Kind Guides will assume that everyone in a combat has a held action on the first turn if a vehicle is involved. Otherwise, characters with vehicles may have an unfair advantage in the first round. This is the free action that every hero gets before having to make a *Speed* roll for initiative, so it's not like the heroes are suddenly getting more actions for nothing.

Either way, heroes in or out of a vehicle can act normally after all the vehicles are done moving.

Crash and Burn

When a vehicle crashes, it takes 1d6+5 damage for every 5 *Pace* it was moving.

If two vehicles collide, figure the damage using their relative speeds. For instance, if two cars are coming at each other at 45 and 65 mph, their relative speed is (45+65=) 110 mph.

If someone's hit by a car, she takes a similar amount of damage, but it's considered massive damage. This kind of injury can really ruin a hero's day.

Crunch!

Each vehicle has a two-number *Durability.* The first is the number of wounds the vehicle can take before it's totally destroyed.

Each time the vehicle takes as many wounds as the second number (or a multiple of that number), add +1 to the Target Number of any *driving* rolls made with it.

> ***Example:*** *A car at* Durability *30/6 can take up to 30 wounds. If takes 15 wounds, add (15÷6=2.5=) +2 to the Target Number of* driving *rolls made with it.*

Sample Vehicle

Vehicle	Durability	Pace	Turn	MPG	Size	Armor	Top Speed	Cost
Chevy Camaro	15/3	100	5	20	10	10/—	120 mph	$30,000

Chapter Seven: Tricks of the Trade

Chapter Seven: Tricks of the Trade

Tricks are special things that a hero can do when he gets extra successes on a die roll. To use a trick, the hero must first know it. During hero creation, each hero is allowed three tricks for free. Other tricks can be learned later at a cost of 10 points each. See Chapter Ten for more about how this works.

If a hero gets lots of extra successes on a roll, he can activate as many tricks as he likes and make sense. The only thing he needs is one extra success for every trick he wants to pull off.

You don't have to declare which tricks you want to use until after you make your roll and figure out how many successes you have to play with.

Combat Tricks

Most tricks are related to a particular skill, but there are a few that are triggered by attack rolls instead. Just like with skill tricks, the hero must know the trick to activate it with an extra success. Otherwise, he's just plain out of luck.

Bull's Eye

For each extra success you get on an attack roll, you can add +1 or take –1 from your roll on the Hit Location Table. Or you can move the hit from one limb to the opposite. Each such move costs a single success.

> ***Example:*** *Rebel throws a rock at a Primer and hits with one extra success on the attack roll. He then rolls 1d6 and checks the Hit Location Table. He gets a 5: arm. He can use his extra success to change his roll by ±1, to either 4: torso or 6: head. Since he knows he gets extra damage for a hit to the head, he changes his roll to a 6.*

Entangling

Some weapons can be used to trap a target instead of hurting him. These include things like, whips, lassos, and nets. If the hero gets an extra success when using a weapon of this sort, the target is not injured. Instead, the victim is entangled by the weapon.

An entangled character is unable to move, attack, or really do much of anything until he disentangles himself. Doing so is either a Challenging (10) *Speed* or *Strength* roll.

Extra Damage

For each extra success on an attack, the hero can add another die to his damage roll.

Grapple

If the hero gets an extra success with a barehanded or blunt-weapon attack, she can grab her foe and put the squeeze on him, holding him in place. First, roll the hit location and damage normally. Then the hero can do her *Strength* in damage to the foe on each of her following actions, including any damage bonus for a head shot.

To get away, the foe has to beat the hero on an opposed close combat roll, which he can try on each of his own actions. Otherwise, the hero can keep up the pressure until she lets go.

Knockback

With each extra success on an attack, the hero can knock a target back 2 inches. If this knocks the target into something hard—like a wall—he must make an immediate stun check, even if he's not wounded. If the surface is more lethal—like spikes or broken glass—it's up to the Guide to set the extra damage.

Knockdown

With an extra success on an attack, the hero can knock a target off her feet.

Ricochet

With an extra success on a ranged attack, the hero can bounce the attack off something hard to get another attack at something else within range. Add +4 to the Target Number for each additional attack. For each additional attack, roll again. The hero can continue ricocheting the attack from target to target if he gets another success on the new attack roll. The modifier is cumulative with each attack, so the third attack (second bounce), for instance, has a +8 modifier.

Be reasonable here. Penetrating attacks can't ricochet off something they hurt. Bullets and knives don't bounce off a victim's chest, for instance, although they might bounce off a suit of armor if they don't do damage.

Something like a thrown club might ricochet off a thug's skull though. If there's a question about this, it's the Guide's call.

This can also be used to take shots against targets with cover by bouncing the attack around the cover. The hero has to attack whatever he's bouncing the attack off of. Add +4 to the Target Number for each bounce. With an extra success, the ricochet hits.

TRAIT & SKILL TRICKS

The following tricks can be used with extra successes on trait or skill rolls. Anyone can pick these, whether or not they have a related skill. Related skills are listed in the trick's header.

Many skills already give bonuses for extra successes. You get those whether you know a trick or not. Only heroes who know a trick can benefit from it. Otherwise, she's just plain out of luck and any extra successes are wasted.

BRILLIANT IDEA — RAW SMARTS

With an extra success, the Guide gives the hero a hint about something he's overlooking. The Guide shouldn't be too blatant. It's up to the player to figure out what she's getting at.

FAST LEARNER — UNSKILLED SMARTS

If the hero gets three extra successes on an unskilled *Smarts* roll, she gets 1 point in the skill for which she substituted the *Smarts* roll. Obviously, this can only be used once with each skill.

FIRST MOVE — RAW SPEED

Extra successes on an initiative roll normally mean extra actions. With this trick, the hero can sacrifice one of those successes—and the action that would have come with it—and use any or all of his remaining actions when his turn comes around.

For example, if the hero has four actions, he can sacrifice one of them and then use his other three actions all at once.

KNOW THE STREETS — STREETWISE

With an extra success, the hero gains *area knowledge* 1 of the area he's in for free.

MAKE AN IMPRESSION — HOSTILE PERSUASION

The person the hero's talking to is really intimidated by her. For each extra success over the opposed roll, add +2 to all future hostile *persuasion* rolls with this person.

THE NATURAL — UNSKILLED SPEED

If the hero gets three extra successes on an unskilled *Speed* roll, she gets 1 point in the skill for which she substituted the *Speed* roll. Obviously, this can only be used once with each skill.

NEW FRIEND — FRIENDLY PERSUASION

The person the hero's talking to considers the hero a new friend. For each extra success over the opposed roll, add +2 to all future friendly *persuasion* rolls with this person.

ON A ROLL — RAW SPIRIT

The hero's having a good day. For each extra success on any *Spirit*-related roll, take –2 from the Target Number of her next roll during this encounter.

PUMPED UP — RAW STRENGTH

For each extra success, the hero can lift and carry 25% more weight than normal, up to twice the normal amount. This lasts for 1d6 rounds. (Roll open-endedly.)

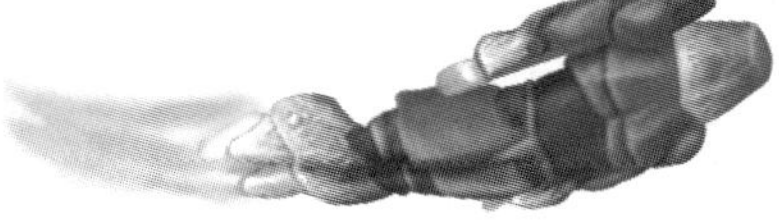

Chapter Eight: What Makes a Delta a Delta

This is where we get to the really cool stuff, the things that separate the deltas from the regs on the street: superpowers.

Deltas Are People Too

The fact is that deltas are just normal, average, everyday folks—people like you or me—that happen to have superpowers. There doesn't seem to be rhyme or reason for who becomes a delta. Whatever higher power—if any—there is that's in the business of handing out superpowers is apparently an equal-opportunity employer.

That's why the biggest part of creating your hero is figuring out who he is as a person. That's what's most important about the hero, not whether or not he can fly circles around a helicopter or rip a car apart with his bare hands.

Of course, when you're done with that part, it's time to get into what makes a delta special: powers of which most people can only dream.

Packaged Powers

Deltas come in all flavors. Some have lots of different kinds of powers—or at least access to them—while others' superhuman abilities are concentrated into a single power. Some of them are similar to each other, and others are wildly different.

A hero's powers don't come in a mix-and-match variety. They come as packages. To use one, all you have to do is pick it and add the package's elements to your hero's sheet. It's that simple.

Each power package tells you what kind of powers the delta has, as well as any kinds of quirks that might come with the package. Some quirks are positive, but others are negative. Either way, these quirks don't cost your hero anything or give her points. They're part of the package.

A delta can only ever have one power package. Once you pick one for your hero, he's stuck with it, so choose carefully.

Look for more power packages in other *Brave New World* books. There are lots of different kinds of deltas out there—more than we could possibly fit into this chapter—and it's going to be a while before we really even do more than scratch the surface.

Still, it's one heck of a surface, so keep watching.

Making Your Own Power Packages

If you've got a great idea for a power package of your own, sit down and discuss it with your Guide. If she likes it, you're all set. After all, it's your game, and you can play it however you like.

If you think your power package is really good, submit it to us. If we think it's got the right stuff, we might even stick it in an upcoming book for the rest of the world to see.

Making a power package is pretty simple. There are no hard and fast rules, but there are some guidelines we can offer.

A power package usually involves one or two powers, although it's sometimes more. If the powers give a bonus to a skill or trait, it's rarely more than +5, and then only if the package only has one power. If there are two or more powers, the bonuses are accordingly less.

More powerful packages can be created, but they need to be offset by negative quirks. See the goliath package for an example of this.

The rule of thumb here is that if the new power package is obviously much better than one already in print, it's probably too powerful. If you propose that kind of package to your Guide, she should shoot it down like a loose balloon.

Alpha Powers

Those of you who've been reading closely should remember that there is a more powerful level of delta: the alpha. You might also notice that there aren't any alpha power packages in this book.

That's because all of the heroes in *Brave New World* start out as deltas, and since the Vanishing, there have been few new alphas.

We'll get to alpha powers and how your hero might get them in a later book. For now, if your hero gets killed, don't throw that hero sheet away. You never know when you might need it again. In the meantime, you should make up a new hero to play with. After all, you need something to do while you're waiting to find out your hero's ultimate fate.

THE POWER PACKAGES

Every power package has at least one entry: powers. Under this, we list what powers a hero gets if you choose this package for her.

Many packages also come with another entry: quirks. When you pick this package, the hero gets these quirks along with the powers.

Last, every package comes with its own tricks. Heroes don't get these automatically. They can pick them as part of their three free tricks (see Chapter Seven), or they can pick them up later (see Chapter Ten).

BARGAINER

Bargainers are a truly unusual kind of delta. They have the power to speak with strange creatures from the nether realms. Your Sunday preacher would call them demons, and you know what happens to people who consort with demons.

The Bargainers aren't worried about their ultimate fate. They know better. A person's final destiny is determined not by what she can do but by what she does. Dealing with demons isn't inherently evil, as long as the Bargainer does so with good intentions. It's a long, slippery slope though, one that's fraught with perils for the soul.

Still, the Bargainers can't seem to help it. It's in their nature to summon up demons and bind them to obey.

Bargainers normally summon a demon into their presence and then force the otherworldly spirit to empower some kind of focus or totem with an unearthly power. Creating a totem is a painstaking process that can go wrong at any time. More than one incautious Bargainer has found himself at the mercy of the very demon he was struggling to bind to his service.

It's not an easy way to make a living.

LEARNING THE TRADE

Unlike most other deltas, a Bargainer has to be taught his trade. After all, it's one thing to have the power to summon demons. Doing it properly is another thing altogether.

There are a few Bargainers who have figured out the whole thing on their own. They had to start somewhere, after all. Most of them, however, have been tracked down and taught the proper use of their power by the members of a mysterious organization known as the Bargainers.

The most well-known Bargainer was the world-famous escape artist Harry Houdini. The legendary magician's flair for performance has colored the way in which the Bargainers look at their power. To this day, Bargainer training includes instruction in stage magic, and most Bargainers feed themselves by means of their more mundane "magic" skills. Many wear the traditional black tuxedo when working their day job, but not all feel so bound by the traditions of the past.

Requirements

As part of their training, Bargainers pick up a few skills. They are required to have the following skills at the minimum listed levels: academia: occult 3, escaping 2, performing: public speaking 2, and sleight of hand 3.

The Totem

The focus of every Bargainer's power is his totem. There are as many different kinds of totems as there are Bargainers. Houdini used a magician's wand, and many of his students follow in his footsteps. After all, nobody ever expects one of those wands to work.

Other Bargainers use large pieces of jewelry or carved stone or wooden images. More modern Bargainers have been known to even use computers.

The key thing about the totem is that it must be noticeable—bigger than a pistol—and it needs to be visible when in use. The casual onlooker doesn't know what's really in the Bargainer's hand, it's a telltale for the less-ignorant.

A Bargainer can have more than one totem—up to one for each point of *Spirit* he has—but he can only use one at a time. Since these are items of great power and require an incredible amount of risk and labor to create, they are guarded jealously. As soon as the totem leaves the Bargainer's grasp, the Bargainer loses its powers.

A Bargainer can only use a totem that he's been attuned to, which requires a tremendous amount of time and effort. Totems can be reattuned to another owner, but this is just as hard.

The number of different kinds of totems would justify an entire book all on their own. For now, we're only going to cover the two most common kinds: the mimic and the delta totem.

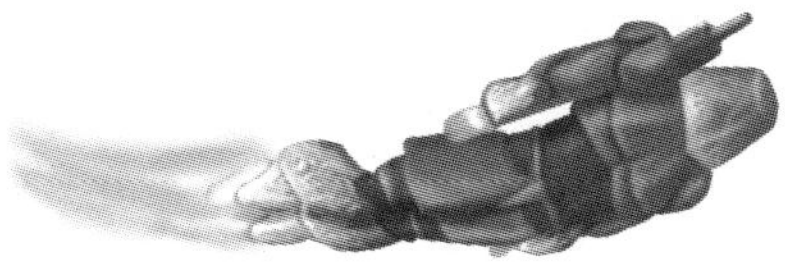

Assume that a starting Bargainer hero has a single totem. If the totem is lost, it takes the hero a week to recreate it. At the end of that week, the hero must make a Phenomenal (30) *Spirit* roll to recreate the totem. If he fails, he's got to start over from scratch.

The hero uses a similar procedure to attune a totem to himself, but the time is cut to three days. Also, he only needs an Amazing (20) *Spirit* roll.

Powers

Bargaining: The hero can summon demons and use them to create totems of power. See page 176 for examples.

Tricks

Jinx: With an extra success on an initiative roll, the hero can try to cause a foe to lose an action. The Bargainer must win an opposed *Spirit* roll too. Either way, the hero uses that success and can't use it for another action.

Make It Look Easy: With an extra success on any Challenging (5) or harder roll, the hero does what she's attempting with style. Afterward, the hero can add +2 to any *persuasion* rolls made against anyone who was watching, until the encounter ends.

Other Tricks: A Bargainer can learn tricks for any power package one of his totems can imitate. When he's not using the totem, though, he doesn't know the tricks either.

The Mimic Totem

A Bargainer with a mimic totem can mimic the power of any other delta.

Of course, there are a few catches.

First, the Bargainer has to actually touch the delta in question with his mimic totem. If the target tries to avoid the Bargainer's touch, this requires a hit in close combat and the Bargainer must win an opposed *Spirit* roll. Skip the roll with friendly deltas.

Second, the Bargainer must copy the other delta's entire power package. No cherry picking .

Third, the totem can only mimic powers for so long: one hour. After the hour's up, the mimicked power package fades away.

Fourth, the totem can only be used to mimic a single power package at a time. If the hero is mimicking a power package and then copies another, the first set of powers leaves him.

Fifth, if the totem leaves the hero's person, the powers do too. If the mimic manages to get his totem back, any powers it was copying are gone.

The Delta Totem

This kind of totem is similar to the mimic totem in that it allows the Bargainer to permanently imbue a totem with any single power package she likes.

The upside is the Bargainer doesn't have to have another delta around. It's not mimicking powers. It has its own. Also, there's no time limit on how long the powers stay with the hero.

The downside is that the hero's stuck with a single power package—at least with this one totem.

Blaster

Some people keep a lot bottled up inside them. Some deltas have the power to let it all out—explosively.

A blaster's hands are basically living guns, capable of firing blasts of energy that can smack into a target like a truck. He can fire an attack from each hand too, doubling his firepower.

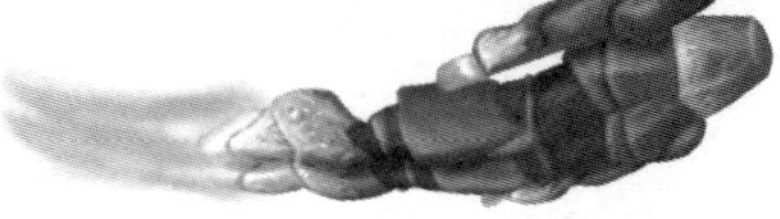

Blasters don't usually bother with other weapons. After all, when your hands are living guns, what's the point?

Whatever source of energy the blaster draws upon toughens his skin too. It doesn't do him as much good as a suit of armor, but it helps to take the edge off that small-arms fire.

POWERS

Armor: 5/—

Energy Blast: The hero can fire an energy blast from each hand. See the Blaster Attack Table for the details on this kind of attack. This blast ignores armor that's not part of the target's skin or power.

TRICKS

Blast Punch: The hero can use his energy blast to open a real can of whup-ass with a punch. If the hero gets an extra success on his close-combat attack roll, he does *Strength*+15 points of damage. Additionally, he can use superblast with his blast punch, but he needs two extra successes to pull that off. If he only gets one, the blast punch works, but the superblast fails.

Superblast: Instead of firing an energy blast, the hero can spend an action to build up her energy. The hero can then add +5 to the damage of a blast for each action she spends powering up a single blast, up to a maximum of +20. For the superblast to work, the hero must also get an extra success on the attack roll. Otherwise, it's just a normal blast. If the hero is stunned while she's building her power, the bonus is lost.

BOUNCER

This hero moves faster than the eye can follow, and he's got a hell of a punch to boot.

With his augmented *Strength*, the hero can do as much damage with his fists as most people can do with a bullet. Lots of bouncers don't bother with weapons. They're a pain to have to carry around, and they're forever breaking, jamming, or running out of ammo.

Other bouncers love weapons. With their extra *Speed*, they're pretty damn good with them after all.

The bouncer's boosted *Speed* also means he's usually going to end up with several actions every round. Since he's so fast, he can use some of these extra actions to dodge attacks against him, waiting for his chance to land a solid blow at the end of the round when everyone else is standing around, waiting for their next actions to come along in the next round. Of course, enough foes can simply overwhelm him, so he's still got to pick his battles wisely.

POWERS

Fast: Add +5 to *Speed* rolls for initiative and *dodging*. Also add +5 to *Pace*.

Strong: Add +3 to *Strength* rolls.

BLASTER ATTACK

Weapon Type	Ammo	Shots	Quickness	Rate of Fire	Range Increment	Damage	Cost
Energy blast	Energy	Unlimited	1	3	10	5d6+10	—

Tricks

Bounce Attack: With an extra success on a close-combat attack roll, the hero can bounce off one foe and attack another, all on the same action. Add +6 to the Target Number of the new attack.

The hero can continue bouncing from target to target if he gets another success on the new attack roll. The modifier is cumulative, though, with each attack, so the third attack (second bounce) would have a total +12 modifier.

Flip-Toss: With an extra success when dodging a close combat attack, the hero flips up into the air and grabs her attacker while she's still in midair. As she lands, she uses her momentum to toss her foe up to 1 inch for each point of *Strength*.

If the foe fails a Challenging (10) *acrobatics* roll, he lands hard on his back. If so, he takes the bouncer's *Strength* in damage, plus damage from anything sharp he fell on.

Flyer

A flyer can soar through the air like a bird on a spring day. This is one of the powers that regs are most jealous of. Who wouldn't want to be able to soar through the skies?

Flyers can speed along in the air at a pretty good clip, or hover in midair. They fly up, down, and sideways at the same rate. Unlike most aircraft, they can even stop and turn on a dime.

Flying apparently energizes the flyer's body in some way, even making her skin tougher, but only so long as she's aloft. Some flyers actually walk around on air to maintain this benefit, but they risk discovery when they do.

A flyer can carry passengers or cargo if she likes, but only as much as she could normally handle on the ground. See page 142 for all about how extra weight affects normal movement. It's the same for a flyer, except if she manages to exceed her limit while in the air, she drops like a stone.

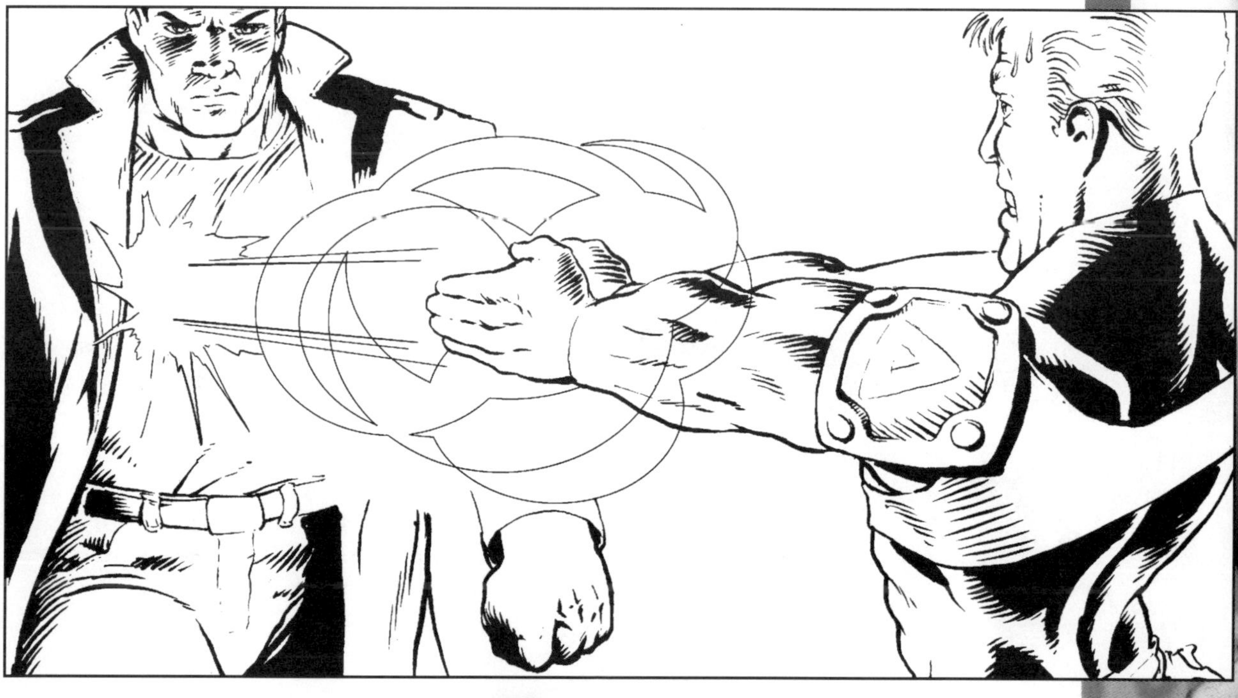

Powers

Armor: 5/— when flying.
Flight: Can fly at a *Pace* of 50.

Tricks

Burst of Speed: With each extra success on an Easy (5) *flying* roll, the hero can add +10 to her flying *Pace* this round. This roll requires an action.

Flying Dodge: With each extra success on a *flying* roll or a *dodge* roll while in midair, any attacks against the hero must add +3 to the Target Number for the rest of the round.

Gadgeteer

Most deltas have obvious kinds of powers. They can fire blasts from their fists, run faster than a car, or even bounce bullets off their skin. Not so with the gadgeteer.

A gadgeteer's power is to be able to build and maintain technological bits of wonder that bend the theoretical laws of physics.

Read that last bit carefully. It's important.

A gadgeteer's power is to build and *maintain* wondrous devices. We call these devices "gadgets." If you're not a gadgeteer, you can still use a gadget, but you can't keep it in working order.

If you look around in *Brave New World,* you'll see things like people walking around in suits of powered armor or dashing about on rocket sleds. These gadgets are obviously far beyond even our most cutting-edge advances in technology. They've been created by gadgeteers.

In a world that focuses on the benefits of mass production, gadgeteers are an anomaly. Nearly all of their creations are one-of-a-kind marvels.

Maintaining a Gadget

A gadgeteer can build as many gadgets as he likes, but he can only maintain one at a time. This makes it impossible to mass-produce gadgets, as they invariably fall apart and stop working soon after they leave the gadgeteer's care.

Maintaining a device requires at least one hour of tinkering with it in a 24-hour period, and an Easy (5) *tinkering* roll.

After a gadget is successfully tinkered with by a gadgeteer, it continues to function normally for 24 hours or until it's tinkered with again. If 24 hours go by without the gadget being tinkered with, it becomes useless—at least until a gadgeteer takes it in for an overhaul.

Overhauling a device, or bringing it back into a gadgeteer's care, takes eight hours of work. At that point, the gadget is back in good working order.

If you're good with numbers, you might realize that a gadgeteer could conceivably have three gadgets going at once. All he has to do is have one gadget working, then spend two eight-hour periods getting two other gadgets up to speed. Then he's got eight hours left before the first gadget he was maintaining gives out.

Of course, a tactic like this means the hero's going to be working on little sleep. The Guide might want to keep this in mind when assigning Target Numbers.

The size of the gadget the hero's maintaining is really irrelevant. This is one reason why most gadgeteers incorporate as many different things into a gadget as they can. This has the effect of putting all their eggs into one basket, but since they can only really carry one basket at a time, why not?

Repairing a damaged gadget can be done, but it takes time. To repair a single wound done to a gadget, it takes an Easy (10) *tinkering* roll and four hours. Each success reduces the time by an hour, down to a minimum of one.

Creating Your Own Gadgets

As the story of *Brave New World* develops, we're going to introduce more and more gadgets for heroes to use. In the meantime, though, here are some guidelines for creating your own gadgets.

Most gadgeteers take the "everything *and* the kitchen sink" approach toward building their own gadgets. That's fine—up to a point. Remember, these heroes are only deltas, and their powers only extend so far. No Death Stars here.

As a guideline, the powers that a gadget confers should be only as powerful as those of a delta who naturally has that power. Any weapons the gadget has should only be as powerful as a standard weapon that anyone could buy.

The real trick with a gadget is it can only bend the laws of physics, not outright break them. Look at the device and see if it makes any kind of sense at all. If the answer's no, then scrap it.

Also, if the gadget would make the hero incredibly powerful, much more so than another delta, it's too much. Scale it back down.

As always, it's up to the Guide to approve any kind of new gadget before it's introduced into the game. Also, the Guide has the option to disallow the gadget at any point if she feels its presence is too powerful or is simply disrupting the game. When that happens, the gadget suddenly fails—hopefully at a dramatically appropriate

moment—and afterward can't ever be properly overhauled, no matter how hard the hero may try.

This way, the player and the Guide can experiment with different types of gadgets until they get a feel for what's appropriate in the game. A word of advice for gadgeteers: Don't get too attached to those gadgets you come up with. You never know when they're just going to stop working for no reason under your control.

Of course, then your hero's got time to come up with a whole new gadget to play with.

Powers

Gadgeteering: The hero can build and maintain gadgets.

Tricks

Fine Tuning: With an extra success on a *tinkering* roll, the gadget the hero is working on doesn't need to be tinkered with for an additional 24 hours.

Smack It: When faced with a gadget that's not working, the hero can give it a good whack and make an Easy (5) *Smarts* roll. For every success he gets, the device works for a single round.

Power Armor

Power armor is just what it sounds like, a powered suit of armor that comes complete with automatic guns, augmented strength, and a jetpack. What more could you ask for?

Well, you might want something a bit easier to carry. Power armor is heavy, not just something you tote around with you like a laptop. It fits in a steamer trunk, but you're not going to be hauling that around with you on your next date. You'd just better hope the thing fits in the back of your car.

Also, it takes a while to put on. With practice, a hero can slip into a suit of power armor in six actions. That's plenty of time for the hero to get her clock cleaned before she even suits up.

Abilities

Armor: 10/3.

Powerful: Add +3 to *Strength* rolls.

Guns: Each wrist has a Triumph 300 firearm mounted on top of it. See the table below for details.

Flight: Can fly at a *Pace* of 40.

Goliath

This hero's just huge. Her skin is hard enough to bounce bullets off of, and she's got enough muscle to toss bowling balls around like acorns. Unfortunately, she's slower than dirt and ugly as sin.

Hey, you can't have it all.

A goliath may not get in as many swings as a bouncer, for instance, but all she's got to do is connect with a single punch and it's lights out!

The real problem with being a goliath is that the hero stands about eight feet tall and weighs in at somewhere around 400 pounds. This

Power Armor Guns

Weapon Type	Action	Ammo	Shots	Quickness	Rate of Fire	Range Increment	Damage	Cost
Triumph 300	Auto	.45	50	1	3	5	5d6+5	—

makes it really hard to disguise the hero's status as a delta. She doesn't really blend in with a crowd.

For this reason, police officers and Delta Primers are constantly hassling the goliath for her registration papers. If she doesn't have them—whether she never registered or has simply misplaced her papers—she's going to have a lot of explaining to do.

Powers

Armor: 10/—.
Big: Add +2 to *Size.*
Powerful: Add +5 to *Strength* rolls.

Quirk

Dirt Slow: Take –2 from *Speed* rolls for initiative.

Ugly: Take –2 from all friendly *persuasion* rolls. At the Guide's option, the hero can add +2 to all hostile *persuasion* rolls.

Obvious: This is the standard –3 quirk.

Tricks

Rock Your World: The hero can attack the floor and set it shaking like a bowl full of jello. Hitting the floor in the right way is an Easy (5) *fighting: barehanded* roll. If successful, the hero has managed to shake the ground enough to possibly knock nearby people off their feet. With a single success, only people within 2 inches of the hero are affected. With each extra success, people another 2 inches away are affected. Anyone affected must make a Challenging (10) *Speed* roll to stay standing.

Superjump: The hero can leap over small buildings in a single bound. The hero makes a *Strength* roll. For every success he gets, he can leap 2 inches straight up and 2 inches in any direction he likes. If the hero tries to land on a foe, treat this as a charge, taking all the hero's movement into account. If the Goliath's *Size* is 4 more than the target, he does massive damage.

Gunner

There are great shots, and then there are *great shots*. A gunner's one of those legendary shootist who can shave the wings off a mosquito at 50 paces. Or at least that's what he'd probably have you believe.

In a country in which nearly everyone carries a gun, some skill with a firearm is often assumed. Just because someone can point a pistol and pull a trigger doesn't mean she's actually going to hit what she's shooting at. With the gunner's power, it's almost assured.

Most gunners don't waste their time just blasting away at a target. They go for called shots to vital areas instead. If they're feeling gracious, they might even pull a Lone Ranger and shoot an opponent's guns out of her hands instead.

Gunners are lightning-fast with their hands too. On a good day, a gunner can actually outdraw and shoot down someone who's already got a gun on him.

With the prevalence of guns in Kennedy's America, most gunners blend right in. Unless they start pulling off tricks most shooters couldn't even dream of, chances of them blowing their cover are pretty small. Of course, if they make use of their talents too often, they might get hauled in on another charge than being an unregistered delta. Shooting people is frowned upon, even in Jack Kennedy's country.

Powers

Crack Shot: Add +5 to *shooting* attacks.

Quick: Add +5 to *Speed* rolls for initiative.

Tricks

Mercy: With an extra success on a *shooting* roll, the hero can reduce the amount of actual damage a shot does by choosing exactly how he wants the bullet to hit the poor target. Roll damage and check for stun normally. After the stun check, though, the victim only takes half the normal amount of wounds.

Pierce Armor: With two extra successes on a *shooting* roll against an armored foe, the hero finds a weak spot in the armor. The armor does not affect this shot. It's the Guide's call as to whether or not the foe's armor actually has a weak spot. If not, the trick does nothing.

Healer

Not all delta powers are entirely destructive in nature. Case in point: the healer.

Healers aren't all fire-and-brimstone televangelists bringing down the favor of God in an ecstatic moment of holy fervor. They come in all stripes. Some are doctors, others are "natural healers," and there are even a few shamans in the bunch.

When a healer lays her hands on a sick or injured person, she can—if she's lucky—cure that person's woes. To use the healing power, the hero puts her hands on the victim's injuries and then makes an Easy (5) *medicine* roll.

Unlike with a standard *medicine* roll, the hero doesn't work on each hit location separately. The healing power is more holistic than that.

For every success the hero gets on the *medicine* roll, one wound on the victim is healed in any hit location or locations of the healer's choice. It's that simple.

A healer can only try to heal a victim's current wounds once. Any wounds that aren't healed after an attempted healing cannot be healed by any means except time or standard *medicine*. A healer can try to cure later wounds normally, but even then, the older wounds cannot be affected.

A healer can try to help as many people as she can reach, but healing isn't as simple as it could be. It's an involved process requiring the healer to mentally peer into the victim's body and carefully push the natural healing process along. Each healing attempt requires a full minute (12 actions).

A healer can work without any medical training at all, but the better she knows the human body, the more success she's going to have with her power.

Powers

Healing: The hero can heal wounds and illnesses. Add +10 to *medicine* rolls when using the healing power.

Tricks

Healing Disease: A healer can try to cure diseases too. See the Healing Disease Table on page 184 for how many successes are required to heal a particular type of illness. If you don't see what you're looking for on the list, it's up to the Guide to come up with the number of successes needed. In most cases, the Guide should guess high.

If the hero manages to get the required number of successes, the disease is healed. Otherwise, the power fails to help at all. At the Guide's discretion, a failed attempt may temporarily help with the symptoms of certain kinds of ailments, but in the end, they're bound to return.

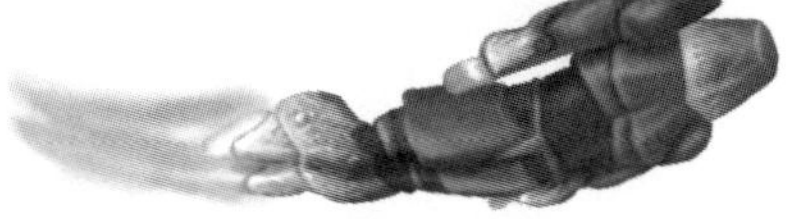

Just as with wounds, if a healer fails to cure an illness, no other power can help. It's up to modern medical science—such as it is—and time. Heroes that have the *illness* quirk are assumed to have had a healer try to help them and fail. This way, they can't easily rid themselves of the *illness.*

Healing Disease

Disease	Successes to Cure
AIDS	8
Asthma	5
Blindness	6
Cancer, early stage	6
Cancer, late stage	8
Cold	2
Deafness	6
Flu	3
Headache	2
Nausea	2
Pneumonia	4
Radiation poisoning	5

Healing Poison: This works just like with healing diseases. With this trick, the hero can cure poisons of varying strengths, as long as she racks up enough successes. See the Healing Poison Table for exactly how many successes you need to roll. If the strength of the poison isn't known, it's up to the Guide to figure it out. If the healer likes, she can actually negate up to a pint of bottled poison instead.

Healing Poison

Poison	Successes to Cure
Poison, mild	3
Poison, medium	4
Poison, severe	5

Scrapper

When there's nothing for it but to wade in with both fists and get your hands bloody, you want a scrapper on your side. Not only are they strong as bulls and tough as nails, they've got healing factors that allows them to quickly recover from all but the worst wounds.

In short, they're just built for brawling.

There's nothing most scrappers like better than getting into a fight—fair or otherwise. Anything else is a waste of their talents. Some scrappers are a bit more careful than that though. Those are the ones who live the longest.

Lots of scrappers have the *bloodthirsty* or *temper* quirks, but just as many are cool customers. What they're buying is victory, and they're ready to pay for it in broken bones and splattered blood.

Powers

Armor: 5/—

Healing Factor: The hero can make a healing roll every hour instead of every day.

Strong: Add +3 to *Strength.*

Tricks

Fast Healer: For every extra success on a healing roll, the hero heals a wound. Combined with the hero's healing factor and his extra strength, this can get him back on his feet in virtually no time at all.

Dirty Fighting: If the hero hits the target in the head or torso with a *fighting* roll, add +2d6 to the damage for every extra success the hero has. For head shots, this adds to the standard damage bonus.

Speedster

When you need to get something someplace in a hurry, the speedster's the way to go. On level ground, they can run faster than a speeding car. Plucking bullets out of the air is beyond them, but not by much.

In a fight, the speedster's favorite tactic is to run up to one target, smack it hard, then run up to another target on the other side of the combat. In some cases, a speedster can zip across a room and knock a foe out before the poor bastard can even squeeze off a shot.

When running long distances, the speedster needs to use the running rules on page 105. It's all a matter of endurance, and smart speedsters build up their *Strength* and their *running* skill as high as they can. Otherwise, they're bound to run out of steam when they should be just hitting their stride.

Speedsters cannot have the *slow* quirk.

Powers

Fast Runner: Add +100 to *Pace.*

Lightning Reflexes: Add +5 to *Speed* rolls for initiative and *dodging*.

Tricks

Afterimages: When the hero makes a *dodge* roll, check how many successes he gets over Challenging (10). For each extra success, the hero leaves behind a separate afterimage of where he was. These images cluster around where the hero really is and follow him around for the rest of the turn. If the attack roll actually succeeds, the attacker must randomly roll to see if the attack actually hit an afterimage instead, missing the hero entirely. An afterimage that's hit by an attack disappears instantly. Of course, this trick is useless against area-affect weapons like grenades or gas.

Burst of Speed: With each extra success on an Easy (5) *running* roll, the hero can add +10 to his *Pace* this round. Making this roll requires an action.

Welcome to
MARS GUN CASTLE!
ARIOUS GRENADES
SLIGHTRY USED KEVLAR
SALE
DeHANZER 99

Chapter Nine: Things Every Hero Needs

Now that you know who your hero is and how his powers work, it's up to you to figure out what kind of gear he's got. Every hero starts out with the basics of modern American life: an apartment, clothes, a radio, a TV, a used car, and so on. Unfortunately, that usually includes a pistol.

Your hero also has $1,000 to spend on things like weapons, ammunition, armor, and other things the average person probably doesn't have. Most of these are listed on the next few pages.

Financing

Heroes can get loans for things that are their own collateral: cars, houses, and the like—not weapons. Getting a loan for up to the hero's yearly salary is a Challenging (10) friendly *persuasion* roll. For each step above the hero's salary on the Starting Money Table that the hero wants to borrow, the Target Number goes up by +2. This means that a hero with *rich* +2 who wants a loan for $500,000 needs a 13 or better.

A hero can only try for a loan every three months. If he fails, he can always try again. If he succeeds, that's all he can borrow until he pays off the loan or refinances up to the same amount.

Starting Money

Status	Starting Money	Yearly Salary
Poor	$100	—
Standard	$1,000	$20,000
Rich +1	$4,000	$40,000
Rich +2	$7,500	$75,000
Rich +3	$12,500	$125,000
Rich +4	$25,000	$250,000
Rich +5	$50,000	$500,000

Pricing Other Gear

We don't have enough space to list prices for everything your hero might want to buy. The solution to this problem is simple. The cost for most items in *Brave New World* is roughly what it is in the real world.

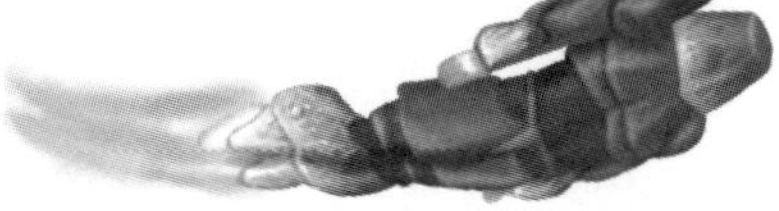

Chapter Nine: Things Every Hero Needs

Ranged Weapons

Weapon Type	Action	Ammo	Shots	Quickness	Rate of Fire	Range Increment	Damage	Cost
Bow								
Compound bow•	Drawn	Arrow	1	2	1	5	*Strength*+5	$100
Longbow•	Drawn	Arrow	1	2	1	5	*Strength*+3	$50
Crossbow•	Drawn	Bolt	1	1	1	5	5d6+5	$100
Thrown Weapons								
Small knife	Throw	—	1	1	1	5	*Strength*+2	$25
Large knife	Throw	—	1	1	1	5	*Strength*+5	$50
Shuriken	Throw	—	1	1	3	5	*Strength*+1	$10
Pistol								
Colt Agent	Revolver	.38	6	1	1	5	5d6+3	$300
Colt Python	Revolver	.357mag	6	1	1	5	5d6+8	$500
Colt 2000	Auto	9mm	15	1	1	5	5d6+5	$600
Derringer	Single	.22	2	1	1	5	5d6+2	$200
Taser	Single	Built-in	1	1	1	5	Stun (9)	$200
Rifles								
Remington M700•	Bolt	7.62mm	5	2	1	10	6d6+8	$500
Barrett M90•	Bolt	.50	5	2	1	10	6d6+10	$1,400
Colt M16A2•	Auto	5.56mm	30	2	3	10	6d6+5	$900
Shotguns								
Double-barreled•	Standard	12 gauge	2	2	2	3	Shotgun	$200
Winchester Defender•	Pump	12 gauge	7	2	1	3	Shotgun	$260
Pancor Jackhammer•	Auto	12 gauge	10	2	2	3	Shotgun	$1,200
Submachine-Guns								
Colt 9mm•	Auto	9mm	20	1	6	10	5d6+5	$800
Ingram M10•	Auto	9mm	32	1	6	5	5d6+5	$400
Machine-Guns								
Saco M60E1†	Auto	7.62mm	90*	1	9	10	6d6+8	$3,000
Browning M2†	Auto	.50	72*	1	9	10	6d6+10	$4,000
Miscellaneous								
Grenade	Thrown	—	1	1	1	5	10d6+10°	$100
Grenade Launcher•	Auto	40mm	3	1	1	10	10d6+10°	$1,500
Rocket Launcher•	Single	120mm	1	2	1	10	10d6+20°	$2,500

*These machine-guns are belt-fed. °These weapons have a Burst Radius of 3.
•These are two-handed weapons. †These weapons are usually mounted on a tripod or vehicle. They could be used as a two-handed weapon by a hero with a *Strength* of 8 or more.

Armor

Type	Armor	Covers	Costs	Notes
Thick coat	1/—	Arms, torso	$100	Adds +4 to *survival* in the cold.
Leather jacket	1/—	Vitals, torso, arms	$75	
Leather pants	1/—	Legs	$75	
Motorcycle helmet	6/—	Head	$75	
Riot helmet	10/—	Head	$200	
Plastic riot shield	6/—	Varies	$200	
Steel riot shield	10/3	Varies	$400	
Kevlar vest	10/—	Torso	$200	Useless against blades, arrows, or bolts.
Power armor	10/3	Entire body	—	Only available to gadgeteers.

Chapter Nine: Things Every Hero Needs

Close Combat Weapons

Weapon	Defensive Bonus	Quickness	Damage	Cost
Ax•	+1	2	*Strength*+5	$20
Bayonet	+1	1	*Strength*+3	$50
Brass knuckles	—	1	*Strength*+2	$20
Cattle prod	+1	1	Stun (9)	$100
Chainsaw•	+2	2	*Strength*+7	$200
Club, big•	—	2	*Strength*+2	—
Club, small	—	1	*Strength*+1	—
Hatchet	+1	1	*Strength*+3	$10
Knife, hunting	+1	1	*Strength*+3	$10
Knife, kitchen	+1	1	*Strength*+2	$5
Lariat•	—	2	None	$10
Machete	+1	1	*Strength*+4	$30
Nightstick	+1	1	*Strength*+1	$40
Sword	+2	1	*Strength*+5	$250
Whip	+2	2	2d6	$45

• These are two-handed weapons.

Vehicles

Vehicle	Durability	Pace	Turn	MPG	Size	Armor	Top Speed	Cost
Chevy Camaro	15/3	100	5	20	10	10/—	120 mph	$30,000
Chevy Metro	10/2	75	7	40	9	10/—	90 mph	$8,000
Dodge Ram	20/4	80	8	25	11	10/—	100 mph	$15,000
Harley-Davidson Sportster	10/2	100	5	50	8	—	120 mph	$20,000
Jeep Cherokee	20/4	80	8	15	11	10/—	100 mph	$35,000

Ammunition

Ammo Type	Cost
.22	10¢/bullet
.38	20¢/bullet
.357 magnum	85¢/bullet
.50	$1/bullet
5.56mm	$1/bullet
7.62mm	$1/bullet
9mm	75¢/bullet
12-gauge shell	$1/shell
12-gauge slug	$1.50/slug
40mm grenade	$250/grenade
120mm rocket	$1,000/rocket
Arrow	$5/arrow
Bolt	$1/bolt
Belt of ammo	$100/belt
AP bullet (AP 5)	10x normal
AP bullet (AP 10)	20x normal
Rubber bullet:	10x normal
.22, .38, 5.56mm (Stun (5))	
.357, .50, 7.62mm, 9mm (Stun 7))	

Miscellaneous Gear

Item	Cost
Binoculars	$100
Computer, full net access	$2,000
Computer, limited net access	Free
False ID papers (poor)	$500
False ID papers (good)	$5,000
Gas	$1/gallon
Handcuffs	$25
Lockpicks, mechanical	$50
Lockpicks, electronic	$5,000
Nightvision goggles (negates lighting modifiers in all but total darkness)	$1,000
Rifle scope, standard (doubles Range Increment when aiming)	$30
Rifle scope, excellent (triples Range Increment when aiming)	$200
Spare gun clip	$10

Chapter Ten: Liberty or Death!

Chapter Ten: Liberty or Death!

So what's it all about? Why is your hero running around, trying to free his fellow Americans from the shackles of martial law?

Simply put, it's the right thing to do—at least from your hero's point of view. One element we explore in *Brave New World* is how differently people can see the same situation.

To a member of the Defiance, it might seem like Delta Prime is an entirely evil organization bent on oppressing the entire country, but others in America don't see it that way. In fact, many Americans believe what they see on TV, what the federal-controlled media and the government itself tell them.

After all, they don't know any better. All they can see is that deltas are destroying the world, and men like John F. Kennedy and the stalwart heroes of Delta Prime are the last line of defense between the common citizen and total anarchy.

As a member of the Defiance, it's up to you to bring them the truth.

Living in Fear

The fact is that most people didn't have their basic civil rights taken away from them by force. They voluntarily gave them up.

That's what happens when people get scared. When they feel like they can't understand the world around them. When they don't know who their neighbors might be. When they fear for the lives of those they love.

When those kinds of things happen, people are willing to make all kinds of sacrifices. If you're that frightened, things like free speech, privacy, and the like don't mean a whole lot.

After all, if you're one of the good guys, what have you got to hide? Let the government come in and poke into every aspect of your life. Let them rip your history apart, tossing through your past for clues to some deeper deviancy, some threat you might pose to the greater whole.

There's nothing suspicious in your past. Is there?

THE ABUSE OF POWER

Of course, even if you're squeaky clean, it's not that simple. Power corrupts, as the saying goes, and in Kennedy's America, the federal government has ultimate power. Sometimes it gets abused.

Innocent people have been disappeared by the feds in the middle of the night, brought in for questioning, never again to see the light of free day. Some of them fester in filthy cells in the country's overcrowded prisons. Others rot in shallow graves or at the bottom of lakes from sea to shining sea. The even-less fortunate end up drafted into the government's service, their loyalty ensured by thinly veiled death threats against the people they know and love.

As a delta, if you hero is captured, that's her fate. If she hasn't registered, she's automatically an enemy of the state. It's up to your hero to avoid those destinies. If, in the course of doing that, you make life a little easier for others in your situation, so much the better.

YOU ARE THE ENEMY

Plenty of deltas have given the public good reason to be scared. The destruction of Chicago is the most notable, but there have been thousands of smaller incidents over the years.

It's in your hero's interest to put an end to this terror. The fewer reasons people have to fear deltas, the less they can hate them. Or so the theory goes.

Some Defiants have taken the low road, using their powers to beat, threaten, and even kill those who disagree with them. That's one way to win the battle, but it's a sure way to lose the war.

Your hero needs to set an example of how a delta should act. He has to help those in need. He has to take down those who would threaten innocents. And he needs to fight for life, liberty, and the pursuit of happiness.

That's a serious responsibility. Ask yourself: If your hero, with all his powers, doesn't take up that cause, who will?

Delta Points

Because your hero's a delta and not just one of the regs, he's got one more power we haven't talked about yet.

He's got fate on his side.

In *Brave New World,* the world belongs to the bold, those willing to step up and take their destiny in their own hands. To reflect that in the game, every delta hero gets 3 delta points at the beginning of each game session.

Your Fate, Your Hands

Your hero can spend a delta point in one of two ways.

First, after making an action roll, the hero can spend a delta point to roll another die and add the result to his current total.

> ***Example:*** *The Rebel makes a last-ditch attempt to clean the Wastoid's clock. Wounded as he is, the Target Number for the Rebel's attack is 9. Marty rolls his hero's* fighting: barehanded, *and his result is 7, not quite enough. Grimacing, Marty decides to spend a delta point. He rolls the die, gets 6, and rerolls it for 2 more. His new result is (7+6+2=) 15, enough for an extra success!*

You can keep spending delta points until you get the result you're looking for or you run out. Each extra die you roll gets added to the total result. The extra dice rolls are open-ended, so if you get a 6, keep rolling!

Delta points can be spent on damage rolls too, but not on things like hit-location rolls or any other table roll.

You can't use delta points to improve a disastrous roll. There's just no way to make that kind of situation better.

Only a Flesh Wound

You can also use a delta point to save your hero's life.

When your hero takes a wound, you can spend a delta point to keep the wound from ever happening. If you take more than one wound from a single attack, you can spend more delta points, but it still takes one delta point to deflect each wound.

The hero still gets hit by the attack. It's just that through some twist of fate it doesn't do the kind of damage it could have.

That's what being a delta is like.

Use 'Em or Lose 'Em

You can't save delta points from game session to session. If you don't use them in one session, they're gone.

If that happens, just count yourself lucky. Heroes who use all their delta points are usually the ones closest to death.

Experience Points

As you play the game, your hero is going to hopefully learn something in the course of her adventures. We're not just talking about figuring out who's behind the latest anti-delta plot or who's threatening the life of the mayor of Crescent City—this time.

Sure, that's going to happen too, but in addition to all that, your hero's just going to get better at doing the things that she does. In the course of the game, the Guide is going to award you points when your hero does the right kinds of things. If the hero helps foil an evil plot or saves the life of an innocent, there are some points in it for her.

We call these things experience points.

USING EXPERIENCE POINTS

You can use experience points your hero's earned in four ways: improving traits, buying or improving skills, buying off negative quirks, or buying new tricks.

Improving a trait costs three times the new score in that trait. Going from 3 to 4, for instance, costs 12 points. And no, you can't skip a score to save yourself points.

Buying or improving a skill works pretty much the same way, except it's cheaper. It only costs you a number of points equal to the new score. Moving from 3 to 4 costs 4 points. Again, you can't skip scores to save points.

You can't buy new quirks, but you can get rid of the negative ones. All you have to do is pay back the cost of the quirk with experience points. Your Guide might give your hero new quirks during play, like a new *enemy* your hero's picked up, but these don't give you any points.

You can also buy new tricks for your hero. Each new trick costs 10 points.

You can save up experience points between sessions. They don't go away until you spend them.

EARNING EXPERIENCE POINTS

It's up to the Guide as to how many experience points he wants to give out. Published adventures—like the one that comes with *Power Shield*, the *Brave New World* Guide's screen—tell the Guide exactly how to handle this, and we cover this in some depth in the Guide's Handbook.

As a player, the only thing you need to know is that if your hero does the right thing, she'll be rewarded for it. Figuring out what's right isn't always easy, but that's part of the game.

EXPERIENCE AND ROLEPLAYING

You should also get experience points for roleplaying your hero well. The more you get into the role you and your Guide have defined for yourself, the better—up to a point, of course. Insert the standard legal disclaimer here.

You remember all of those quirks you picked out for your hero? Those are the kinds of things that help you flesh out your hero, to make her into a realistic character, a person. Keep those in mind when playing your hero, and don't be afraid to ham them up a bit. Guides tend to reward those players who do.

HAVING FUN

At the end of the day, *Brave New World* is a game, and games are all about having fun. Of course, fun comes in more than 31 flavors, and it's up to you and the rest of your team to come up with your own definition of the kind of game you enjoy.

Make jokes. Or be dead serious if you like. Describe how your hero launches himself into a room with both guns blazing like he just burst straight out the screen during a John Woo movie. Get into your hero's character, and play her to the hilt.

These are your friends you're playing with. You're there to entertain them as much as they're there for you. Do what you can to make each game a memorable experience.

We've got one other treat for you. To encourage you to make things better for everyone, the Guide also gives out experience points for heroes who make the game more fun.

As if you really needed another reason.

The Guide's Handbook

Chapter Eleven: Guiding the Game

Being a Guide—or a Gamemaster, as some games call it—is definitely the biggest responsibility in *Brave New World*. It's up to the Guide to come up with the adventures, figure out who all the extras are, get together a group of players, and then run the game.

The Guide's Job

It's not a job for the faint of heart. As Guide, you're part writer, part referee, part actor, and part entertainer. It's up to you to make sure that the game runs smoothly and—most importantly—that everyone has fun—including yourself!

Don't worry. We're here to help you.

The Guide's World

As the Guide, you're the ultimate power in your game. You are your players' eyes and ears into the realm of *Brave New World*. Without your descriptions of the people the heroes meet and the places they go, they're deaf, dumb, and blind.

Sure, the players can read all the *Brave New World* books they like, but those are just books, not the actual game. If they want the full roleplaying experience, they need a Guide.

It's up to you to take the words we publish in these books and breathe life into them. To make the heroes hate the villains. To make them care enough about it all to want to save the world.

In short, when you're playing *Brave New World*, it's your game, not ours. We can't be there looking over your shoulder and cheering you on.

No. You're on your own.

The Guide's Power

That doesn't mean we're just going to leave you twisting in the wind. If you think you've got what it takes to run a good game, then we're here for you. Here's your first gift:

As Guide, your word is final.

When you say that something happens in your game, that's exactly what happens. There's no arguing about it.

Well, the players can always try to convince you of the error of your ways, but at the end of the day, it's your call. When you've heard enough, you can also end a discussion about any ruling you make. Like we just said, your word is final.

That's really all you need. It's a lot of power, and you've got to be careful how you use it.

THE GUIDE'S DUTY

Someone once said, "With great power comes great responsibility." Just because you're in charge of your game doesn't mean you can abuse that power.

It's your job to make sure the players are all enjoying themselves. There's one easy way to tell if you're succeeding or not.

If the players aren't having fun, they'll quit.

Now, people are going to come and go from your game for lots of different reasons, but if you suddenly find yourself alone on every game night, you need to take a long, hard look at yourself and see if it's something you did as Guide. If so, you can always give it another try, but if you do so, make sure to change your ways.

ASSEMBLING A TEAM

As a Guide, one of the first things you've got to do is get together a group of players to take part in your *Brave New World* game. That part should be easy. Just tell some of your friends about the game and invite them to play.

Roleplaying games usually do well with smaller groups of players, especially if you're new to running a game. As Guide, you need to pay attention to each of the players during the course of the game, making sure each of their heroes gets some time in the spotlight.

No one likes sitting around watching other people enjoying themselves. No, they want to get into the fun too! The easiest way to do that is to start small.

We recommend starting out with only three or four players—not counting yourself. That way, you know you're going to have enough time to devote to each of them.

Once you've run the game a few times and you're comfortable with both the game system and running a game, you can add more players. Do this slowly. If you're careful, you'll spot your limit before you go over it. An experience Guide may be able to handle up to eight players, but more than that is often unmanageable.

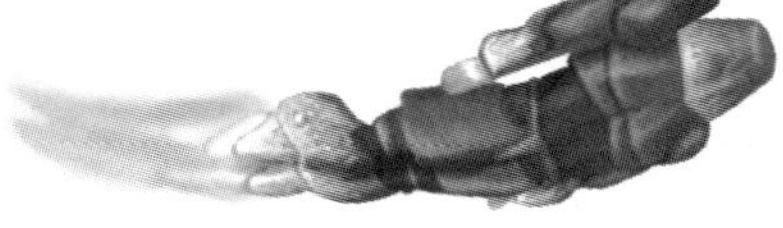

A Team Effort

Sure, it's ultimately your responsibility to make sure the players are having fun, but help is close at hand. Your players can pitch in too.

When you sit down with the players to make up their heroes, first talk about what kind of game you'd like to play. Do you want to concentrate on paramilitary combat or political intrigue or something else entirely? Are the players more interested in rolling dice or roleplaying?

There's no right or wrong here, but it helps if you can come up with some kind of consensus. If you've got several people who are all trying to play in a different type of game, they're not going to be able to work together.

We call a group of heroes a team for a reason. When a team's at its peak, it functions as a unit, a well-oiled machine. For this reason, start out with heroes that all have the same status quirks. For most games, this means they should be unregistered deltas with secret identities.

An accomplished Guide can handle a disparate group. In fact, the tensions in the team can add to the roleplaying experience. If the players aren't extremely mature and friendly about it, though, it can lead to some serious friction, which can destroy a team.

That's not fun.

If you can come up with even an overall consensus before the heroes are created, then you're a step ahead of the game. When the players come up with their heroes' personalities, they should be thinking about how each of the heroes is going to work as part of the larger whole. With any luck, this should translate to a closer-knit team and happier players who can have fun together.

Running an Adventure

A roleplaying game is different than most kinds of game because there are no winners or losers. The players all just get together to have fun, pretend to be different people, and entertain each other. If everything works like it's supposed to and a good time is had by all, then everyone wins.

Just like some of your favorite fictional stories in films, novels, or comics, the saga might have a definite beginning, but it doesn't ever have to end. As long as the players keep having fun, you can keep getting together for session after session for as long as you like or the sun goes out—whichever comes first.

The Saga

An ongoing game of *Brave New World* is called a saga. The saga is made up of several different stories or adventures that link together into a greater whole. Some of the stories might have a deeper meaning when seen in the context of the saga's ongoing tale, while others might just be temporary tangents.

Each time you and your players sit down to play *Brave New World*, we call that a session. When you call a halt to the game until you can meet again, the session is over. It can take several sessions to finish a story, or just one.

As Guide, you need to think about your game in terms of both the saga and the stories. The easiest way to do this is to just start playing through whatever stories you like. As time goes on, you can look back and see all the things the heroes have done—all the people they've saved and all the enemies they've made. Suddenly you've got a saga.

Alternatively, you can set up each of your stories ahead of time to link into the overarching saga. As the heroes go from story to story, they pick up on larger themes and possibilities, and eventually they realize there's something larger going on here, a major plot in which they've now found themselves embroiled.

You can go either way you like. Better yet, you don't have to decide now. If you like, you can just start out playing whatever kinds of stories you like. Later you can start up a more integrated saga, or you can even weave elements of the earlier stories into a new whole.

Creating Your Own Stories

Coming up with your own stories can be tough, but we've got help for you there too. *Power Shield* is the Guide's screen for *Brave New World*. It's a colorful cardboard screen you can hide your secret notes behind while you run the game, but it also comes with an introductory adventure, perfect for launching any *Brave New World* saga.

As time goes on, we're going to be releasing more and more sourcebooks for *Brave New World*, exploring different aspects of its people and universe. Most—if not all—of these are going to come with an adventure too. Many of these are designed to be generic enough for you to be able to slot into many different types of sagas.

Even if you never use any of the published adventures in your saga, they still serve as excellent examples of how a story is constructed. If you're just starting out, we strongly recommend you try one of the published adventures.

Story Structure

Once you move on to creating your own stories, we're still there for you. Here's the basic structure of any *Brave New World* story.

The Backstory

Most times, the heroes don't come in at the beginning of a story. Instead, they stumble onto or are led into something that's been going on for a good while already. The tale of what's happened up until the heroes get involved is called the backstory.

You need a good backstory so you can quickly figure out what happens if the heroes wander off in a different direction than you might have predicted.

Take our word for it: This happens all the time! There's no predicting exactly what a team's going to do, so you need to be prepared.

The Setup

Once you know what's going on, you've got to get the heroes involved. In this section, you figure out how the heroes might first discover what's going on.

You also need to think about why they might want to get involved. Sure, you can say, "They're heroes! They'll lend a hand." But it's not always that simple.

Think about who the heroes are and what motivates them. Is it love? Money? Patriotism? An overwhelming sense of responsibility? Figure out what the heroes' buttons are and push them.

Hard.

If you can't quite figure this out, let the players give you a hand. Have them come up with their own reasons.

Chapters

Stories are generally broken down into chapters. Short stories might only have a single chapter, while mini-sagas could be a dozen or more chapters long.

In each chapter, describe a single scene and who might be encountered there. This is where you list the full profiles of any goons or villains the heroes might run into. You should have an idea of what's supposed to happen here, and some contingency plans in case things go awry.

Moving Right Along

If you want to keep things moving along, you also need to stick in clues or contacts to lead the heroes onto a later chapter. If the chapters simply lead from one to another, you've got a linear adventure. If the heroes deviate from the plotline you've developed, there's no telling where they might end up.

To make the story less constrictive, try having two or three different directions in which the heroes might go after a chapter. Most adventures have a single climactic scene that the heroes need to get to in order to succeed, but that doesn't have to be true. You can even come up with multiple endings if you like. This can be a truly rewarding kind of adventure, but it's a lot more work, so tread carefully in this territory, especially if you're new to it.

Rewards

At the end of each chapter, you should list the rewards the heroes' get if they have a successful chapter. These usually come in the form of experience points, but they can also be new friends, enemies, gear, or even cash. It's up to you.

Awarding Experience Points

Part of being a hero in *Brave New World* is the challenge. You've got to be careful about giving out too many experience points. At the end of a chapter, a hero who did well might earn 1 or 2 points, and that's it. If it's a really important chapter—like the climactic one—the hero might get 3 or even 4 points, but no more.

Delta Points

If you want to reward the hero for being clever or keeping everyone entertained, give him a free delta point instead. If you give this out during play, it can only be used in this session. If you give it out at the end of play, it has to be used during the next session. Unused delta points simply disappear.

The Guide's Shortcuts

As the Guide, you've got a lot going on. Not only do you have to know what's happening at any given point in the game, you've got to keep track of both the players and every extra in the game. That can quickly overwhelm even the most experienced Guide, so we've got some tried and true shortcuts to make your life that much easier.

Handling the Extras

First, let's separate out the extras into two different types: minor and major.

Minor extras (called goons) are those people who aren't too powerful or who aren't going to have much of an affect upon the game. They're pretty much a dime a dozen, at least as far as the game is concerned. Sure, they've all got families and jobs and real lives and all of that, but in terms of the heroes' interaction with them, we can ignore a lot of the finer details.

Major extras (some of which are the big villains) can affect the heroes' lives in big ways. This runs from the local chief of police to the head of the terrorist organization threatening to blow up Crescent City—this week.

To make things easier on you, you can handle minor and major extras in different ways.

Profiles

A profile for a major extra needs to be complete, often requiring as much thought as creating a hero. A minor extra, on the other hand, doesn't require as much attention. You can just list down their trait scores and only the skills that might come up in the course of meeting one of the heroes.

Sure, that cabbie might have a *contact* in Delta Prime, or maybe he's fluent in 12 languages, but since you can pretty much bet that's not going to come up in the course of the story, don't worry about it. That much detail just bogs things down.

As a baseline, the average person has a score of 2d6 in each trait, plus a score of 2 in any skills she might need to have. You can bump this up to a score of 3 in skills the person specializes in. That cabbie above, for instance, would have a *driving: personal vehicle* of 3, while his *language: English* would be 2. You can usually ignore any quirks.

In the case of major extras—who have a tendency to crop up again and again, even when the heroes think they're dead—you need to have a full profile. After all, you never know what the heroes are going to put him through.

If you get caught flatfooted and suddenly need to know an extra's score for any trait or skill, just roll 1d6. If it's a goon, cut the results in half. Either way, it's not an open-ended roll, so the highest the score can be is 6.

Initiative

The first thing you're going to need is a bit of scrap paper to keep track of everyone's initiative roll. Be sure to write down each players' result as well the extras'. You're going to need to keep track of them all, and having them right in front of you works a lot better than having to ask players to repeat themselves all the time.

When rolling initiative for a major extra, it works just like with the heroes. Just roll her *Speed*. Since the extra works for you though, you don't have to announce the result. Keep it to yourself and keep the players guessing.

With minor extras, you've got two options. You've usually got lots of these goons fighting at once, so you don't want to have to keep track of initiative rolls for each of them. It can get ridiculous pretty quickly.

First, you can just not roll for any of the goons. Depending on who they are, just set an initiative number for them and go. If they're a bunch of really minor extras, their result is 4. This means they each only get one action. If they're a bit tougher, their result is 7, giving them two actions each.

Alternatively, you can make a single *Speed* roll for each type of goon involved. Since each type of goon has the same profile, use the *Speed* listed on that profile for the initiative roll.

If you get a really great roll (10 or higher) or a disastrous roll, assign that result to one of the goons and then roll again for the rest.

Injuries

Villains and goons get separated once more when it comes to sucking up those wounds.

Major extras take wounds just like heroes do. For each point of *Strength* they have, they can take one wound in each of the six different hit locations.

For all intents and purposes, minor extras don't have hit locations. Let the heroes roll for hit location anyhow. If they're lucky, they might get some extra damage dice after all.

When applying the wounds to a goon, they all go to a single spot. Once the goon takes more wounds than his *Strength*, he's been knocked unconscious. If he takes double that amount, he's dead.

If this makes the hero into an accidental killer, show some mercy. The goon isn't really dead, but he's going to be spending the next few weeks of his life eating hospital food.

Of course, if the hero's got a mean streak and she's trying to kill the goon, let her go right ahead. Just remember, that goon's a real person, and the law doesn't look kindly on killers.

Maps and Miniatures

If possible, get yourself a dry-erase map or board. During play, you can sketch layouts of rooms and areas so the players can see exactly what's going on.

Better yet, with a map drawn roughly to scale, you can use miniatures—metal figurines about an inch tall—to keep track of exactly where every hero and extra is. *Brave New World* is designed to make easy use of miniatures. *Pace*, for instance, is listed in inches, so get yourself a ruler, and you're all set.

Chapter Twelve: Brave New Secrets

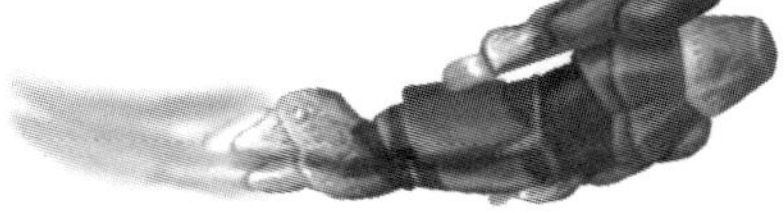

Chapter Twelve: Brave New Secrets

Hey, buddy! Come here. We got something for you. Something we don't tell those player-types about.

That is, if you're a Guide.

This part of the book is for Guides only. If you don't qualify, you'd better flip back to the earlier parts of the book before your Guide sees you.

If you don't have a Guide yet and you're just wandering around, that's fine—to a point. If you're thinking about being a Guide, come on in and poke around a bit. See if this Guide gig's for you.

If that's what you're doing, though, we recommend you go back and read Chapter Eleven and leave the rest of the book until you're absolutely sure.

The Cone of Silence

The fact is that this chapter and Chapter Thirteen are full of all sorts of secrets that only the Guide should know about. If you're not pretty darn sure you're going to be a Guide, leave now.

Why? First, we asked nicely. Second, as a player you're going to eventually learn about most if not all of the secrets, but in the course of playing the game. Be patient.

Sure, it might seem cool to get your hands on all the secrets ahead of time, but you're really just spoiling the fun. It's like waking up on Christmas and knowing who really put those presents under the tree and what's in them. It takes half the fun out of it.

The Guide's Duty

If you are a Guide, then the warning about keeping things secret goes double for you. Don't go wandering around with loose lips. Even if your players have already figured out some of *Brave New World*'s secrets, you can bet not every player has. For their sake, keep the faith.

Just to keep you honest, we're keeping some of the most important secrets to ourselves—for now. That way, you can join in the unwrapping of those presents too.

What's Really Happening

Now that it's just you Guides reading, we can finally kick off our shoes, lie back, and get down to the truth. Right?

Not so fast.

Sure, as a Guide, there are certain secrets we just have to let you in on. Otherwise, we'd be hampering your ability to do your job. But we're not quite ready to blab about everything all at once. Not quite yet.

As we publish supplements for *Brave New World*, you can look forward to learning more and more about what's really going on behind the world. Eventually you'll be able to piece together the whole story.

In the meantime, we've got some pretty darn juicy bits in this chapter for you, so don't blink. You never know what you might miss.

Truth in Our Time

The woman known as Truth is actually Marta Alonso, a reporter for the *Crescent City Star*, one of the city's two daily newspapers. She's worked there for several years, as an investigative reporter—and a damn good one.

Unfortunately, Marta's editor refuses to print the best stuff she comes up with for fear of having the federal government come in and shut the paper down. This has happened five times in the past decade, and if it happens again, it might be the last anyone will ever see of *The Star*.

Because of her job, Marta knows a lot more about the world than ever sees print in *The Star*. She uses this to her advantage when she moonlights as Truth, the editor and publisher of *The Delta Times*.

As delta powers go, Truth's are pretty subtle. When she listens to a person's voice, she can instantly tell whether or not he's being truthful. Unfortunately, that doesn't always get her a whole lot closer to the truth of the matter. It just lets her know when she's being fed a line of bull.

Some people have been able to get around Truth's power by telling her the truth, but not all of it. Her finely honed reporter's instincts often let her know when someone's being evasive with her, but they're not always foolproof.

The upshot of all of this is that the materials printed in *The Delta Times* are usually pretty darn trustworthy, but not always. Smart heroes check their facts before they rely on them. Of course, this is a lesson your team might have to learn the hard way.

The Defiance

Here's the flip side of Truth's powers. Sure, she knows the truth, but she's a damn good liar too. You can't always trust this seasoned reporter to be as straightforward as you might hope.

Case in point: the Defiance Movement. From reading Truth's diatribe about the Defiance, you might come away thinking it's nothing more than what the deltas who spat on the DRA call themselves.

That's not entirely true.

Sure, any delta who refuses to sign up with the feds can call himself a Defiant, but there's more to it than that. There are pockets of resistance in the country in which the Defiance is actually pretty together, and there's a secretive higher level to the organization that actually thinks it's got a shot at kicking Kennedy out of office.

It might be right.

When the heroes join the Defiance (as most heroes will), all they really know about the Defiance is what they read on the website. As opportunities present themselves to test the heroes' loyalty's they'll receive assignments from one of the higher-ups in the Defiance—often from Truth herself.

WORKING WITH THE DEFIANCE

At the early stages of membership, the heroes are rarely ever trusted with any information that might prove potentially harmful to other Defiants. They're simply presented with a situation and asked to resolve it.

The heroes might be asked to rescue a young delta from Delta Prime before she gets hauled in, for instance. Or they might be asked to investigate a series of crimes that are being blamed on the Defiance. Or maybe they're given a way they could hamper the activities of Delta Prime.

In any case, the benefits of these test cases are usually pretty obvious. The Defiance isn't into running people around like idiots until they decide they can trust them. No, they're more about the field test.

If the heroes manage to complete these test with flying colors, they're given more important assignments. This continues until the heroes are completely trusted by all levels of the organization.

For more about how this might work in the case of your team, check out the background in *Ravaged Planet* and the upcoming *Defiance* sourcebooks. For now, the information you've got here should be plenty to get you started. If in doubt, the Defiance treats the heroes like mushrooms. They keep them in the dark and feed them manure.

GETTING BOOTED

Of course, not all heroes are going to succeed at the tasks the Defiance puts in front of them. If they blow enough of them, the Defiance kicks them out.

If this happens, the heroes are officially deemed untrustworthy by the Defiance. That means the most they can do is get on the website to read about whatever details Truth has decided she's willing to release to the general public. Unless the heroes do something on their own to redeem themselves in the eyes of the Defiance, they're never going to have much to do with the organization.

This means that when the heroes need a hand, they're not going to have anyone to call on. Since they're unregistered deltas, though, they should be used to that by now, right?

Where Delta Powers Come From

The fact is no one knows for sure where delta powers come from. In the old days, there were a lot of cornball theories about alien implants, mad scientist experiments, and strange visitors from other planets.

None of that ever panned out.

Of course, just because there's no proof of any of those theories doesn't mean that there aren't lots of people who believe them. In fact, some of those people have positions of great power in both the Defiance and Delta Prime.

The point is that there are idiots everywhere, and people generally believe what they want to believe. Even some of the seemingly smartest and most connected people buy into these crackpot notions.

Of course, these days there's another crackpot notion that's gotten more attention than any of the others. It's helped by the fact that it's grounded in science.

The Delta Factor

With the advent of the Human Genome Project, scientists have managed to map large portions of humanity's DNA. While the project is far from complete, the scientists have made a few astonishing discoveries.

A good portion of the human population has a unique sequence in its DNA that doesn't appear in any other creature on the face of the earth. In fact, a good portion of the human population doesn't have it at all.

In deltas, this same sequence has been altered—some say mutated—radically, and often in new and unpredictable ways. Scientists believe that this mutable DNA is the source of delta powers. Being the prosaic kind of people they tend to be, the eggheads call this sequence the delta factor.

As is usually the case, this discovery raises more questions than it answers. The first of these is both the easiest to ask and the hardest to answer: Where did this sequence come from?

You Say You Want an Evolution

There are lots of guesses and little in the way of proof.

Some people think the delta factor is simply the next stage in evolution. Those who have this sequence in their DNA are part of a new race of people known as—all adolescent jokes aside—homo delta.

Those who subscribe to this idea predict that eventually regular people will either die off or be bred into the

delta population. When that happens, every person in the entire world will have the potential to become a delta.

Others suspect something with results that are just as pervasive but with far more sinister origins. They claim that this "rogue" DNA sequence was somehow implanted into the human genome.

The more paranoid among those who tout this theory believe that whoever did this will one day trigger a subsequence of the gene that will allow them to control every delta on earth. These same people often claim that the Nazis or Soviets are behind such an effort. Pointing out that the first recorded deltas were discovered during World War I doesn't seem to dent their fervor for their beliefs.

Then there are those who point out that the easiest way to introduce a new genetic sequence into a population is by breeding. When this notion hit the papers, all sorts of wackos crawled out of the woodwork, claiming they'd been abducted by aliens and impregnated with their delta-factor-tainted offspring. None of these stories has ever been proved.

Then there's the Delta Cult. Some cultists believe that the deltas are the long-lost descendants of the ancient gods of myth and legend. They worship deltas as "children of the gods," and they say that the great-great-great-whatever grandparents of these deltas will come back to reclaim their offspring soon.

Of course, they can't agree on when. Some DCs think it's all going to happen on January 1, 2000. Others bet on 2001. Of course, the ancient gods never heard of the Gregorian calendar, but they're gods, so they can do whatever they want, right.

Like we said, no one really knows.

The Great Tragedy

There is one secret we can reveal to you in no uncertain terms.

John F. Kennedy is dead.

In fact, he died on that fateful November day in Dallas back in '63.

Obviously, that's not what the general public—including the heroes—believes. Here's what really happened.

A Moment Too Late

Superior was on the scene moments after the Dreadnaut strike team began its attack. He mopped the floor with the killers, swept the President up in his arms, and zoomed off toward the nearest hospital.

On his way to Dallas' Parkland Hospital, Superior quickly realized that the President was beyond help. He was well and truly dead.

Superior wasn't the sort to accept any defeat gracefully. He didn't let the Nazis win World War II, and he was damned if he was going to let the forces of terror believe they'd won this round as well.

Superior turned around and zoomed toward Washington, DC, instead. Within minutes, he was knocking on the door of a man called Facade.

Not much is known about this mysterious figure. He's an alpha with a single, incredible ability: He can impersonate anyone.

By that, we don't mean Rich Little was looking over his shoulder. No, the Facade could actually take on the appearance, voice, and mannerisms of anyone he'd studied. For all intents and purposes, he could become any other person he studied, lacking only their knowledge.

You can guess what Superior had in mind.

THE BIG SWITCH

Within moments, the Facade agreed to Superior's plan. Minutes later, Superior flew into Walter Reed Memorial Hospital with the Facade in his arms. Of course, everyone else mistook him for President Kennedy as planned.

Superior explained to the healers at the hospital that he had taken Kennedy directly to Dr. Joel Abrahams, the best-known alpha healer in the country. Dr. Abrahams had been able to repair most of the damage done to Mr. Kennedy, but the President was going to need to recuperate in private until his personal physicians could arrive.

After he handed the Facade over to the doctors at Walter Reed, Superior dashed off to Dr. Abraham's home to get him on board with the deception.

Dr. Abrahams had served in Delta Squadron alongside Superior back when he'd been known as Sparky. He knew the man that the boy had become, and he trusted him entirely. Although he had some reservations, he shoved them aside and put his faith in Superior's judgment.

THE RUSE

When the Facade woke up in Walter Reed, he feigned memory loss from the healed head injury he'd suffered in the assassination attempt. This gave him a chance to adjust to his new role as President.

In later days, the ruse served the Facade well. Anytime someone asked him about something Kennedy should have known about, he blamed his forgetfulness on the head wound.

Over the years, a few people have gotten close to the truth. They were either brought on board or—if Superior or Kennedy didn't feel that they could be trusted with so enormous a secret—eliminated.

When Superior originally pitched the idea to the Facade, he had imagined the deception would only be a temporary one. At some point in the future, the President would "die" peacefully, and the Facade would be free to return to his old life.

That never happened.

Superior got the idea for the Delta Registration Act and had the Facade push it through Congress. After that, it was only a few short steps to martial law.

Suddenly, the Facade found himself as the sole ruler of the most powerful nation on the face of the Earth, and Superior played the part of the power behind the throne.

It couldn't last.

THE BICENTENNIAL BATTLE

When Chicago disappeared in that burst of white light back in '76, the world drew a collective gasp. In one fell swoop, over 80% of the alpha heroes were gone.

Superior was, of course, among them. This was no coincidence.

The Devastator got the technology for his amazing bomb directly from the Supplier, the head gadgeteer at Evil Unlimited, the most pervasive criminal organization on the planet. The Supplier got the technology from a freelance gadgeteer looking to make a quick buck off his latest invention.

The freelance gadgeteer was secretly a member of Delta Prime, giving the tech to the Supplier under the orders of the President himself.

It all boils down to this. The Facade has gotten used to holding the reins of power, and he wasn't willing to risk ever having to give them up to anyone. He wanted to get rid of Superior and any other alpha who might someday challenge his authority.

When Chicago disappeared, the Facade got exactly what he wanted. Since that fateful day, he's had plenty of opportunities to regret his actions. It all falls under that age-old lesson: Be careful what you wish for.

Either way, with one decisive move, the Facade cemented his position as President for life. There are few who remain who he might even consider fearing. Sure, the Defiance is always making rumbles about tossing him out of office in some kind of coup, but he's got that angle covered too.

As for the remaining alphas, they're all either on the run, in his pocket, or so far away from Washington that the false President doesn't even think about them.

WHERE HAVE ALL THE ALPHAS GONE?

The strangest effects of the Devastator's bomb is the one that no one ever talks about. Ever since the moment that device went off, shaking the country and even the planet to its core, no delta has become an alpha.

Sure, there are still some alphas out there—the ones who were either in prison at the time, protected from the Vanishing by the power-dampening fields—but no new ones.

Every now and then, a delta steps up and calls himself an alpha. She might even really believe it. But it's not true.

The fact is that deltas still get into the kinds of situations that might cause one to transform into an alpha. It's just that when they get into these near-death situations, most of them die. Those who survive just count their lucky stars—along with their fingers—and move on. But they're not alphas.

Of course, not all of the bodies of those dead deltas are always recovered. That's not anything strange, in and of itself. Lots of times, deltas get themselves into incredibly dangerous situations in which they risk not only death but not having much left of themselves to fill a coffin.

Still, it's suspicious, and those inclined to come up with paranoid theories have lots of answers for these kinds of questions.

DRAWING BACK THE VEIL

Of course, the heroes (and the players) don't know any of this stuff. It's up to you to make sure it stays that way—at least until we say otherwise.

The information in *Brave New World* is released on a need-to-know basis.

We'll tell you when you need to know.

Chapter Thirteen: The Usual Suspects

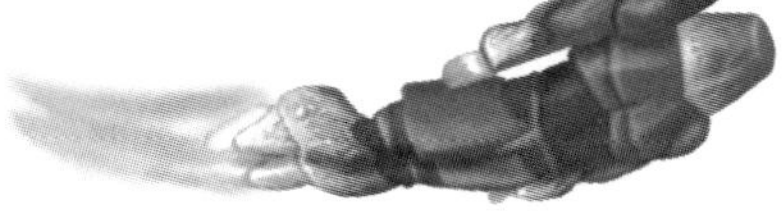

Chapter Thirteen: The Usual Suspects

All right. The players know how to create their heroes. You've got the straight dope—or at least part of it—on what's going on. You even know how to run the game.

Now all you need is something for the heroes to do.

Well, we've got that covered too. What's a hero without a villain after all?

Fighting Foes

The following pages describe seven different types of extras for the heroes to face off against. This should be enough to get you started in your saga, but don't worry, we've got lots more on the way.

Just about every *Brave New World* supplement is going to feature new adversaries for your heroes. Delta Prime, for instance, is going to get an entire book all to itself, devoted to dealing with the Defiance's sworn enemies in depth. Evil Unlimited is scheduled for its own book as well.

Using Foes

When you're reading the profiles of the people and creatures in this chapter, you might think to yourself, "These guys aren't so bad. My team's going to mop the floor with them."

True enough, in a toe-to-toe fight, a delta team is going to make quick work of a beat cop or a wiseguy, but that's not usually how it goes down. Sure, the heroes might occasionally run into the lone police officer, but that cop's got lots of well-armed friends he can call in for backup on a moment's notice.

The same's true of just about any of the rest of these opponents. They're not monsters that popped out of a videogame, and they're not just going to stand there and let the heroes beat on them. They're smart, and they've got connections. The leaders of these organizations aren't going to be found walking alone down a dark alley. They've got bodyguards. They've got fortress-mansions.

And they're ready and waiting.

Aquarians

The Defiance isn't the only illegal organization of deltas in the nation. It's just the largest. Another notable group calls itself the Aquarians.

These people are apparently deltas who have the ability to live and breathe underwater. They can be found nearly all over the planet, but there's a particularly large settlement of them living in the bottom of Chicago Bay, right below where the Sears Tower used to stand.

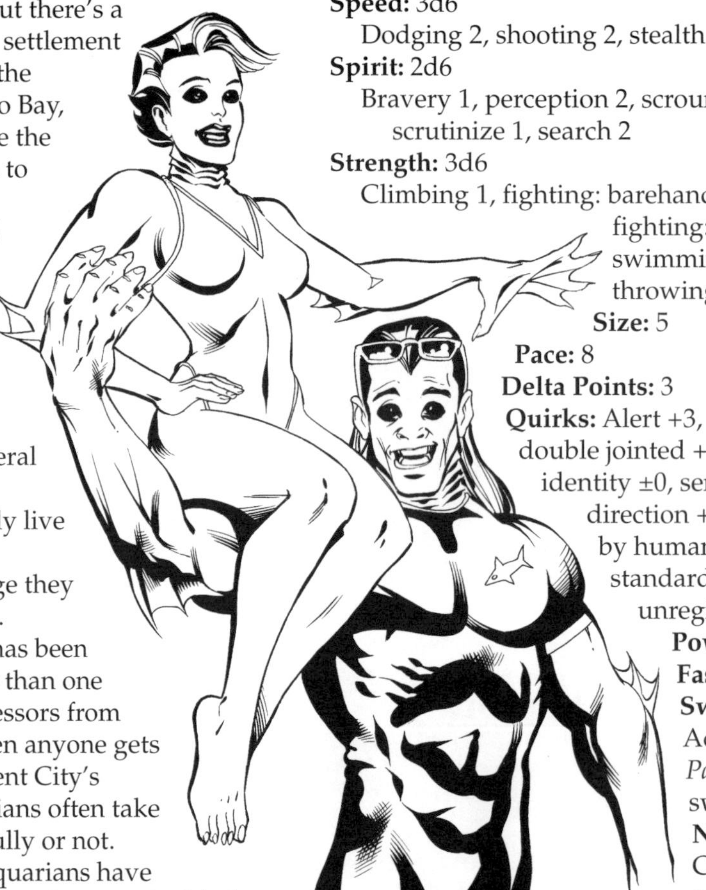

The Aquarians are fairly reclusive. Their stated goal is the founding of a full-fledged Aquarian city in Chicago Bay. Several dozen of the Aquarians actually live there now in an underwater village they call New Atlantis.

New Atlantis has been attacked on more than one occasion by aggressors from Delta Prime. When anyone gets killed near Crescent City's docks, the Aquarians often take the blame, rightfully or not.

Some of the Aquarians have decided to live up to the terrorist label they've been given by the *Crescent City Star.* Others argue for peace, but they're hardly willing to start a civil war over protecting a group of people who are persecuting them.

Aquarians look pretty much like normal humans, with a few notable exceptions. They have small gills located just below their ears, and their toes and fingers are webbed. Most notably, their eyes are entirely black.

Profile

Smarts: 2d6
Area knowledge: Chicago Bay 2, area knowledge: Crescent City 1, language: English 2, navigation 2, survival: underwater 2
Speed: 3d6
Dodging 2, shooting 2, stealth 2
Spirit: 2d6
Bravery 1, perception 2, scrounging 2, scrutinize 1, search 2
Strength: 3d6
Climbing 1, fighting: barehanded 2, fighting: club 2, swimming 5, throwing 1
Size: 5
Pace: 8
Delta Points: 3
Quirks: Alert +3, delta ±0, double jointed +1, public identity ±0, sense of direction +1, ugly –1: by human standards, unregistered ±0
Powers:
Fast Swimmer: Add +20 to *Pace* when swimming.
Nightvision: Can see normally in the dark
Water Breathing.
Tricks: Bull's eye and first move.
Breach: With an extra success on a *swimming* roll, the Aquarian can leap up to 20 feet from the water.
Gear: None.

EVIL UNLIMITED

Not every unregistered delta is a misunderstood freedom fighter looking to live free. Some are actually the horrible criminals that Kennedy would have the American people believe all rogue deltas are. They kill, rape, pillage, loot, and rob. Sometimes they've even got delusions about ruling the planet—or at least some small corner of it.

In short, they're bad people.

The fact is, there's no higher percentage of bad deltas than there are bad people. The DRA, though, instantly criminalizes many deltas, and the fact is that when a delta decides to go bad, people notice.

When a delta criminal needs help, she knows who to turn to: Evil Unlimited. EU is an underground organization of loosely affiliated deltas and regs who have the common aim of supplying people who want to cause destruction.

Evil Unlimited employees work for a mysterious central office from which they take their orders and to which they relay requests for personnel and ordnance. EU sales reps come in all different flavors, but they share one common trait. They're all a lot more dangerous than they look.

EVIL UNLIMITED SALES REP

Smarts: 2d6
Area knowledge: Crescent City 2, language: English 2, profession: sales 4

Speed: 2d6
Dodging 1, driving: personal vehicle 2, shooting 3, stealth 1

Spirit: 4d6
Perception 2, persuasion: bluff 3, persuasion: charm 4, scrutinize 3, search 2

Strength: 2d6
Climbing 1, fighting: barehanded 2, swimming 1, throwing 1

Size: 5

Pace: 7

Delta Points: None

Quirks: Arrogant –3, contact +4: Evil Unlimited's board of directors, greedy –2, reg ±0, self-confident +2,

Gear: Colt 2000 and 45 rounds of armor-piercing (AP 10) ammo in spare clips, Kevlar vest, hidden Derringer with 2 rounds of ammo, explosive briefcase (Damage: 10d6+40, Burst Radius: 5), cell phone, pager, palmtop computer, and $2,000.

DEADERS

Since anyone with the delta factor in his genes can become a delta, the Primers have a saying: "Don't believe someone's dead until you see the body." Even then, you can't always be sure.

With deaders, though, you can pretty much count on their being deceased. Their rotting flesh is a "dead" giveaway.

The first deaders were created by a gadgeteer who figured out a way to create a device that could stimulate a dead brain with electric pulses sent from a central control unit—which is the actual gadget—giving a corpse a semblance of life. Since then the technology has become common knowledge among the more morbid gadgeteers.

With a little makeup and cologne, a deader can pass for human. They don't tend to talk much, although they can if they have to. The chips that give them life also force them to follow their creator's orders to the letter. Some deaders take malicious glee in abusing those orders, but most readily comply, since if they fail in their mission, all that awaits them is a return to the grave.

PROFILE

Smarts: 1d6
Area knowledge: Crescent City 2, language: English 2
Speed: 4d6
Dodging 4, driving: personal vehicle 2, shooting 4, stealth 4
Spirit: 2d6
Perception 2, persuasion: intimidation 4, scrutinize 1, search 2
Strength: 4d6
Climbing 1, fighting: barehanded 4, fighting: club 4, swimming 1, throwing 1
Size: 5
Pace: 9
Delta Points: None
Quirks: Bloodthirsty –2, clumsy –3, double-jointed +1, reg ±0
Powers:
Undead: A deaders doesn't suffer wound-effect modifiers and doesn't have to make stun checks. It's only truly dead when its head is pulped.
Weaknesses:
Chipset: A deader's chip can be destroyed with a single wound to the back of the head. The location is covered with an armored plate (Armor 10/—), and attackers add +8 to hit the location with a called shot. If a deader is shot in the head, roll 1d6. On a 6, the shot hits the plate.
Tricks: None.
Gear: None.

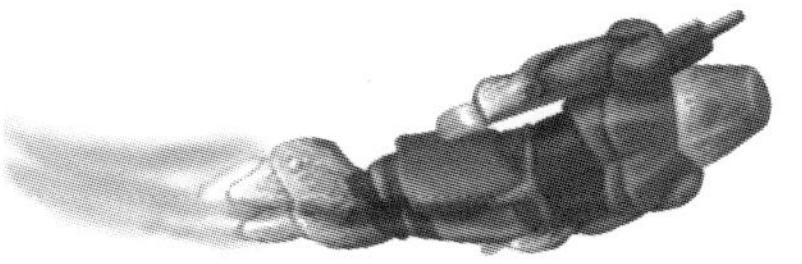

Delta Prime

If a hero registers as a delta, she's off to either Delta Academy or Delta Squadron. From there, most registered deltas move on to Delta Prime.

Delta Primers are some of the most feared people on the planet, and they're legendary in the United States. The appearance of a single Primer is enough to strike fear into the heart of any Defiant.

Those who tell you different are either lying or dumb.

Perhaps the most feared Primers are those chosen to wear the DP's legendary power armor: the Armorgeddon suit. The fact is that most of the people in the Armorgeddon suits aren't even deltas. They're highly trained soldiers making use of a suit that's maintained for them by a gadgeteer assigned to them as both their mechanic and mentor.

Armorgeddon Pilot

Smarts: 2d6
Area knowledge: Crescent City 2, language: English 2, navigation 2, tactics 3
Speed: 5d6
Dodging 4, flying 4, martial arts: barehanded 5, martial arts: club 5, martial arts: blade 5, quick draw 3, shooting 5, speed-load 3, stealth 3
Spirit: 2d6
Bravery 3, leadership 2, perception 4, scrutinize 2, search 2
Strength: 3d6
Climbing 1, fighting: barehanded 2, fighting: club 2, persuasion: interrogation 2, persuasion: intimidation 5, swimming 5, throwing 1
Size: 6
Pace: 10
Delta Points: None
Quirks: Authority +3: Delta Primer, contact +3: suit's gadgeteer, duty +5: Delta Prime, reg ±0, tough +2
Gear: Armorgeddon suit: Armor 10/3, add +5 to *Strength* rolls, shoulder cannon (see below), fly at a *Pace* of 40.

Armorgeddon Guns

Weapon Type	Action	Ammo	Shots	Quickness	Rate of Fire	Range Increment	Damage	Cost
Shoulder Cannon	Auto	.50	50	1	3	5	5d6+10 (AP5)	—

The Police

The people most Defiants are going to get the most hassles from are the cops on the beat. These men and women are on the front lines of Kennedy's "war on Defiance." They're the first on the scene to investigate any kind of disturbance, so the heroes are likely going to run into them from time to time.

For the most part, police officers are just men and women who believe in their government and are just doing their jobs the best they can. Not all of them share the sentiment that the only good Defiant is a dead Defiant, but given the choice, they tend to err on the side of shooting first and letting their sergeant ask the questions later.

Smart Defiants do their best not to face off against the police. It's hard enough having to put up with Primers chasing you all over town, much less having the cops taking an active hand. Also, most officers are just struggling to keep the peace, something most Defiants should be in favor of.

In most cases, you should use the police as a goad. If you want to pressure the heroes to move along, let them hear approaching sirens or have them get spotted by a beat cop who immediately reports in on his radio. Most cops are just ordinary people who don't have much of a chance against a delta, and they know it. Their strength is in numbers, and they're not afraid to use it.

Profile

Smarts: 2d6
Area knowledge: Crescent City 4, language: English 2, language: Spanish 1, navigation 1, tactics 2
Speed: 3d6
Dodging 2, driving: personal vehicle 2, shooting 2, stealth 2
Spirit: 3d6
Bravery 1, perception 2, persuasion: bluff 2, leadership 1, persuasion: intimidation 3, scrutinize 2, search 2, shadowing 3
Strength: 3d6
Climbing 1, fighting: barehanded 2, fighting: club 2, swimming 1, throwing 1
Size: 5
Pace: 8
Delta Points: None
Quirks: Alert +3, authority +1: beat cop, duty +3: police department, loyal –3, patron +3: police sergeant, reg ±0
Gear: Colt 2000 with 15 bullets and 15 armor-piercing (AP 5) bullets in a spare clip, riot shield (in car), Kevlar vest (Armor 10/—), nightstick, five hand grenades (in car), patrol car, Winchester Defender with 14 shells (in car), and a set of handcuffs.

THE MAFIA

When the President declared martial law back in 1963, he took a lot of steps to ensure that he would remain in power. After all, without popular support, he was going to have a hard time maintaining his authority. One of the most important initiatives he took was deciding to work with the Mafia rather than against it.

With the Cosa Nostra (and many labor unions along with it) in Kennedy's pocket, most of America works like Chicago used to before it was blown off the face of the planet: It's extremely corrupt but oddly efficient—as long as you're on the right side of things.

The Defiance has put taking down the mob at the top of its list. Defiance leaders have long suspected the secret connection with the White House, and if they can prove it, they'll strike quite a blow against the President's public image.

In the meantime, the Mafia runs much of the country like a well-oiled, money-making machine. Crimelords line their pockets with profits made on drugs, prostitution, racketeering, construction, garbage collection, and others of the seedier facets of modern American life.

PROFILE (WISEGUY)

Smarts: 2d6
Area knowledge: Crescent City 3, language: English 2, language: Italian 1, tactics 2
Speed: 3d6
Dodging 1, driving: personal vehicle 2, shooting 2, stealth 1
Spirit: 3d6
Perception 2, persuasion: bluff 2, persuasion: intimidation 3, scrutinize 2, search 2
Strength: 3d6
Climbing 1, fighting: barehanded 2, reg ±0, swimming 1, throwing 1
Size: 5
Pace: 8
Delta Points: None
Quirks: Duty +4: the family, loyal –3, patron +3: local mob boss, reg ±0
Gear: Colt Python with 12 bullets and 6 armor-piercing (AP 5) bullets, a big, black car, and $1,000.

VAMPIRES

It seems that deltas aren't the only strange things in *Brave New World*. Apparently monsters of myth and legend also crop up from time to time. Case in point: the vampire.

Some people claim these creatures are actually just a strange form of delta. This theory is supported by the supernatural abilities the vampires display, but no other deltas have to drink blood in order to survive. Still, there's really no way to be sure.

Modern vampires share some traits with their mythic ancestors, but they've come down out of the mountains, so to speak. They cruise large cities at night, looking for fresh blood on which to feed. Then they congregate in all-night dance clubs after hours, and by day they sleep in coffins scattered throughout the city, often in some of the most exclusive, high-rent districts.

There's never been as good a time to be a vampire—except for the deltas who hunt them down.

Those in the know find the vampires' efforts to be "pathetically hip" their greatest weakness. By clinging to their human egos, they open themselves to all sorts of attacks by those who would hunt the hunters of human prey.

The truly dangerous vampires are those who've left their humanity far behind. There's no reasoning with such beasts, and it's difficult to predict their activities.

There's a theory that the vampires that have cropped up lately are actually deltas who got their demented powers in the wake of the bombs that destroyed Atlanta and San Francisco. In truth, there is an unaccountably very high concentration of bloodsuckers in the regions around these towns. Of course, it's just a theory, and there's no way to prove the link.

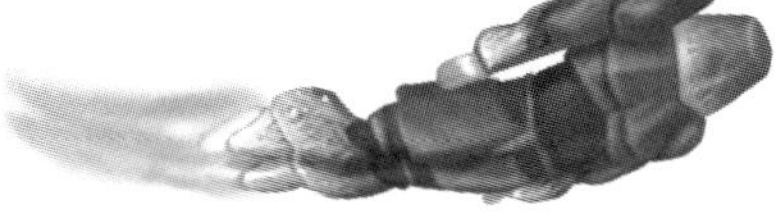

Profile

Smarts: 2d6
Area knowledge: Crescent City 2, language: English 2
Speed: 3d6+5
Dodging 2, shooting 1, stealth 3
Spirit: 2d6
Perception 2, persuasion: seduction 3, scrutinize 1, search 1, shadowing 3
Strength: 3d6+5
Climbing 5, fighting: barehanded 2, throwing 1
Size: 5
Pace: 13
Delta Points: 3
Quirks: Arrogant –3, beautiful +1, bloodthirsty –2, dark secret –5: vampire, heavy sleeper –1
Powers:
Become Mist: With a single action, can turn to mist or become solid again.
Mesmerize: Add +5 to *persuasion: seduction* rolls.
Morph: With a single action, the vampire can become a huge wolf or a bat or return to human form.
Nightvision: The vampire can see in total darkness and ignores lighting modifiers.
Undead: Don't suffer wound-effect modifiers and don't have to make stun checks. It's only truly dead when its head is pulped.
Vampiric Healing: When biting a foe, for each wound the vampire does, she can heal one wound on herself.
Weakness:
Bloodthirst: The vampire must drink a living being's blood at least once a day. Lower forms of life will do in a pinch, but most of these bloodsuckers prefer the human vintage.
Holy Water: Vampires can't stand the stuff. This does 1d6+1 damage per ounce. Large amounts of it do massive damage.
Religious Symbols or Garlic: The vampire can't approach within 1 inch of these. Of course, these days vampires don't limit themselves to using their teeth. More than one of the living dead has been known to carry high-caliber pistols for just this kind of situation.
Sunlight: At the start of every round a vampire is exposed to sunlight, he takes 3d6+5 points of massive damage, ignoring his *undead* ability. Armor does nothing against this.
Wood: Wooden weapons ignore the *undead* power's abilities.
Tricks: Bull's eye and first move.
Vampiric Grapple: With an extra success on a *fighting: barehanded* roll, the vampire can bite its opponent for *Strength*+2 points of damage.
Gear: None.

Bat Form

Smarts: 2d6
Area knowledge: Crescent City 2, language: English 2
Speed: 4d6+5
Dodging 4, stealth 3
Spirit: 2d6
Perception 3, scrutinize 1, search 1, shadowing 3
Strength: 1d6
Fighting: barehanded 1
Size: 1
Flying Pace: 14

Wolf Form

Smarts: 2d6
Area knowledge: Crescent City 2, language: English 2, tracking 4
Speed: 3d6+5
Dodging 3, stealth 5
Spirit: 2d6
Perception 5, scrutinize 1, search 3, shadowing 3
Strength: 3d6+5
Fighting: barehanded 3
Size: 5
Pace: 13

INDEX

INDEX

WAIT, THERE'S MORE!

Come on, we weren't going to get you all worked up about *Brave New World* and then just leave you hanging. If you liked this book, there's a lot more where that came from!

RAVAGED PLANET: THE BRAVE NEW WORLD PLAYER'S GUIDE

Now that you've got your feet wet, it's time to jump on in! *Ravaged Planet* features coverage of the delta situation all across America and even the world. Plus, learn the final fate of Patriot! There are even 10 new power packages for you to build your heroes with.

This deluxe, hardcover book is one you cannot afford to miss.

Written by Matt "Brave New World" Forbeck, with a stunning cover by Paul Bonner.

160 pages, 16 in color! *SKU# 7002* *$25.00*

POWER SHIELD THE BRAVE NEW WORLD GUIDE'S SCREEN

Now that you know the game, it's time to actually play it. No more fumbling through the book looking for that crucial table. They're all here in an easy-to-reference format on the inside of this dazzlingly colorful, trifold screen, the perfect place to keep your secrets behind.

Power Shield also comes complete with *The Ripper*, the first *Brave New World* adventure. It's a great launching point for your very own *Brave New World* saga.

Written by Shane "Deadlands" Lacy Hensley.

48 pages, plus screen! *SKU# 7001* *$15.00*

DEFIANTS: THE DEFIANCE SOURCEBOOK

The battle for *Brave New World* rages on. This book draws back the veil of secrecy that surrounds the most powerful group of rebels in America: the Defiance! Learn the truth about Truth and the organization she's behind.

Defiance also comes with six brand-new power packages for use in your game. No good Defiant would be caught without it!

Written by Matt "Brave New World" Forbeck, with a hot cover by Brian DeSpain.

128 pages, softcover *SKU# 7003* *$20.00*